STARTUP CAPITALISM

STARTUP CAPITALISM

New Approaches to Innovation
Strategies in East Asia

Robyn Klingler-Vidra
Ramon Pacheco Pardo

CORNELL UNIVERSITY PRESS   **ITHACA AND LONDON**

Thanks to generous funding from King's College London, the ebook editions of
this book are available as open access volumes through the Cornell Open initiative.

First published 2025 by Cornell University Press

Library of Congress Cataloging-in-Publication Data

Names: Klingler-Vidra, Robyn, author. | Pacheco Pardo, Ramon, author.
Title: Startup capitalism : new approaches to innovation strategies in East
    Asia / Robyn Klingler-Vidra, Ramon Pacheco Pardo.
Description: Ithaca : Cornell University Press, 2025. | Includes
    bibliographical references and index.
Identifiers: LCCN 2024023171 (print) | LCCN 2024023172 (ebook) | ISBN
    9781501780295 (hardcover) | ISBN 9781501781391 (paperback) | ISBN
    9781501780301 (pdf) | ISBN 9781501780318 (epub)
Subjects: LCSH: New business enterprises—East Asia. |
    Entrepreneurship—East Asia. | New business enterprises—Government
    policy—East Asia.
Classification: LCC HD62.5 .K58 2025 (print) | LCC HD62.5 (ebook) | DDC
    658.1/1095—dc23/eng/20241010
LC record available at https://lccn.loc.gov/2024023171
LC ebook record available at https://lccn.loc.gov/2024023172

Contents

Acknowledgments

The subject of startups and their societal role has grown in salience over the years we wrote this book. Yet, public debate about what, exactly, startups are meant to contribute to society has not proliferated. Given the decline in business dynamism and simultaneous uptick in public support for startups in the twenty-first century, a comprehensive understanding of the aims and means of startup-fueled innovation has never been more important. With this book, we hope to inform public debate about why governments support startups—the first essential step in designing impactful policy.

We owe much to the ecosystem analysts, founders, investors, and policy makers who shared their time and insights. Their views helped to shape the empirics and the narrative on which this book stands, and we hope that we have done justice to their shared experiences and wisdom. Three anonymous reviewers offered constructive feedback that helped shepherd the book's analysis. Jacqulyn Teoh, our editor at Cornell University Press, is to thank for this project having the analytical precision that it does. Jackie, thanks for believing in startup capitalism and for investing your sharp editorial eye, which no doubt made the book stronger.

Our work benefited from interactions with many colleagues and friends. Our academic community at King's College London provided instructive feedback throughout. The book has been improved thanks to valuable comments we received in response to presentations at the International Studies Association annual conventions in Baltimore (2017) and San Francisco (2018), the Society for the Advancement of Socio-Economics annual conventions in Kyoto (2018) and New York (2019), an Economic and Social Research Council and National Natural Science Foundation of China networking event in Shanghai (2016), a workshop at the Korea Institute for International Economic Policy (2018), the Key Issues in the Current Global Political Economy conference at UC Berkeley (2019), Brussels Korea Forum (2022), British International Studies Association in Glasgow (2023), Asia in World Finance workshop in Frankfurt (2023), and a virtual workshop led by the World Bank Seoul Center for Finance and Innovation in March 2024. Conversations, and in some cases collaborations, with the following scholars were essential to shaping the project in various ways: Vinod Aggarwal, Adam William Chalmers, Koo Min Gyo, Steven Jiawei Hai, Kathryn Ibata-Arens, Michiko Izuka, Yu Ching Kuo, Juanita Gonzalez-Uribe, Nahee Kang, Chun-Yi Lee, Chen Li, Ye Liu, Johannes Petry, John Ravenhill, Lena Rethel, Elizabeth

Thurbon, Robert Wade, Jing Wang, and Henry Wai-chung Yeung. Our research assistants, Xinchuchu Gao, Saeme Kim, Asha Naradate, Mitch Shin, Frida (Ziyi) Shui, Huang Wei, and Ester Zatkalikova, helped compile the historical policy data. Conversations with Anwar Aridi (World Bank Seoul Center for Finance and Innovation), David Hong (Plug and Play Taiwan), Rodrigo Mahs (former 500 Global), and James Mawson (Global Corporate Venturing) sharpened the book's framing. Thanks also to Sasindu Silva for her excellent job designing the radar chart figures.

Financial support provided by the Chiang Ching-kuo Foundation for International Scholarly Exchange, through a Research Grant (RG013-U-18), enabled fieldwork and research assistance. We also received support from several units within King's College London, including the Department of European and International Studies, School of Social Science and Public Policy, and King's Business School.

Undoubtedly our greatest debt is to our families. They were gracious when we traveled and generous with feedback when we discussed the book. For this and much more, Robyn thanks her husband, Eze, and their children, Rafi and Maya, and Ramon thanks his wife, Mina, and their daughter, Hannah.

Abbreviations

AI	artificial intelligence
AWS	Amazon Web Services
BATs	Baidu, Alibaba, and Tencent
CBRC	China Banking Regulatory Commission
CCEI	Center for Creative Economy and Innovation
CEPD	Council for Economic Planning and Development
CME	coordinated market economy
CPC	Communist Party of China
CSRC	China Securities Regulatory Commission
EAFC	East Asian Financial Crisis
EPB	Economic Planning Board
ERSO	Electronic Research Service Organization
FDI	foreign direct investment
FoF	fund of funds
GFC	global financial crisis
GPIF	Government Pension Investment Fund
HIDZ	high-tech industries development zone
ICT	information and communications technology
III	Institute for Information Industry
IP	intellectual property
IPO	initial public offering
ITRI	Industrial Technology Research Institute
JAFCO	Japan Associated Finance Co. Ltd.
JETRO	Japan External Trade Organization
JFC	Japan Finance Corporation
JST	Japan Agency of Science and Technology
KAIST	Korea Advanced Institute of Science and Technology
KISED	Korea Institute of Startup and Entrepreneurship Development
KIST	Korea Institute of Science and Technology
KMT	Kuomintang
KONEX	Korea New Exchange
KOTRA	Korea Trade-Investment Promotion Agency
KRW	Korean Won

KVIC	Korea Venture Investment Corporation
LME	liberal market economy
LP	limited partnership
MEST	Ministry of Education, Science, and Technology
METI	Ministry of Economy, Trade, and Industry
MEXT	Ministry of Education, Culture, Sports, Science, and Technology
MIC 2025	Made in China 2025
MIIT	Ministry of Industry and Information Technology
MoEA	Ministry of Economic Affairs
MoF	Ministry of Finance
MOFCOM	Ministry of Commerce
MOHRSS	Ministry of Human Resources and Social Security
MoST	Ministry of Science and Technology
MSS	Ministry of SMEs and Startups
NDRC	National Development and Reform Commission
NIS	national innovation system
NPS	National Pension Service
OECD	Organization for Economic Co-operation and Development
OSTI	Office of Science, Technology, and Innovation
PBOC	People's Bank of China
PRC	People's Republic of China
R&D	research and development
RMB	Renminbi
SAIC	State Administration for Industry and Commerce
S&T	science and technology
SAT	State Administration of Taxation
SBIC	Small Business Investment Companies
SBIR	Small Business Innovation Research
SEI	Statute for the Encouragement of Investment
SEZ	special economic zone
SMBA	Small and Medium Business Administration
SME	small- and medium-size enterprises
SMIC	Semiconductor Manufacturing International Corporation
SMRJ	Organization for Small & Medium Enterprises and Regional Innovation, Japan
SOE	state-owned enterprise
SSTC	State Science and Technology Commission
STI	science, technology, and innovation
SZSE	Shenzhen Stock Exchange
TITAN	Taiwan Innovation and Tech Arena

TSMC	Taiwan Semiconductor Manufacturing Company
TSS	Taiwan Startup Stadium
VC	venture capital
VLSI	Very-Large-Scale Integration
VoC	varieties of capitalism
WTO	World Trade Organization

Introduction

In June 2017, at the Seoul Centre for the Creative Economy and Innovation located right next to the South Korean capital's most important former royal palace, our interviewee explained why the government was bankrolling his center: "The government wants conglomerates to gain innovative DNA by working with startups." What we heard was that the center—which assists startups by providing coworking space, access to coaching, and mentorship and networking—was not necessarily designed to bolster startups. Instead, investment in startups was a means of injecting "innovative DNA" into Korea's large firms. This was the first time we grasped that startups were considered to be resources to boost, not challenge, the competitiveness of big business.

This interview stands out as a crystalizing moment. Until then, we had understood that government efforts like the center were fundamentally *for* startups that, in this book, represent new, high-growth, and often technologically oriented firms. It was surprising to hear that this flagship startup initiative positioned startups as a *resource for* other firms. We had thought that headlines of East Asian governments' investment in startups represented a break with their developmental past, which was centered on relations with, and investment in, large firms. Our intention was to write a book about how even quintessential developmental states were succumbing to the global trend of adopting a Silicon Valley–styled approach.

That moment came to symbolize our finding that government policy often conceives of startups as innovation resources for big businesses, not as the ultimate beneficiaries. The finding that startup largesse is not necessarily serving startups is important because economic growth, national security, and public health are dependent on a state's innovative capacity. The contemporary innovation imperative has been evident in the US-China trade war (Zhen 2023) and the race to develop a vaccine against COVID-19 (Neate 2021). There is no question that we are living in an epoch that can be called *startup capitalism*: startups play a central role in market economies' techno-industrial competitiveness. However, many questions about the *how* and *why* of startup capitalism remain unanswered. Businesses, governments, and wider society need to understand what drives today's cutting-edge innovation, and what role startups and corporations play in advancing national innovation capacity. Does startup capitalism involve startups as disruptive engines of innovation or resources fuelling established firms' innovativeness?

In this book, we answer this question by debunking two myths. The first myth is that startup promotion is intended for startups. A Silicon Valley–styled version of startup-led innovation where new firms disrupt industries is considered the gold standard. We instead find that government policy often conceives of startups as resources for—not challengers to—conglomerates. Startups inject new ideas, talent, and ways of working to enable the future competitiveness of lead firms that must compete with foreign rivals. This is a model that directly challenges the stylized Silicon Valley approach.

The second myth is that startup promotion is merely a means of entrepreneurship or employment policy. While startup policies do aim to boost employment, especially among the youth, they are a contemporary form of industrial policy. Targeting specific sectoral and technological capacities, industrial policy endeavors to bolster national economic and industrial competitiveness. Historically, industrial policy emphasized the use of financing to enable the productive capabilities and export activities of established firms operating in strategic industries. Today, we argue that startup promotion is a growing tack that sees startups (David), working with (or even for) large firms (Goliath), fueling national capabilities at the world's technological frontier. As a result, high-technology entrepreneurs and accompanying venture capital markets are part of today's high politics; they fuel countries' prowess in critical technologies, informing national economic competitiveness and security. Thus, the nature of the industrial-military complex in the twenty-first century is not only about big-scale government contractors; it also hinges on national supplies of startups' cutting-edge technologies and disruptive thinking.

Our finding that startup policy is not necessarily *for* startups is something of a puzzle. For comparative capitalism (Hall and Soskice 2001; Schneider 2013; Witt et al. 2018), startup-centric approaches *should* indicate a liberal market economy (LME) model in which disruptive entrepreneurs, with their accompanying equity financiers and flexible labor markets, fuel radical innovation. From this perspective, East Asian governments' startup capitalism would signify convergence on the Anglo-American LME, and as such, movement away from a coordinated market economy (CME).

In a similar vein, for developmental state scholars, startup largesse *should* infer the death of the developmental state that was characterized by its coordination with and directing of credit to large firms. In the classic developmental state, big businesses held central positions as employers and innovators.[1] On the face of it, startup-centric initiatives, such as Korea's CCEI and Japan's J-Startup Initiative, should represent a break with that large firm–centric model. These policies should instead signify that these countries are converging on operating as entrepreneurial states (Tiberghien 2007; Mazzucato 2013) and startup nations (Senor and Singer 2009). For evolutionary economists, policy to encourage innovative startups *should* indicate an adherence to a paradigm in which economic growth and revolutionary innovation are driven by startups disrupting existing technologies and the positions of existing firms (Aghion et al. 2021; Akcigit and Van Reenen 2023). So, policy to boost startups should indicate that startup capitalism manifests as startups posing existential threats to incumbent firms' competitive positioning.

In contrast to these expectations, state initiatives for startups do not necessarily constitute a break in governments' close relationships with big business. In this book, we show how and why *startup capitalism*, which we define as an economic and political system in which startups contribute to employment, innovation, and growth, can take multiple forms. Startup capitalism can manifest according to contrasting logics—some that align with the notion that startups disrupt existing industries and some that fit better with open innovation models in which established firms leverage startups to benefit their competitive positioning. We argue that policy makers simultaneously draw on opposing Schumpeterian logics; they see startups as both disruptors *and* resources for big businesses.

With this book, we advance debates in a few important ways. First, we contribute to political economy scholarship by showing that startup capitalism does not necessarily signify the death of the developmental state nor convergence on a neoliberal paradigm. Instead, startup capitalism can exemplify the persistence of CME complementarities and the developmental status apparatus. We show how startup policies often strive for both creative destruction *and* the augmenting of incumbent firms' innovation capacity. Second, we offer new evidence that may help explain why government policies targeting startups are not delivering results. Economic research has found that since the start of the twenty-first century, productivity and business dynamism have been declining in major advanced economies, including in the United States (Decker et al. 2016a; Philippon 2019). The reason being that government efforts that are ostensibly striving to cultivate disruptive innovation are, in fact, oriented toward expanding the innovation capacity and competitive positioning of established firms. We contribute to evolutionary economics by extending Schumpeterian understandings of the patterns of innovation into the context of startup capitalism.

This book's focus is on East Asia. Japan, Korea, Taiwan, and China offer archetypal cases of state-led development and a mix of market economy types, which is helpful in challenging the notion that embracing startup capitalism is synonymous with a declining developmental state or convergence on an LME. In addition to the region's analytical significance, there is its empirical importance. China is the second largest VC market in the world and is second to only the US in terms of its number of unicorns (Chen 2023);[2] Japan ranks highest globally for the number of innovation outposts in Silicon Valley (JETRO 2019); Korean corporations (Kakao and Samsung) are among the world's most active VC investors (CB Insights 2019); and Taiwan—long construed as the small firm–centric developmental state—has a single firm (Taiwan Semiconductor Manufacturing Company, or TSMC) that leads the world's semiconductor manufacturing (Ryan 2022) and has been said to be the world's best example of a state-engineered VC market (Gulinello 2005). In other words, East Asia is an ideal region for studying continuity and change in governmental efforts to boost startup-fuelled innovation.

We find that there are varieties of startup capitalism in East Asia. Japan and Korea's startup capitalism is best seen as a continuation of their developmental state models, which are persistent in efforts to network startups with big businesses. However, this is now done in the guise of an "open innovation" mode (Chesbrough 2003; Weiblen and Chesbrough 2015). In these cases, provision for startups can best be understood as a key tool in a broader arsenal of means for bolstering the technological innovation of established firms. While remaining mostly in line with its early depiction as a small firm–oriented developmental state dubbed the Silicon Valley of Asia, Taiwanese policy continues to be dedicated to widening pools of entrepreneurs in emerging technologies. As the China chapter reveals, the country's engagement with startups is a complex one, with a mix of support for disruptive startups and efforts to challenge the dominant positions of select industry giants.

In all cases, startups are construed as resources for big businesses in areas considered critical, or emerging, technologies, such as artificial intelligence (AI), quantum computing, robotics, and semiconductors. This aligns with notions of a techno-nationalist state (Plantin and de Seta 2019), a techno-security state (Cheung 2022), and a national security state (Weiss 2014) and the role of creative insecurity (Taylor 2016) in marshaling investment into startups as part of military-industrial complexes around the world (see Nicholas 2019). Building a venture capital state has been motivated under the guise of boosting national security (Klingler-Vidra 2018). Startups—the recipients of venture capital funding—are engines for critical technology prowess.

Startups are often engaged in a means of boosting large firms' ability to compete with other national champions. Even markets considered quintessentially neoliberal—like the United States—include entrenched companies as crucial innovation partners. For instance, the US National Science Foundation partnered with Amazon Web Services, IBM, and Microsoft in 2022 to boost quantum computing capabilities, a field in which the United States is locked in competition with China and other leading economic powers. The NSF also partnered with Microsoft to offer cloud computing credits to startups participating in its Big Data Regional Innovation Hubs in 2016. The incumbents benefit directly from this integration into public startup policies, as they lock in swaths of startups as users.

Big (tech) companies are key partners in startup policies in Europe, too. In 2021, for instance, Nesta, an innovation agency headquartered in the United Kingdom, and the European Commission's Startup Europe Partnership launched a new ranking for Europe's 25 Corporate Startup Stars, which included BMW, Microsoft, and Telefonica, to further celebrate corporation-startup interactions (Dunsby 2021). German efforts to boost Dresden and the surrounding area as Silicon Saxony include the US$11 billion spent on attracting a TSMC chip plant, a key element in the European Union (EU) Chips Act, in order to link industry leaders such as TSMC to growing European producers (Blanchard and Escritt 2023) while limiting unwanted foreign investments in the technology sector (Chazan 2019). Meanwhile, the Macron administration's 2019 aim for France to produce 25 unicorns was reached in 2022, with tailwinds coming from clusters built around the French government's handouts to Taiwanese firms such as ProLogium in Dunkirk (*Economist* 2023a). By partnering with startups, these companies are praised by policy makers for not perishing as Blockbuster and Kodak, two former multinationals whose respective business models and technologies became obsolete, did.

Is this approach best for the economy and society as a whole? Seminal academic theory, in the form of Joseph Schumpeter's work on patterns of innovation, suggests no. Over the course of the first decades of the twentieth century, he distinguished two industrial paradigms—one in which startups served as essential disruptors and one in which large companies fostered innovation and growth, owing to their ability to mobilize their significant resources. While both modes of innovation were separately valid, he posited that they did not occur simultaneously. He studied which mode could best drive innovation in a particular industry at a given time.

In this book, we hope to reinvigorate this exercise to ascertain how startup capitalism can effectively drive business dynamism and innovation. This is an important debate, as research has revealed a dearth of competition as big businesses increasingly dominate many industries in the twenty-first century (Tepper 2023). Studies show that there has been a decline in business dynamism and entrepreneurship in the United States since 2000 (Decker et al. 2016b). Thus, it has never been more important to understand how countries can best engage startups as engines of economic growth and national security.

Basis for the Puzzle

The existence of institutional similarities and differences across economies is now well established. Many scholars agree that the global economy is not converging on the so-called US style of neoliberalism and that different economic models coexist, even in the context of innovation-oriented activities (Boyer 2005). Among the different strands of literature discussing these similarities and differences from a comparative perspective, the varieties of capitalism (VoC) approach, first established by Peter Hall and David Soskice (2001), has become dominant. Using an institutionalist approach, Hall and Soskice's edited volume theorized a dichotomy between LMEs, such as the United States and the United Kingdom, and CMEs, typified by Germany and Japan.

VoC delineates why LMEs and CMEs differ in the way that firms behave. Both market economy types possess complementarities across the institutional arenas of labor organization, the nature of interfirm relationships, corporate governance, the availability of information, and models of financing. These institutional complementarities are internally coherent and self-reinforcing and, according to the authors, shape how their firms compete in global markets.[3] In the case of LMEs, market mechanisms define the arm's-length relationship between firms accompanied by equity finance and fluid labor markets. As for CMEs, nonmarket mechanisms in the form of strategic interactions among firms underpin this relationship, with reinforcing debt-based patient capital and rigid labor markets.[4] LMEs, owing to their institutional logics, are expected to excel in radical innovation, while CMEs are expected to lead in incremental innovation. While the LME and CME varieties are "ideal" models that, in practice, operate differently from country to country, they have become popular anchors to describe and analyze how market economies operate.

Underpinning much of the research on the East Asian region is the developmental state concept, which refers to late industrializing economies, with the state at the center of capacity upgrading and economic growth.[5] The developmental state can be summarized as a focus on long-term (decades-long) strategic goals driving socioeconomic development, the existence of a quasi-autonomous bureaucratic apparatus staffed by talented officials seeking to maximize benefits for society as a whole, and the use of institutionalized mechanisms for public- and private-sector cooperation (Amsden 1989; Wade 1990; Evans 1995). The developmental state offered support to specific sectors or firms in a bid to advance technological capabilities, move up global value chains, and thus provide economic growth, steady employment, and national security (Woo-Cumings 1999). Largesse included the mobilization of citizens' banking or postal savings accounts, which were used to bolster corporations' productive capacity through access to credit (Calder 1990, 2017; Vogel 2018). In return, these large firms would create steady and relatively well-paid jobs to employ the country's abundant labor force (Johnson 1982; Okimoto 1989). The developmental state, in these different constellations, encouraged domestic firms to manufacture and export goods that relied on Western technology, at least in the initial phases (Westney 1987), acting as a guardian for the economy and society (Tate 1995).

Synthesizing this depiction, we understand the four key defining characteristics of the developmental state as: (1) central or strong long-term state intervention in economic policy planning and implementation; (2) a perceived importance of quality employment for socioeconomic purposes; (3) a preference for bank-based financing conducive to the existence of patient capital; and (4) relatively high levels of ownership concentration, whether family- or state-dominated. A crucial aim was to accumulate technical capacity, initially in catch-up technologies but ultimately at the world's technological frontier, thus escaping the middle-income trap (Lee 2013). This depiction has been reiterated across the economics literature, which finds that countries initially achieve growth through technology transfer and adoption and later move toward innovating at the technological frontier (Acemoglu et al. 2006; Peters and Zilibotti 2023). The literature thus draws our attention to systemic coordination and institutional complementarity often centered on large firms as drivers of technical capacity advances and suppliers of well-paid, stable employment.[6]

Whether the developmental state is dead or alive has been much debated. Some argue that crises such as Japan's Heisei Era bubble burst, the East Asian Financial Crisis (EAFC), political shifts such as democratization, and the states' economic successes, have led to a death or decline of state-led orchestrating of techno-industrial output (Lim and Jang 2006; Pirie 2018). Others point at the structural changes in the global economy that have been underway since at least the 1980s as having diminished the role for the region's developmental states in fostering industrial capabilities (Wong 2004; Yeung 2016). Globalization and the neoliberal Washington Consensus have also been said to have eroded the role of the state in economic policy making (Wade 2018).

Others contend that the developmental state is very much alive—or evolved—given relatively unchanged normative contexts and institutional structures. Scholars argue that the underlying mindset that drove the developmental state has persisted (Thurbon and Weiss 2006; Stubbs 2009; Thurbon 2016). They assert that policies continue to be implemented in the context of a deeper entrenching of state interventionism in the economy (Lee 2024). In fact, beyond the East Asian setting, there's growing awareness of, and acceptance for, states' pursuit of industrial policy aimed at boosting techno-industrial capabilities (Aiginger and Rodrik 2020; Juhász et al. 2023). In other words, state interventionism has not disappeared in East Asia; rather, like a chameleon, its characteristics and modalities have changed, and have grown in global popularity.

To explore the ways in which startup capitalism constitutes continuity and change, we draw on Schumpeterian understandings of industrial dynamics that foment technological innovation. Neo-Schumpeterian economics posits that innovation is the main driving force behind economic growth (Hausman and Johnston 2014; Perez 2002, 2016). In the wider literature on evolutionary economics, scholars examine the relationship between firm size, market dynamics, and systemic technological change (see Nelson and Winter 1982). This tradition has conceptualized two distinct modes of how firms, and the characteristics of accompanying industrial systems, shape innovation activities. These two modes are referred to as Mark I and Mark II.

In what is referred to as Mark I, the emphasis is on Schumpeter's (1934) espousing of the benefits of new entrants—*startups*, in today's parlance—in instigating processes of creative destruction. Creative destruction is understood as the dynamic in which startups revolutionize "the economic structure *from within*, incessantly destroying the old one, incessantly creating a new one" (1942 [2010], 73). Startups "continually arrive to compete with existing firms," and their new technologies "render existing technologies obsolete" (Aghion et al. 2021, 1; Akcigit and Van Reenen 2023, 1). In this mode, creative destruction poses a threat to established companies to revolutionize a way for new firms and technologies to boost productivity and, as a result, drive economic growth. The Mark I policy implication is that public policy needs to remove constraints to innovation for high-potential entrepreneurs, including access to market entry and growth inhibitors imposed by large firms and their nonproductive strategies (Hanusch and Pyka 2007; Baslandze 2023). Said differently, Mark I startup policies should encourage the widening of entrepreneurial pools so that would-be disruptors are able to form and grow.

In contrast, Mark II, emanating from Schumpeter's *Capitalism, Socialism and Democracy* (1942), emphasizes the productive role of large firms as innovators in the first decades of the twentieth century. Oligopolistic competition dynamics endow big businesses with the financial means to invest in new products and technologies. To compete with the other dominant firms, these lead firms invest in research and development (R&D) at scale. In this context, industry giants are the engines of transformative innovation. The public policy imperative is to enable established firms' access to resources. This aligns, in some ways, with the developmental state paradigm in which industrial policies ensured access to credit, organized consortia, and more.

By considering startup capitalism in both Mark I and II terms, this book represents a departure from seminal work on the developmental state. Rather than seeing startup policy align with either Mark I or II ideals, we find hybridity. Startup capitalism can strive for widening pools of entrepreneurs and startups can be perceived as a means of enabling innovation capacity among oligopolistic firms (see Sandulli et al. 2012; Dahlander et al. 2021). In this way, policies encourage oligopolistic firms to leverage startups as open innovation system resources (Pacheco Pardo and Klingler-Vidra 2024). This differs from the Mark II ideal type in which large firms did innovation in-house.

Our findings also challenge expectations that the rise of startup capitalism is evidence of the region subscribing to a universal convergence on a LME logic. Rather than seeing startup capitalism strive for Mark I's creative destruction dynamics, we find that startup policies that do align more with Mark I tend to emphasize emerging industries and technologies, but not disruption. They are fostered as argonauts advancing a new frontier rather than being seen as a challenge to existing businesses.

Startup capitalism either avoids confrontation with big businesses or pursues collaboration with incumbents whose innovation capacity will benefit from interactions with startups. To analyze these variations systematically, we map startup capitalism in terms of the institutional logics of VoC (employment, finance, innovation) and the developmental state (firm relations and social purpose). In doing so, we strive to understand startup capitalism in wider political economy terms and to investigate which means of engaging startups is optimal for society, given industry patterns and life cycles in the twenty-first century.

Argument: The Rise of Startup Capitalism

We argue that startup capitalism strives to both harness the disruptive power of startups for creating new markets *and* benefit big businesses. Policy makers even sometimes publicly speak about their intention to concurrently create cohorts of unicorns while simultaneously injecting innovative ideas and talent into incumbents. This thinking constitutes a best-of-both-worlds logic.

If startup capitalism aligned with Schumpeter's Mark I creative destruction paradigm, established firms would go into bankruptcy, get acquired, or shift to other industries. In the Mark I understanding, it is the fear of new entrants posing an existential threat, not only their actual activities, that is essential to boosting big companies' innovative prowess. But the startup policies closest to the Mark I ideal aim to enable startups competing in emerging technologies, *not* to incentivize startups that are challenging incumbents.

This existential threat is certainly absent in the Korean Center for Creative Economy and Innovation (CCEI) example we shared at the beginning of this book. Each CCEI has a chaebol designated as the core corporate partner (Klingler-Vidra and Pacheco Pardo 2020). These centers provide entrepreneurs with consulting services, marketing assistance, prototyping help, and access to investors. In return for their contribution, the chaebol gain access to the startups' ideas, talent, and technologies. Rather than threatening the destruction of the big businesses, the CCEIs fuse startups together with the chaebol to deliver mutual benefits. This offers innovative DNA to large firms.

Korea's CCEI and chaebol are not alone in this. Corporate accelerators around the world speak of their efforts to foster "disruptive startups," as Intel gushed in the September 2023 announcement of their London-based Ignite program (Intel 2023). The startups in the accelerator programs are perceived as customers, operating based on the firm's services and technologies, be it Intel's chips or Amazon's cloud computing. Startups are complementary to big business, not disruptors. This does not align with Schumpeter's Mark I paradigm in which startups are propelling creative destruction.

Likewise, our observation of startup capitalism closer to the Mark II ideal type does not align with Schumpeter's conventional understanding of oligopolistic firms as standalone innovation leaders. Instead, we contend that today's startup capitalism activities closest to Mark II are consistent with open innovation practices, as epitomized by the CCEI example. Startup policy, in this twenty-first-century variety of Mark II, conceives of startups as external resources for established companies to leverage in a bid to advance their competitive positioning. Incumbent firms benefit from open innovation through the injection of new ideas and access to talent and by acquiring new sales distribution channels and direct customers (Klingler-Vidra and Pacheco Pardo 2022). Corporations engage with startups for the purpose of boosting their own innovation (Weiblen and Chesbrough 2015). Patents and temporary secrecy do not serve as "protecting devices" (Schumpeter 1942, 77); in fact, open innovation systems may endow significant information and talent advantages to entrenched businesses and thus act as a barrier to startups' ability to achieve scale. Thus, we see a variation of Mark II in which oligopolistic firms engage startups to benefit their innovation prowess instead of relying on internal R&D and consortium links with other lead firms.

There are good reasons why startup capitalism often takes this open innovation variety. Direct state largesse for incumbents has become increasingly unsalable to a public that scrutinizes government spending ever more closely and worries about dominant firms' shaping of their daily lives. Examples of the prevalence of public sentiment against big (tech) business include a June 2023 *New York Times* essay whose title begins "Big Tech Is Bad" (Acemoglu and Johnson 2023). Jonathan Tepper (2023) asserts that the *Myth of Capitalism* in the United States is propagated by the oligopolistic firms that benefit from their dominant positions in their respective markets. This sentiment aligns with research that recognizes that "vested incumbents are incentivized to do what they can to slow down the process of creative destruction" (Baslandze 2023, 559). The *Economist* (2023b) covered the June 2023 World Bank arbitration ruling that describes the Korean state's meddling in a Samsung merger as "cozy relations between government and business" and the chaebol as "too close for comfort." There are challenges to this prevailing negative framing of big business, however. Notably, Robert Atkinson and Michael Lind's (2018) best-selling book, *Big Is Beautiful*, pleads for a reassessment of the (positive) role of large firms as employers and innovators.

Policy Implications

Should the aim of public policy vis-à-vis startups today be one of instigating unfettered capitalism, with the expectations that creative destruction will propagate society's technological advances? Or should big businesses build protective moats—including the accelerators and corporate venture capital funds that underpin their open innovation—to boost society's innovation prowess and corresponding improvements in quality of life? Can startup policies that enable the continuance of incumbent dominance help explain declining business dynamism trends?

In contrast to Philippe Aghion and Peter Howitt's (1992) modeling of creative destruction in endogenous growth theory, we contend that startup capitalism operates according to variations on conventional understandings of both modes. On the one hand, policies closer to Mark I aim to foster new cohorts of unicorns in emerging industries. On the other hand, startup policies engage big businesses in part to enshrine their innovation capacity. What is more, some startup policies strive to do both simultaneously—create unicorns and boost the competitive position of established companies. This conflates—and, we argue, undermines—the distinct logics of Mark I and II patterns of innovation. According to Schumpeter, both are superior at a given place or point in time. For instance, Franco Malerba and Luigi Orsenigo (1996) argued that alignment with Mark I or II is technology specific.

In the context of startups as an engine for incumbent-centered open innovation, there are several questions. For one, the ontology of open innovation is one of firm-level or microeconomic performance. Open innovation, according to Henry Chesbrough (2003), offers an updated counter to the five forces that Michael Porter and other management scholars depicted as essential to firms' competitive strategy. Startup policy that strives to benefit big businesses should be clear that its premise is that open innovation is optimal for the economy, not only for the big corporations.

There are several reasons why the open innovation variety of Mark II could be perceived as superior. System benefits from corporate venture capital, for example, show that value is created for the corporation *as well as* the new venture firms (Bugl et al. 2022). Research shows that as investors in startups, incumbent firms offer access to their networks, market knowledge, and sales and distribution channels (Alvarez-Garrido and Dushnitsky 2016), which can help startups grow. In addition, startup policy acknowledges that large firms can offer an important means of exit by trade sale or acquisition for many startups. These win-win scenarios likely motivate the pursuit of startup policy enabling open innovation systems.

Yet, it is essential to also distill the potential risks involved in bringing big businesses into startup policy. For one, the ultimate winner of such startup backing may be the corporations rather than the wider economy or society. Incumbents engage in open innovation systems for both inbound and outbound purposes, with startups serving in a range of capacities, from external R&D provision to sales opportunities (Dahlander and Gann 2010). In addition, the response to open innovation startup policies may be tepid, as startups may limit how much they engage with large firms due to concerns that their efforts and ideas will be appropriated. Incumbents may "try to win the market with productive strategies" (such as accelerators) in which they integrate startup ideas and technologies or "rely on nonproductive strategies" that enable them to maintain their market position through patent portfolios and anticompetitive acquisitions (Baslandze 2023, 558). Corporations may also leverage their political connections and power, employing "different forms of lobbying" and thus integrating themselves as essential partners and benefactors of startup-led innovation (Bombardini et al. 2023, 538).

Many also worry that high-growth startups and burgeoning unicorns fall victim to the national champions that can either copy their technologies and mass produce them more cheaply or use their market dominance to prevent the distribution of new products by smaller firms. In the United States, big companies, including big tech firms, have been accused of exploiting startups' ideas, forcing early acquisitions, and applying predatory pressures that constitute kill zones (*Economist* 2018a). This concern has been realized in East Asia. In Korea, for example, some analysts believe that, "immensely wealthy and historically backed by government support, the chaebol have a tradition of establishing their own affiliates to compete and undercut startups instead of acquiring the new technology through M&A [mergers and acquisitions]" (Harris 2019). As an example of the alleged downside to open innovation, there are "delivery wars" in Korea, as the chaebol are looking to "snatch market share from the delivery startups that cultivated the industry" (J. Kim 2020). Some analysts worry that they wield so much power that they can acquire teams—or whole businesses—on the cheap, allowing them to hoover up talent, ideas, and products without having to hire or build such capacity in-house. While this characterization of chaebol-startup relations is contested, policy makers' intention is certainly not to exacerbate this predatory potential.

It is not only startups that risk negative outcomes from open innovation activities. Research has shown that incumbents may fail to capture value from engagement—across accelerators, investments, and more—due to ineffective integration, IP management, and knowledge spillovers (Dabic et al. 2023). There is also the risk of open innovation engagement serving what Steve Blank (2019) calls "innovation theater" rather than big businesses conducting substantive innovation.

From a societal perspective, there are concerns about the equity of gains and societal welfare resulting from variations of startup capitalism. Startups are high-risk, high-failure businesses that are—if dynamism and disruption forces exist—unlikely to be in existence long enough to provide long-term employment and social benefits (Klingler-Vidra and Pacheco Pardo 2019). The firms targeted by startup policy are epitomized by VC-backed companies. These companies raise early-stage equity investments due to their potential to achieve remarkable scale, but they often face binary fail-or-succeed outcomes. A sobering statistic comes from a study of two thousand VC-backed companies in the United States between 2004 and 2010 that had each received at least US$1 million in funding; Shikhar Ghosh from Harvard Business School found that 75 percent failed completely, never returning cash to their investors (Gage 2012). Similarly, Bob Zider (1998) found a high potential for failure, with only one out of ten companies in a VC portfolio likely to succeed and half failing. These failure rates hardly instill confidence that high-growth entrepreneurship can provide steady jobs, let alone employment for life, as the chaebol and keiretsu offered in the post–Korean War and post–World War II eras, respectively. In addition, job creation through tech-intensive startups that pursue scale by automating human tasks—thus allegedly reducing the need for human labor—has a fundamental tension with the provision of employment opportunities.

As Schumpeter (1942, 119) acknowledged in his exploration of innovation paradigms, access to high-performing entrepreneurship is not available equally to all members of society. Certain demographics, based on disability, ethnicity, gender, and socioeconomic attributes, may struggle to participate (Zehavi and Breznitz 2017; Klingler-Vidra and Liu 2020). What is more, technology-fueled automation can cause certain groups to suffer more acutely from job losses. Automation also has the potential to deliver greater returns to the capital owners than labor, benefiting from lower labor costs and higher productivity on account of scalable technologies and as a result accentuating inequality (Klingler-Vidra et al. 2022). The gains reaped from high-growth startups are amassed by entrepreneurial founders who may or may not make investments that benefit local communities or their wider society. And on top of that, companies can domicile in tax-efficient locales and operate online, enabling them to pay little tax and hire few (local) employees.

In this way, startup capitalism's focus on job creation is wrought with challenges and contradictions. Policy that encourages startups as job creators will necessarily transfer more risk onto citizens than policy that favors large firms providing permanent employment. The financial reward of startup employment may be greater for the individual than a steady salary, but the risk of losing one's job as well as social benefits is also substantial (Acs et al. 2016).

There is also the question of which of society's challenges are being targeted by startups. In *Big Is Beautiful*, Atkinson and Lind (2018) make the Mark II argument that large, well-resourced companies are more likely to take on big societal challenges and thus invest substantial resources that could drive widespread impact. According to this rationale, oligopolies, with their significant balance sheets and workforces, can best take on and advance on technologies that could address society's more pressing problems. As a contemporary example, in a May 2016 TED talk, Astro Teller, the head of Google X—which Alphabet (Google's parent company) describes as a moonshot factory—outlines the team's approach to solving complex challenges that affect all countries, such as the need for sustainable food and transportation.[7] The X team was working on vertical farming as a way of producing (more) food without needing more agricultural land and on a lighter-than-air, variable-buoyancy ship. X, as Teller explained, invested many man-hours and tens of millions of dollars to develop and test prototypes before deciding how, or whether, to continue. The X example underscores Schumpeter's contention that it is large firms (in his day, US Steel, for instance) that can take on these major challenges.

In the East Asian developmental state context, national champion firms often worked in tune with societal needs and at the behest of government bureaucrats. State-society priorities, in the (Japanese and Korean) developmental state's heyday, were channeled into consortia initiatives, with the state setting the agenda and funding the technologies that were to be developed. In a decentralized system, in which each entrepreneur works on different opportunities, the ability of startups to serve the social purpose of wider society may be muted. With that said, the state's use of tax incentives and direct funding for startups can instigate activity in line with state priorities. China's startup competitions, for instance, offer a good example, identifying certain societal issues and emerging technologies that contending entrants should focus on (China Innovation and Entrepreneurship Competition 2020).

Collectively, startup capitalism entails trade-offs and challenges. Each variety aligns better with different aims and at distinct points in technological cycles. Policy makers are now pursuing a hybrid approach in which they strive for both unicorn births and big business successes. This combination may be optimal in the twenty-first century. If Schumpeterian logic does hold, though, then this hybrid approach would not deliver optimal results, as it does not wield the power of either paradigm. Future innovation performance of the region will reveal whether hybridity is producing results or is inadvertently undermining the power that either mode could achieve.

Research Design

In our analytical framework, we conceive of startup capitalism in terms of degrees of continuity and change from antecedent settings. We draw on theories of gradual institutional change (see Mahoney and Thelen 2010; Acemoglu et al. 2021). Our framework delineates five institutional components that constitute our synthesis of the developmental state and varieties of capitalism frameworks. To analytically account for the continuity and change underpinning the countries' evolving approaches, we explore: (1) the size of firms expected to drive this (capability at the technological frontier); (2) the employment market's character, as a continuum of permanent employment to more fluid; (3) sources of finance, spanning (main) banks distributing lines of credit to capital markets that issue equity; (4) the nature of the innovation sought, from catch-up toward the technological frontier; and (5) the primary social purpose underpinning policy efforts.

The book draws on a novel assessment of startup policies and the media coverage of those policies across four East Asian countries: Japan, Korea, Taiwan, and China. Policy information was collected in English as well as in Mandarin, Japanese, and Korean; when we translated materials into English, we strove for consistency with the language used by the government (in that era). In total, we analyzed startup policies employed from the beginning of each country's developmental state era (1948 for Japan, 1961 for Korea, 1949 for Taiwan, and 1979 for China) through 2023.

We study startup policy within the wider rubric of science, technology, and innovation (STI) policies. Broadly speaking, innovation policies are those that strive to advance "new combinations," as Schumpeter (1934) would say. There are numerous classifications of STI policies according to the intention and the instruments used (e.g., see Nee and Opper 2012; Edler and Fagerberg 2017; Schot and Steinmueller 2018). State-of-the-art classifications of innovation policy employ a tripartite classification according to the policies' intentionality as either "mission-oriented" or transformative; "invention-oriented"; or national innovation system (NIS)–oriented (Edler and Fagerberg 2017; Schot and Steinmueller 2018).[8]

As a specific variety of NIS policy, the aims of startup policy are often defined as striving to advance the quantity and quality of high-technology oriented entrepreneurial ecosystem actors, such as VCs and accelerators, as well as the informal or intangible factors, such as a risk-taking and creative culture (Engel 2014; Autio et al. 2016; Klingler-Vidra and Wade 2020). The focus on startups as a target of NIS policy stems from the truism that new firms expand "the technology frontier," a crucial aim of innovation policy (IMF 2016, 39).

Existing research on startup policy has conceptualized the policy aims and forms in several ways. The first is in terms of different life-cycle stages (e.g., antecedent, founding, behavior, and outputs) and the interventions needed at those different points (Audretsch et al. 2020). A second way of categorizing startup policies is by delineating the types of entrepreneurship targeted, delineating efforts focused on innovative new entrants from the broader category of entrepreneurship policy enabling new, small firms (Acs et al. 2016). A third way is based on the nature of the policy instruments used—such as funding, tax incentives, or regulatory changes—as a means of boosting startup activity (Pacheco Pardo and Klingler-Vidra 2019). In addition, scholars have aligned startup promotion expectations with levels of economic development, contending that creative destruction is more likely to be present and more impactful as economies develop. The argument is that in developing contexts, innovation initially takes the form of adopting technologies from abroad (Acemoglu et al. 2006; Peters and Zilibotti 2023).

In this book, we coded startup policies according to the instruments used rather than other taxonomies.[9] We did this to be comprehensive in our understanding of a startup, distinguishing it from the broader category of small- and medium-size enterprises (SME) but not focusing on any one point in a startup's life cycle or on specific innovation or employment strategies. The eight startup-centric policy types are as follows: (1) Funding; (2) Taxation; (3) Regulation; (4) Clusters, Networks, Institutes; (5) Attracting Talent and Investment; (6) Stock Market Access; (7) Technology Infrastructure and Government Procurement; and (8) Education and Training. Table 1.1 summarizes each policy type.

To identify the startup policies enacted in each country, we used two means. First, we searched for startup policies on governmental websites and search

TABLE 1.1. Startup policy types

	SPECIFIC POLICY TOOLS
1. Funding	· Startup investment · Grant funding · Guarantees · VC funds · Fund of VC funds
2. Taxation	· Incentives for investors, particularly VCs and business angels · R&D tax incentives · Preferential tax rates by firm age, size, and founder attributes
3. Regulation	· Bankruptcy laws · Intellectual property rights · Investor structures · Pension fund portability · Regulatory sandbox
4. Clusters, networks, institutes	· Accelerators and incubators · Co-working spaces · Innovation centers · Science and hi-tech parks
5. Attracting talent and investment	· Programs to entice (foreign) entrepreneurs to startup locally · Provisions to calibrate for, or incentivize participation by, foreign investors
6. Stock market access	· Establishing stock markets serving startups · Startup-friendly rules for stock market listing and facilitating foreign exchange dual listing
7. Technology infrastructure and government procurement	· Incentives to award government contracts to startups · Infrastructure projects (e.g., 5G) · Open data provision
8. Education and training	· Entrepreneurship skills training (e.g., business plan and pitching) · STEM education

Note: Details on each policy type are sketched in terms of their alignment with conventional understandings of Mark I and II modes in chapter 1. Further explanations of policy instruments can be found in Klingler-Vidra 2014, Pacheco Pardo and Klingler-Vidra 2019.

engines. We canvassed government sources, international policy databases, and web sources to identify policies implemented across the period in each country. We began with government sources such as Japan's Ministry of Economy, Trade and Industry (METI) website and then covered international policy databases, namely the Global Entrepreneurship Network Atlas as well as the Startup Genome's Global Startup Ecosystems Reports. Our next step was to cover wider web sources, which we did by conducting a Google search consisting of the country name (e.g., Japan) and startup policy language (see Klingler-Vidra and Chalmers 2023). Second, we canvassed the body of developmental state, comparative capitalism, and Asian business systems scholarship to ensure we captured the most comprehensive picture of startup policies across the eight instrument types. This second step helped us check for discrepancies and missing policies.

Once we collated the startup policies for each country, we analyzed them in terms of the size of firms targeted as the participants and intended beneficiaries, the equity/debt nature of finance, lifetime or fluid employment strategies, the type of innovation targeted (radical or incremental), and the underpinning social purpose. To assess the social purpose, we examined the objectives as laid out in the policy documents themselves. We then conducted a Google search of each policy to find media communications around its launch. We coded media statements made by senior policy makers and politicians with respect to why they were pursuing the policy and what aims they hoped to achieve with the initiative. Finally, we complemented the policy analyses with semistructured interviews with national, provincial, and local policy makers as well as innovation system actors, including startup founders and venture capitalists, conducted between 2016 and 2023.

Collectively, we present a political economy account of startup capitalism across three archetypal developmental states—Japan, Korea, and Taiwan—and the juggernaut of China, which combines state-owned enterprises, established private firms, and entrepreneurs quickly advancing to the world's technological frontier. Invariably, despite the extensive research published on East Asian industrial policies, to date, there has been insufficient investigation of each state's startup promotion efforts. We hope to address this gap in a way that establishes startup policy as an industrial policy arena within comparative capitalism, developmental state, and neo-Schumpeterian literature.

Plan for the Book

The book is organized as follows. Chapter 1 advances the analytical framework. It conceptualizes the institutional arenas that are fundamental to studying startup capitalism. The five components are: (1) the size of firms (large or small) targeted to drive innovation prowess; (2) the fluidity of labor markets; (3) financing for innovation, as credit- or equity-based; (4) the type of innovation as either catch-up or striving to compete at the technological frontier; and (5) the social purpose. We examine how these five institutional arenas have changed in step with startup policies in terms of a continuum framed by Mark I and Mark II ideal types. Chapters 2 through 5 offer analytical narratives for each country by providing a brief distilling of the antecedent period through to a more extended analysis of the contemporary period. Each chapter closes with a discussion of the extent to which continuity or change is observed and delineates the case's variety of startup capitalism in terms of the Mark I and II modes.

We begin the case analyses by focusing on Japan in chapter 2, the quintessential developmental state that serves as a least likely case for policy makers pursuing Silicon Valley style, given the widespread depiction of the state as coordinating large-firm consortia and working with main banks to offer the keiretsu steady credit lines (Jackson 2003; Pempel 1998). We find that the Japanese developmental state apparatus has, since the onset of the Heisei recession that began in 1990, supported startups as a means of fueling open innovation systems. This has been in line with an open innovation variety of a Mark II pattern, as the keiretsu and main banks are key partners, investors, and beneficiaries of Japan's startup capitalism. In fact, even high-profile startup programs, such as the J-Startup Initiative and Startup Ecosystem Consortium, involve the keiretsu and main banks in selecting startups for participation. Then–Prime Minister Fumio Kishida's 2022 "Startup Development Five-Year Plan" explains that "large, existing companies . . . can stay in business if they engage in open innovation" (Cabinet Secretariat 2022, 1). The open innovation aim is evident in the Japanese government's articulation of social purposes of encouraging startups, which we see as threefold: first, to provide high-quality jobs and thus increase creative talent for the keiretsu; second, to boost technological capacity of the established firms; and third, to collectively drive technological prowess and economic growth.

Chapter 3, Korea, also offers a state-led case in which development was fostered in partnership with national champions: the chaebol. Our research reveals how high-profile, startup-centric initiatives have been pursued, such as President Park Geun-hye's creation of the Creative Economy Action Plan and former President Moon Jae-in's establishment of the Ministry of SMEs and Startups (MSS) in July 2017. Both efforts have seen funding, tax incentives, and a variety of government-led programs aimed at startups as well as startup-chaebol partnerships. We reveal how startups are often perceived as advancing large firms' technological capabilities, consistent with a Mark II open innovation variety of startup capitalism. While startups are publicized as key targets of innovation policy in Korea, the chaebol are often essential partners and beneficiaries. Startup policies strive to provide innovative ideas and talent to the chaebol while also aiming to diversify the economy away from the giant firms and encourage an entrepreneurial mindset.

Chapter 4 examines the Taiwan case, which begins from a different origin in many ways. In political economy research, Taiwan stands out for its early orientation toward high-growth small firms. From the 1970s onward, the Taiwanese state increased its high-growth startup initiatives such as Hsinchu Park. Our research reveals that Taiwan has broadly remained consistent with a Mark I approach in the sense that it is focused on widening pools of entrepreneurship in emerging technologies. Startup policies do not conceive of the fledgling firms as resources for large firms. Dominant companies, like TSMC, have pursued their own open innovation strategies, though not in collaboration with the government, let alone as part of the startup policy mix. However, Taiwan's brand of startup capitalism does not align with a conventional understanding of Mark I, as startups are not creative destruction engines; instead of disruption, they are only construed as advancing emerging technologies.

Chapter 5 focuses on China as the last case study, given the later timing of its developmental advance and reflecting its position as distinct from the "classic" developmental states. The chapter establishes how China, from 1979 to 2000, exhibited antecedents of its assistance for startups as an alternative growth and employment mechanism. China's political economy has often been depicted as antithetical to the neoliberal United States, with the state marshaling resources into national champions operating in select sectors and critical technologies. However, we find that China's brand of startup capitalism began with and continues to be characterized as having noticeable contradictions consistent with versions of both Mark I and II patterns of innovation. In some ways, only Taiwan exhibits more characteristics that align most closely with Mark I in the sense that startups are not construed as resources for big businesses. Also, unlike policy makers in the other cases, those in China have demonstrated some willingness to threaten the oligopolistic positioning of giants such as Alibaba (Deng 2022).[10] In addition, the Ministry of Industry and Information Technology (MIIT), National Development and Reform Commission (NDRC), and other Chinese policy makers have mostly steered clear of closely involving incumbents, which is a signature of the open innovation–style Mark II tactics taken in Japan and Korea. Overall, the Chinese case experienced moves toward Mark I but remains a unique mix of the two modes.

The conclusion chapter first compares the four countries. Across the cases, there are movements toward the Mark I end of the spectrum but also degrees of path dependence. The earliest two startup capitalism cases—Japan and Korea—have mostly continued their Mark II developmental state approach that centers on big business largesse as a means of driving economic competitiveness and employment. The third case, Taiwan, in contrast, has mostly retained its version of a Mark I model in which policies aim to encourage a wide pool of startups in emerging technologies. Finally, we distill how China's evolution is again different from the others, as it combines elements of both modes. In China, startups are positioned as a means of competing at the frontier in critical technologies and as a provider of (mass) employment. While there is evidence of policy to support incumbents in critical technology areas, such as around the Semiconductor Manufacturing International Corporation (SMIC), its national champion technology firm, in other sectors, the Chinese case also resembles a pared-back version of a Mark I understanding of startup backing—widening entrepreneurial pools but not necessarily disrupting markets.

The conclusion then brings these insights back to the developmental state dead-or-alive debate. Developmental states were defined according to their dedication to upgrading industrial capacity, fostering firm relations, and providing necessary access to finance. In this respect, we argue that developmental states persist, as startup capitalism can take the form of an open innovation paradigm, with start-ups enabling big businesses' innovation capabilities. Developmental states, even when using the language of Silicon Valley ambitions, can still be essential enablers for established firms, which continue to serve a crucial socioeconomic role. Thus, startup capitalism does not constitute the death of the developmental state but an open innovation version of Mark II.

We show that startup capitalism has varieties and, as such, can approximate *both* opposing ideal types of VoC: LME and CME. The LME version is more consistent with creative destructive logic, in which new entrants are viewed as crucial growth engines. However, we argue that comparative capitalism and entrepreneurial state research often assume that this Mark I variant is *the* rationale and aim, and so evidence of it has shown an inevitable convergence on a Silicon Valley–styled LME. We contend that startup capitalism can also comprise open innovation approaches in which public policy strives to benefit both incumbents and startups by fostering their interactions, which necessarily subverts creative destruction. This Mark II variant aligns with CME logics in terms of close large-firm relations and relatively permanent or inflexible labor markets. Thus, the persistence of a CME-styled variety of startup capitalism suggests that rather than convergence on the Anglo-American LME occurring, different models persist.

Finally, we close the book by returning to our opening question: Are startup policies clearly designed to foster either creative destruction or oligopolistic leadership of innovation? We argue that startup capitalism does not align with either ideal type and that the pursuit of hybrid logics could help explain declining business dynamism in the twenty-first century. We reveal the implications of governments engaging startups as resources, not (only) disruptors. We underscore why policies often posit startups are enabling the growth and survival of East Asia's large firms that must compete with American and European rivals. Finally, we weigh in on how the open innovation version of startup capitalism challenges the Silicon Valley approach and may be allowing East Asia to be at the forefront of the global technology competition.

ANALYTICAL FRAMEWORK

Our analytical framework enables the study of institutions and their change over time. Our point of departure from existing political economy approaches is our conceptualization of market institutions in the context of Schumpeterian patterns of innovation. Institutions are the "rules of the game" and "constraints on human behavior" (North 1990; Rodrik et al. 2002; Acemoglu et al. 2021, 365).

We distill two bodies of scholarship to identify the institutions central to our analytical framework. The first of these is comparative capitalism—specifically, VoC—which focuses on institutional complementarities across finance, labor, firm relations, and modes of innovation (Hall and Soskice 2001). The two main varieties are the LME and CME that comprise distinct combinations of institutions. The LME variety has equity-based finance, fluid, generalist labor markets, and arm's-length firm relations and, as a result, excels in radical innovation. The CME, in contrast, draws on debt-based financing, specialized employment, and close firm relations and, owing to these complementary elements, shines in incremental innovation. In addition to the LME and CME types, scholars debate the extent to which there are regional variations.[1] Second, we draw on the developmental state literature that depicts a strong state centered on the bolstering of catch-up technological capabilities, access to long-term debt finance, and permanent employment (Woo-Cumings 1999; Kohli 2004).[2] The formula is centered on state-labor-society coalescing around an export-led model in which growing firms are the engines and, in exchange for state assistance, welfare providers.

Based on the institutions delineated in VoC and developmental state research, our analytical approach focuses on five institutional components: (1) the size of firms expected to drive this innovation capability at the technological frontier; (2) labor markets in terms of their fluidity or permanent employment characteristics; (3) sources of finance for innovation, spanning (main) banks distributing lines of credit to capital markets that issue equity; (4) the type of innovation sought, from incremental, catch-up technologies toward radical innovation at the technological frontier; and (5) the domestic and external social purposes underpinning efforts.

We extend historical institutionalist tools, developed by James Mahoney and Kathleen Thelen (2010) and Daron Acemoglu and James Robinson (2006), to assess *how much* change has occurred. Change is conceptualized as a continuum, ranging from no change, to "strategic stability," to change that is path dependent (Acemoglu et al. 2021). Ideational and organizational institutions are expected to be relatively "sticky," while change at the level of the instrument is common (see Hall 1993 and Lenschow et al. 2005 for more). Like Elizabeth Thurbon (2016), we allow for contingency at the policy and institutional levels, expecting specific instruments and institutional configurations to naturally change over time. We also draw on the developmental state's approach to studying institutional change.[3] While some speak of change in extreme terms—either dead or alive (Wade 2018)—many scholars conceptualize degrees of change. This includes the developmental state as adaptive (Wong 2004), declining (Pirie 2008), degraded (Hundt 2014), disembedded (Carroll and Jarvis 2017), evolving (Koh 1997; Dent 2003; Stubbs 2012), in its last stage (Kalinowski 2008), and transformed (Lim 2010). Researchers have also conceptualized change as "institutional layering" to depict ways in which new activities are grafted onto long-established institutions (Debanes 2017).

To evaluate the degree of continuity or change in each country, we conceptualize the transitions between two ideal types of startup capitalism. These ideal types are based on our linking of VoC and developmental state institutions with Schumpeterian framing of Mark I and II patterns of innovation. The first is the startup-centric Mark I variant, which is most akin to VoC's LME type and most distinct from the classic developmental state. According to the economic logic of Joseph Schumpeter (1942) and then Philippe Aghion and Peter Howitt (1992), Mark I centers on the process of creative destruction, a means of constant renewal in which new entrants disrupt the positions of established firms and their corresponding technologies. The second type is an open innovation variety of what is conventionally depicted as Mark II, which emphasizes oligopolies as central innovation actors and is more akin to a CME and quintessential developmental state. The open innovation variety of Mark II still conceives of oligopolistic firms as central innovation agents. But whereas oligopolies conducted their activities, especially R&D, in-house in Schumpeter's Mark II, established firms in the twenty-first century leverage external resources, including startups. In this variant, startups help incumbent firms access new ideas and emerging technologies, which big businesses then leverage to bolster their innovation capacity and competitive positioning.

The Mark I and II types are depicted in terms of the size of firms central to innovation and then their complementarities, which include the equity or debt nature of financing, employment as flexible or permanent, and innovation as radical or incremental. Extending logic from developmental state scholarship on the social purpose of innovation, we conceive of the social purpose encompassing domestic priorities, such as employment, economic growth, and social inclusion, as well as externally focused challenges, primarily the national security imperative associated with technological competitiveness.

Figure 1.1 synthesizes the five institutional attributes of the two ideal types on a radar chart. Each of the five institutional areas is depicted on a 0 to 5 scale. The extremes of the scale—0 and 5—correspond to complete dominance or absence, respectively. The size of firms central to innovation see a score of 0 in command economies in which only dominant firms operate and a score of 5 when there are only startups in the market. Similarly, for financing, a score of 0 implies that no equity funding is available, whereas a score of 5 corresponds to only equity investments with no provisions of debt in the financing of innovation.

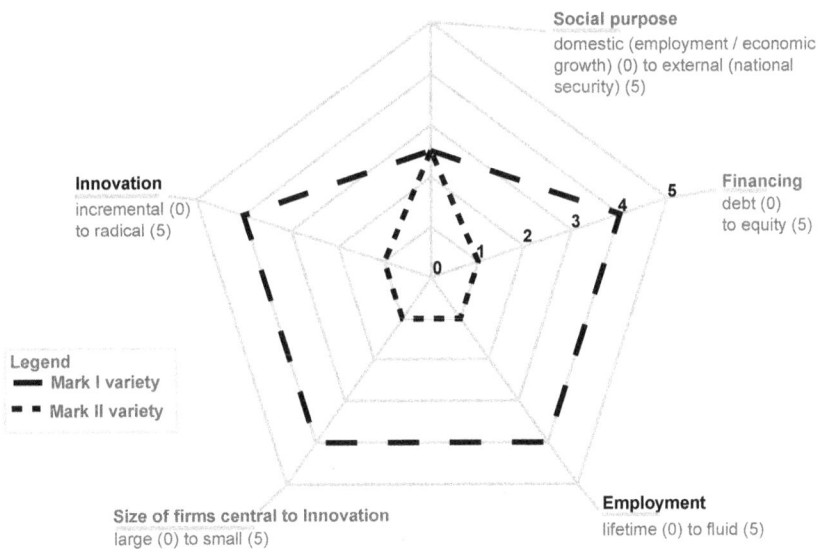

FIGURE 1.1. Startup capitalism: Mark I and II varieties

The Mark I and II varieties—as dotted and dashed lines, respectively—are visualized on this radar chart. The developmental state and CME are depicted as primarily comprising incremental innovation, debt financing, lifetime employment, and large firms being central. As such, the Mark II type scores close to 1 for most attributes. Mark I attributes are closer to the 5-point end of the scales. As such, the Mark I variety is scored as a 4 in terms of radical innovation, equity financing, fluid employment markets, and startups essential to innovation. Figure 1.1 also illustrates the social purpose ranging from domestic to external factors. The score of 3 reveals the expectation that both the Mark I and II varieties are motivated by a blend of external and domestic motivations.

Instead of viewing the rise of startup promotion as an inevitable departure from the developmental past, we investigate shifts in terms of this scale. Certainly, no country is expected to fully fall into the Mark I or II ideal types. This categorization allows us to analyze the extent to which the developmental state is dead or alive by presenting a benchmark against which to analyze the institutional change underpinning the rise of startup capitalism.

Firm Size

Mainstream accounts of the developmental state's phenomenal economic success center on the essential role of large firms in innovation activities (Johnson 1982; Woo-Cumings 1999). The state–big business relations formed the backbone of technological upgrading that was essential to development, and the lead companies were also crucial providers of high-quality, permanent employment that generated social stability. Historically, in China, Japan, and Korea, catch-up technology capabilities were often expected to come from the lead companies because small firms were less productive and less technologically savvy (Kim 2012; Vogel 2018). In Japan, large firms comprised conglomerates—the horizontally integrated keiretsu or the vertically linked pre–World War II zaibatsu (think Mitsubishi and Sumitomo). Astute readers will think of the consortia that the Ministry of International Trade and Industry (MITI) organized to advance semiconductor, then supercomputer and machine-learning capacity from the mid-1970s. These R&D consortia consisted of major electronics firms such as Fujitsu, NEC, and others (Callon 1995). In a similar way, in Korea, the chaebol were construed as central to technological upgrading and employment and were afforded government assistance accordingly (Amsden 1989; Kalinowski 2008).

This big business–centric developmental state model, which best corresponds to Japan and Korea, is akin to Schumpeter's Mark II. This mode emphasizes oligopolistic firms as essential innovators and focuses on "the industrial R&D laboratory for technological innovation and the key role of large firms" (Malerba and Orsenigo 1995, 47). Monopoly power, which enables access to finance and human capital, endows incumbents with superior innovation prowess (Nelson and Winter 1982; Malerba and Orsenigo 1996).

Analysis of the developmental state in the twenty-first century continues to emphasize the centrality of big businesses. Henry Yeung (2014) maintains that East Asian governments seek to work more closely with their respective country's most internationalized firms. In the case of China, Richard Appelbaum and coauthors (2011), Erik Baark (2016), and EunYoung Cho (2021) concur that the state seeks to work with established firms to foster cutting-edge innovation, especially in critical technologies such as semiconductors. Meanwhile, Joe Wong (2011) suggests that the alleged failure of East Asian developmental states in fostering a world-leading biotech sector—despite decades of investment—can at least partially be attributed to a limited focus on big companies.

In international business and strategy research, however, scholars contend that structural shifts in the global economy have changed the way large firms innovate. Big businesses, under the guise of open innovation, increasingly draw on external resources such as startups, R&D support, universities, and public institutes (Heurgo and Moreno 2017; Dahlander et al. 2021). Open innovation, as a concept, was established in a *Harvard Business Review* book by Henry Chesbrough (2003). In *Open Innovation*, Chesbrough refers to the dynamics whereby firms increasingly rely on external resources and logics to innovate. Changes in the techno-industrial paradigm in the second half of the twentieth century have meant that firms need to engage external resources rather than rely on in-house R&D. Incumbents can harness ideas from startups through partnerships with them, by promoting startup ecosystems, and through investment and acquisition (Chesbrough et al. 2014). The means of engagement with external organizations range from acquiring and sourcing (inbound innovation) to selling and revealing (outbound innovation) (Dahlander and Gann 2010, 700).

Given this proliferation of open innovation, we conceptualize contemporary Mark II as emphasizing big businesses whose capabilities benefit from interactions with startups. In this respect, startup capitalism sees startups infused into incumbent-led innovation systems.[4] State championing of open innovation strives for the deepening of established firms' capabilities. For this reason, the Mark II variation is given a score of 1 in figure 1.1. Open innovation, like conventional Mark II understandings, perceives of large firms as the key drivers of transformative advances. However, their prowess now depends on the involvement of startups to boost their innovation capacity.

The other ideal type of startup capitalism, a variety of Mark I, focuses on new entrants. New entrants—what we today call startups—offer strong innovation potential and create opportunities through creative destruction (Schumpeter 1934) by challenging incumbent firms and technologies. This creative destruction dynamic is an essential driver of economic growth and innovation (Fontana et al. 2021; Akcigit and Van Reenen 2023). Creative destruction is said to set "the stage for a permanent conflict between the old and the new," necessarily involving established firms to "perpetually attempt to block or delay the entry of new competitors in their sectors" (Aghion et al. 2021, 5). Startups pose an existential threat to incumbents; this threat, according to Schumpeter, is the mechanism by which new entrants bring systemic value.

The startup capitalism version of Mark I is given a 4 for the size of firms central to innovation in figure 1.1. This is because policies encourage new entrants rather than the entrenchment of big businesses, but policies do not explicitly aim to disrupt big firms. Taiwan is the salient example here, given its long-standing emphasis on small firms (then called SMEs) as essential innovators and disruptors to world technology markets.[5] The thrust of these policies is on new and different entrepreneurial pools. Conflict between incumbents and new firms—the central tenet of creative destruction—is absent.

We analyze the size of targeted firms by assessing the nature of how both big businesses and startups are included in policies. Efforts that focus on startups as beneficiaries and strive to boost their high-growth potential align with the variety of Mark I. Initiatives that involve big businesses as partners, judges, and investors may augur for a Mark II pattern, because the initiative may seek mutual benefit. Startup policies may implicitly—and even sometimes explicitly—say that oligopolistic firms are core engines of innovation and economic growth and should thus benefit from the ideas, talent, and technologies that startups can offer. For instance, in 2020, Japan's Cabinet Office worked with regional governments to establish the Startup Ecosystem Consortium, bringing startups and keiretsu together in a bid to boost each city's existing innovation capacity (Osaka Innovation Hub 2020).

Initiatives include coordinating an open innovation system with startups as a crucial resource to drive incumbent-led innovation. In addition, big businesses are enlisted by governments to provide mentoring, funding, exit options, and more to startups. In exchange, the incumbent firms seek to benefit from the infusion of startup mindsets, practices, and technologies. For instance, similar to the CCEI quote we opened the book with, in a fieldwork interview, a science and technology (S&T) policy adviser to the Presidential Office in Korea explained that startups are essential to "bring new blood to *chaebol* DNA" (Klingler-Vidra and Pacheco Pardo 2020: 346). Thus, we study the size of firms central to innovation by exploring the extent to which startup policies ultimately aim to boost startups in their bid to deliver creative destruction (Mark I) or the capabilities of big businesses (Mark II).

Employment

We examine employment in innovative sectors as a continuum from rigid to fluid labor markets. Employment contracts affect the extent to which labor is funneled toward permanent employment at established firms fosters an environment in which it is typical to make career movements across firms and thus encourage entrepreneurship. In the classic developmental era, large firms provided society with high-quality, lifetime employment. The state, then, did not need to provide a direct social welfare system because its backing of big businesses fostered a workfare system. Across the region, the social safety net comprised the provision of jobs from big internationally competitive exporting firms supported by the state (Choe 1998; Vogel 2018). In fact, unemployment insurance was only introduced in Korea in 1996.

In many ways, this developmental state depiction is akin to Mark II labor markets, which involve incentives for talent to join and then remain at incumbent firms. Employment policy prioritizes job retention and protection in times of crisis. Pension-fund regulations in the form of nonportable pensions encourage permanent employment and, relatedly, discourage midcareer movement (Dore 1986). Nonportable pensions refer to regulations in which a worker who leaves a firm forfeits their accumulated pension fund savings (Calder 1990, 2017). Nonportable pensions reinforced the lifelong employment nature of the Japanese and Korean systems (Zeitlin and Herrigel 2000; Jackson 2003; Schoppa 2006). These policies align with a conventional understanding of the Mark II mode of innovation because employee retention contributes to an "accumulated stock of knowledge in specific technological areas" among the large firms' "researchers, technicians, and engineers" (Malerba and Orsenigo 1995, 47). Mark II employment institutions, in the context of twenty-first-century open innovation, can offer mechanisms for longtime employees to gain experience in other settings. Notably, secondments—when employees spend a period working for an external firm, including a startup or research lab—can help established firms' employees gain access to ideas without the risk of leaving their job. In figure 1.1, the labor market character for the Mark II mode is scored with a 1, reflecting this orientation toward lifetime employment.

In contrast, the Mark I mode leans toward fluid labor markets in which employees can make career moves and pursue business ventures. As such, the Mark I ideal type is represented with a score of 4 in figure 1.1. Employment in the Mark I type consists of policies that encourage the widening of entrepreneurial pools, resulting in the creation of new firms and jobs. This includes efforts to encourage antecedent conditions for startups, including "mitigating the obstacles faced by entrepreneurs when starting new firms" (Audretsch et al. 2020, 1).

Policies that reverse pension-fund portability boost fluidity. Entrepreneurship tax incentives are another instrument that can help widen the pool of would-be founders (Rigby and Ramlogan 2013). Tax incentives for startups can impact the size of the entrepreneurial pool, because the establishment and growth of new businesses depend "strongly on the fiscal environment that a country provides" (European Venture Capital Association 2013, 10).[6]

Another means of employment-themed intervention is the provision of entrepreneurship training and incentives to attract startup talent. Entrepreneurship skills training includes idea generation, business plan writing, product development, and fundraising competencies. Entrepreneurship education can be offered directly through a variety of government agencies and can also be delivered via partnerships with intermediaries.[7] Accelerators and incubators can provide for direct management of the programs by civil servants or teams assembled by government or through the procurement of a private company, such as 500 Startups, Plug and Play, Techstars, or Y Combinator, to manage the program. Entrepreneurs, armed with skills to establish and scale their business, are more likely to start up. Similarly, bankruptcy reforms can allow business owners to close failing ventures, which can aid labor market flexibility as would-be founders are both more likely to take an entrepreneurial risk in the first place (because they know they can wind it down without damaging their personal finances) and more able to walk away from unproductive activities (e.g., zombie firms).

Relatedly, Mark I policies, from a fluid employment perspective, can strive to encourage the immigration of talented professionals and entrepreneurs as another mechanism for widening the pool of startups. Japan's X-Hub inbound program, run by JETRO and the Tokyo Metropolitan Government, hosts cohorts of international startups in Tokyo to do just this. In a similar way, the Start-Up Chile program, created in 2010 by the Commerce Ministry, offers a well-known model of programs designed to attract foreign entrepreneurial talent (Gonzalez-Uribe and Leatherbee 2018). Changes to immigrant regulations can also make it easier for foreign talent to change jobs—increasing flexibility in the labor market and helping to de-risk their entrepreneurial venture. Japan, for instance, now allows foreign trainees on a technical program to change jobs within the same sector after one year of immigrating (Yuasa 2023).

Finance

We analyze whether funding for innovation prioritizes equity or debt instruments. This debt/equity binary is consistent with developmental state research, which portrays the state as providing credit to fuel growth and R&D (Amsden

1989). In comparative capitalism scholarship, CMEs are depicted as debt-centric financing systems that offer patient capital, enabling incremental innovation.[8] LMEs, in contrast, rely on equity-based capital markets to finance high-risk, high-reward, innovations. The equity-based financial system is construed as boosting the creation and scaling up of startups. Comparative capitalism scholarship conceptualizes this relationship between high-functioning stock market–based capitalist systems and the advance of radical innovation, as the equity markets provide both finance and pressure to outperform. Equity-based financing does not require regular repayments, which is an attractive attribute given the (often negative) cash flow realities of fledgling firms.

The intuition of the debt-based CME and equity-focused LME is that the financial systems are complementary to the other institutional arenas (e.g., employment) and thus enable their distinct advantages in incremental (CME) and radical (LME) innovation. We conceive that these financial systems broadly, although not perfectly, align with our startup capitalism understanding of the Mark I and II types. In figure 1.1, Mark I is represented with a score of 4, reflecting its equity focus, while Mark II is scored at 1 to illustrate the centrality of debt.

In the Mark II variety, the expectation is that preferential access to credit is essential to large firms' innovation activities. Intense pressure to perform, at least on a quarterly (equity) earnings basis, augurs for radical innovation, whereas long-term access to credit suggests innovation on a more incremental basis. In the classic developmental state model, state credit was the staple means of financing big businesses' activities. Such credit could take the form of loans for product development as well as working capital lines. In the archetypal Japanese case, the state would coordinate consortia and work with main banks to offer the keiretsu steady credit lines (Johnson 1982; Pempel 1998). This aligns with depictions of CME contexts in which patient capital is provided by main banks for firms' R&D and product or geographic expansion. The result is that established firms excel in incremental innovation.

In contrast, the role of the state in encouraging Mark I–styled finance approaches involve shaping equity markets in which investors buy shares in high-growth companies. By enabling a range of stock markets, the state provides critical exit venues for high-growth innovative startups (Gilson and Black 1998). The launching of a Nasdaq-like technology stock market that is friendly to startups in terms of the number of years in which operating profits are required before the company can list and the assurance that paperwork requirements for listed firms are simple would indicate a stock market–focused effort to bolster startups' growth. Allowing a second-tier listing scheme helps avail startups' access to a major exit opportunity.[9]

Private equity, in the form of venture capital (VC), is central to the availing of equity financing for startup-centric settings. VC comprises investments in young, high-growth, and often high-technology firms in exchange for equity stakes in the company. Colin Crouch (2005) asserts that VCs maintain close relationships to monitor firm performance, which is distinct from the traditionally arm's-length nature of stock market investing in LMEs. In a similar way, John Zysman (1983, 64) asserts that VCs are akin to German universal banks in their closeness and patience. The thrust of VCs' hybrid features emanates from their serving as smart money (Lerner and Nanda 2020; Mallaby 2022), meaning the financiers bring operational expertise, professional networks, and technical insights that help founders navigate the multitude of product and operational uncertainties encountered when building their businesses. VCs work closely with the startups in which they invest, as they (can) receive board seats and various voting rights (e.g., veto rights) (Alemany and Andreoli 2018).

It is interesting to note that as VC markets have developed in different countries, they have taken on varied characteristics. In some settings, they have manifested as equity-based investments in very early-stage, high-risk technology businesses, which gives them more of a LME flavor, whereas in others, they have sometimes been disseminated as a combination of credit and equity offered for more mature businesses (see Ahlstrom and Bruton 2006). For these reasons, comparative capitalism scholarship conceives of VC as a hybrid form of financing. For us, its provision sits squarely within Mark I, given that the investment target is a startup—not a big company—and because of the emphasis on large-scale growth.

Another Mark I–oriented approach is the use of limited partnership (LP) legal structures. LP fund structures incentivize risk-taking, since the investors' personal assets are not held as collateral. With the LP structure, investors in VC funds are only liable to lose the capital they have invested, not their personal assets. Regulations around the issuance of preferred stock is also a helpful feature in enabling VCs to have economic and control rights, such as veto and voting rights, that allow them to mitigate risk while maximizing their potential return (Feld and Mendelson 2013).

In a related way, startup capitalism's Mark I–styled approaches involve boosting cohorts of early-stage equity-based investors, such as angels and VCs, through direct investments in high-potential entrepreneurs. Government efforts to grow VC markets range from funding a set of professional investors to more surgically striving to grow the volume of VC in a specific investment stage (Da Rin et al. 2005; Alperovych et al. 2020; Bai et al. 2022). To fund a domestic VC market, the state forms funds of VC funds, whose investment mandate is to invest in several privately managed VC funds (Klingler-Vidra 2018). These VC funds then each go on to invest in portfolios of startups. There are many examples of funds of VC funds across the globe, with the touchstone version being Israel's Yozma fund, which was created in 1993 by the Office of the Chief Scientist to foster a professional domestic cohort of Israeli VCs (Avnimelech and Teubal 2006). Through the Yozma fund, Israel created a bench of local VCs that startups could raise early-stage equity financing from before trying to raise funding from US venture capitalists and, ultimately, list on Nasdaq.

The relative mix of debt and equity becomes essential to assessing how this institutional logic contributes to the nature of innovation. As such, we examine the ways in which policy engages with debt and equity financing for startups and big businesses.

Innovation

In Schumpeterian industry life-cycle terms, radical innovation occurs in the Mark I variety.[10] "When technology is changing very rapidly, uncertainty is very high and barriers to entry very low, new firms are the major innovators" (Malerba and Orsenigo 1995, 48). In contrast, the Mark II context is characterized as a time when an industry has developed, there are "well-defined trajectories, economies of scale," and "financial resources become important in the competitive process and large firms with monopolistic power come to the forefront" (Malerba and Orsenigo 1995, 48).

Bringing developmental state trajectories, comparative capitalism, and Schumpeterian economics together, we posit that the classic developmental state period best aligns with the conventionally understood Mark II mode, as big businesses were leading incremental advances, especially in manufacturing and established technologies. Reflecting this emphasis on incremental innovation, Mark II is scored with a 1 in figure 1.1. In contrast, Mark I is aligned with radical innovation and is thus illustrated as a 4 on the continuum. It is in these radical innovation settings that startups are essential to innovation, as they challenge the existing technological paradigm and threaten to disrupt the position of incumbents.

The developmental state model centered on incremental innovation, as it centered on adopting foreign technologies and subsequently producing them locally at a lower cost. It started with labor-intensive light industries, such as textiles, garments, and footwear; continued with capital-intensive industries, including steel, petrochemical, shipbuilding, or car making; then followed with higher-value-added, technologically more complex industries such as electronics or semiconductors. As capabilities advanced, governments across East Asia were unafraid to invest in new sectors, attempt to pick winning sectors (Aoki et al. 1998), and boost domestic capacity in critical technologies. This was already seen in the 1970s, with Japan's MITI supercomputer consortium (Callon 1995). MITI's boost of semiconductor prowess for Japanese firms in the 1970s was motivated by a desire to match what Japanese businessmen had seen at IBM and Bell Telephone Laboratories (now known as Bell Labs) while visiting the United States (Anchordoguy 1989).

By the 1990s in Japan, subsequently in Korea and Taiwan, and then later in China, the catch-up ambitions of innovation policy shifted toward competing at the technological frontier (Lee 2019). In comparative capitalism terminology, this shift can be understood as moving from incremental innovation, in which process advances were *the* primary value added, toward radical innovation, in which the aim is to develop new, disruptive technologies (Taylor 2004). The policies used to boost prowess in the context of the incremental innovation phase emphasized securing access to foreign technologies and then championing local firms capable of producing along those lines. Innovation policy making at the technological frontier instead emphasized the development of novel products and services that had not previously existed. This required new ways of thinking; more creativity and greater risk-taking were needed than they were for process-based advances.

The four countries analyzed in this book—Japan, Korea, Taiwan, and China—now compete at the frontier across several critical technologies. Firms from these countries are at the cutting edge of sectors such as electric batteries, electric vehicles, green shipping, renewable energies, robots, and famously, semiconductors. Therefore, their innovation approach has had to move away from the catch-up mentality of previous decades. As a result, radical innovation is not a policy option anymore; it is a necessity. Without radical innovation, these four East Asian countries cannot compete against themselves or against other innovation powerhouses such as Germany, Israel, Sweden, Switzerland, or the United States. Perhaps the best known of these world-leading technology ambitions is the Made in China 2025 initiative, which explicitly named being the best in the world in specific technologies as its objective. As of 2024, evidence suggests success in some of these verticals, with China being the world's largest electric vehicle exporter (*Economist* 2024b).

Social Purpose

The last institutional arena we examine is social purpose in terms of a continuum of domestic and external aims. We define *social purpose* as "the social aim of policy efforts, which is rooted in substantive (input) and performance (output) legitimacy" (Klingler-Vidra and Pacheco Pardo 2020, 337).[11] East Asian policy making has been predicated on variants of a clear social purpose in which the government propels economic prowess as a means of providing economic growth, shared prosperity and stability, and national security. At the highest level, social purpose involves the state providing stewardship over the economy and security and, in return, the corporate sector providing well-paid, stable jobs. The dual purpose of domestic and external aims has been documented. For example, Elizabeth Thurbon and Linda Weiss (2006, 2) assert that the Korean government's primary goal in the postwar era was to "promote rapid industrialization for national security and domestic legitimacy purposes."

Domestically, the developmental state social purposes comprised economic and technological advances that enabled various improvements in terms of the quality of work, housing, and infrastructure. Even though the goal of the state was not to create jobs directly, its social purpose included creating the conditions for (high-quality) job opportunities to grow. For example, Chisung Park and co-authors (2015, 320) argue that historically—especially prior to democratization—the Korean regime "tried to secure its legitimacy by ensuring output-oriented effectiveness . . . [Strong] economic development was essential for output-oriented legitimacy." In a similar way, Richard Whitley (1992, 112) explains that the Korean ruling elite's legitimacy claims were symbolic, as "the general identification of leadership [was] with moral authority"; the source of legitimacy changed from 1961 onward, as "state legitimacy rests significantly upon rapid economic development."

External concerns focus on the ways in which economic competitiveness and capabilities in critical technologies foster security against external threats. A country's ability to compete in key technologies in international markets is a long-recognized social purpose for innovation policy (Stubbs 2009; Weiss 2014; Taylor 2016). Tai Ming Cheung (2022), for instance, conceives of China's innovation policies as being fundamentally motivated by "techno-security." Gerard Roland (2023, 521) gives the example of the launch of the Sputnik satellite in 1957, which saw the "more than tripling of the National Science Foundation budget" in the US bid to overcome the Soviet system in the space race. Capabilities in critical technologies include semiconductors, which are identified as essential to national security and thus a basis for contemporary policy making (Samuels 2008, 2019; Klingler-Vidra and Kuo 2021; Huang 2023).

This link between technological competition and national security—called *economic statecraft* (Aggarwal and Reddie 2021; Thurbon and Weiss 2021)—is increasingly ubiquitous in motivating startup efforts in the twenty-first century. Particularly salient to the nexus between economic and national security, the United States and the European Union both adopted chips acts—the United States in 2022 and the European Union in 2023—indicating their dedication to advancing domestic semiconductor chip capabilities. The EU Chips Act states that dependency on a small number of international actors poses an important challenge in the critical technology of semiconductors; accordingly, the act aims to strengthen European design and manufacturing capabilities through several levers, including largesse for startups and scale-ups. These interventions are presented in terms of enabling economic growth, job creation, and national security.

Given this expectation that startup policies are motivated by a convergence of domestic and external purposes, we examine degrees of continuity and change in the stated objectives articulated when startup policies are launched. To do so, we analyze objectives as laid out in statements by senior policy makers and politicians as well as in official government outlets. We assess how the policies are motivated—whether they are intended to affect domestic (employment, economic growth, and social inclusion) or external (national competitiveness and, by extension, national security) aims. Our expectation, in terms of this mapping onto the Mark I and II startup capitalism types, is that both varieties comprise a combination of domestic and external social purposes. This expectation is reflected in the fact that both types are scored as 3 in figure 1.1. Our point is that the prioritization of technological capabilities for national security purposes does not fundamentally align with *only* startups fueling creative destruction (Mark I) or enabling big business (Mark II). The dual purpose of domestic and national security imperatives can instigate either or both modes of innovation.

Plan for the Case Studies

This book adopts an institutionalist approach to analyze startup capitalism, questioning whether governments view startups as disruptive innovators or essential resources for big companies. We explore policies in Japan, Korea, Taiwan, and China, drawing on VoC and developmental state literature to identify how key economic policy-making paradigms change over time. This chapter develops our analytical framework for studying the continuity and change underpinning East Asian states' startup capitalism, in accordance with Schumpeter's Mark I and II typologies. In it, we conceive of five institutional arenas to study: (1) firm size; (2) employment; (3) finance; (4) innovation; and (5) social purpose. We explore each of these institutional areas across the startup capitalism varieties of Mark I and II. This helps us understand how startup policies strive to deliver entrepreneurial pool-widening aims (Mark I) or large firm–led advances (Mark II).

The application of the institutional framework helps us to identify degrees of continuity and change, particularly with respect to the ways in which each state's developmental state model persists. Ultimately, we examine the extent to which institutional change augurs for disruptive startups or the fostering of established firms' capabilities. This approach offers an updated understanding of the big business–centered developmental state and a challenge to the presumption that the entrepreneurial state is distinct. We evaluate the boundaries between industrial policy and economic statecraft in the lens of startup capitalism by exploring external (e.g., national security) and internal (e.g., economic growth and job creation) social purposes underpinning startup capitalism.

2

JAPAN

At a September 2022 speech at the New York Stock Exchange, Prime Minister Fumio Kishida emphasized that his government "place[s] particular emphasis on startups" (METI 2024). This follows initiatives to help develop unicorns as part of Japan's vibrant and globally linked startup ecosystem. Notably, in 2018, Hiroshige Seko, Minister of Economy, Trade, and Industry launched the J-Startup program, which would foster a cohort of 20 unicorns and promote the overseas development of Japan's startups (Ikeda 2018). The Ministry of Economy, Trade, and Industry (METI)—the contemporary version of the MITI that is credited with steering the country's postwar economic miracle—created the J-Startup initiative in order to "encourage society overall to cultivate entrepreneurship, a mindset motivating people to establish a company and take on new business" (METI 2018). There is a twist, though. Startup promotion, as explained at the Tokyo launch, is a means to an end; startups are vehicles for boosting creative talent and high-tech innovation capacity to aid the continued competitiveness of Japan Inc.

Since 2021, Japan's promotion of startups, which first began in the early 1990s, has been construed as part of the new capitalism that strives to graft startup-centric innovation onto Japan's existing economy. In 2022, the Kishida administration even announced the creation of a cabinet post to promote startups across ministries and agencies as part of this new capitalism push (Takeuchi 2022). Already in the 1990s, Japan's attempt at reinvention (Schaede 2020) and a profound transition toward techno-preneurship (Whittaker 2001) were underway, which augured for a move away from its Mark II orientation. But it was only after Japan's first unicorn was born in 2018 that startup capitalism takes center stage. While the increasing prioritization given to startup promotion may suggest a clear trend toward Mark I logic, in Japan's new capitalism, big businesses are not to be dethroned but rather are to act as crucial partners. In many respects, incumbents are involved as beneficiaries of the innovation prowess—particularly the power to integrate information technologies—that startups generate. Thus, Japan's invoking of startup capitalism, as this chapter reveals, retains significant alignment with its Mark II antecedents in which large firms (its keiretsu) are essential innovators.

Creative destruction is not the dominant logic. In fact, Japan's big businesses encourage new entrants to innovate and engage with them. This constructive engagement was well evidenced in 2022, when the Keidanren, Japan's Business Federation, announced their aim for Japan to "become home to 100 unlisted startups worth $1 billion or more by 2027" (Sugihara 2022). If the keiretsu that make up the Keidanren feared creative destruction, they would certainly not ask for government help to create a hundred unicorns; they instead see startups as resources to aid their competitiveness. As another example of this symbiotic mantra, in April 2023, the vice chairperson of the Keidanren made the case for globally minded startups and the necessity of attracting foreign talent to Japan to help boost the startup ecosystem (Nagata 2023).

This chapter examines the extent to which Japan's startup capitalism mode suggests continuity with its Mark II–consistent developmental state model or whether Japan's startup promotion involves a significant shift toward the creative destruction-centric Mark I mode.

Japan is an interesting case to begin with, as political economy literature offers a widespread—though contested—depiction of "Japan Inc." as an archetypal CME centering on conglomerates gaining access to long-term credit and steadied by a system of permanent employment (Aoki et al. 2007).[1] The model became enshrined in political economy doctrine by developmental state scholars such as Chalmers Johnson's (1982) account of MITI's role in partnering with keiretsu and main banks to orchestrate Japan's postwar economic miracle.[2] Thus, Japan has been construed as the quintessential relational market economy (Keller and Samuels 2003). There has also been analysis of the Japanese government's efforts to "facilitate venture formation and venture capital, and public campaigns to foster entrepreneurial spirit," among other boosts to innovation capacity since the 1990s (Vogel 2018, 106).

Therefore, there is a case for exploring how and why startup initiatives may intend to benefit rather than challenge established firms. We analyze how Japan's postwar institutions, including forced savings and conglomerate coordination, have incorporated startup-centric innovation. As the chapter reveals, these so-called developmental state strategies—even the use of public pension funding, famously a source of patient capital for the keiretsu—are now construed as a key funder of Japanese startups. Yet, the chapter reveals continuity in Mark II approaches, with the keiretsu and main banks remaining essential partners and even beneficiaries of startup capitalism. The shift reflects the embrace of open innovation logics, moving away from internal R&D and large-firm consortia toward the leveraging of startups for ideas and talent. Thus, Japan has adopted Mark I characteristics in terms of equity financing and flexible employment but shows continuity in the imperative of established firms as its essential innovators.

Antecedents: Japan (1948–1990)

The Japanese postwar model was "premised on the sustained success of large manufacturing firms" in export-led growth (Streeck and Yamamura 2003, 7). The interlocking keiretsu–main bank, permanent employment system ensured economic growth as well as equitable economic growth and social stability (Aoki and Patrick 1994; Dore 2000; Inagami 2001). In line with conventional Mark II characterizations, these self-reinforcing institutions limited "new entrants so as to preserve orderly competition that will keep incumbent firms alive" (Anchordoguy 2005, 64). Norms are said to have blunted "the process of creative destruction" in which "competition clears out firms that fail to adjust to change by adopting new technologies and organizational structures" (Anchordoguy 2005, 10).

Research was "performed in large corporate laboratories that focus on improvements of those technologies in which incremental learning trajectories promise considerable payoffs" (Kitschelt 1991, 482). This enabled competences in manufacturing and engineering, a Mark II context, rather than success in arenas that are highly complex and unpredictable and in which bold new configurations occur, wherein Mark I logics excel. This was because Japan Inc. based their production system on foreign patents and then long-term relational contracts with their affiliates to produce those patented products more efficiently (Gerlach 1992). In this way, Japan's postwar mode best aligns with the Mark II mode in the sense that big businesses led process-based advances in maturing industries.

The emphasis on large firm–led R&D was reinforced by a labor market characterized as providing lifetime employment. The permanent employment that firms offered came in "exchange for wage moderation and cooperation in raising productivity" (Vogel 2006, 16). Workers and managers were committed to one another, such that jobs were secure, but performance was based on seniority rather than (out)performance and with the understanding that wage reductions were desired over job losses (Holzhausen 2000). As Kathryn Ibata-Arens (2005, 1) explains, "incremental innovations are rewarded with incremental seniority-based wages eked out over decades of service." Regulations around pension fund portability reinforced the permanent employment system. Japan's pension funds were nonportable, meaning that a worker who left a firm forfeited their accumulated pension fund savings, as they could not take the savings with them (Schoppa 2006). This, unsurprisingly, encouraged lifetime employment, as employees waited until retirement to obtain their pension and so remained with the same company across their career.

With the keiretsu at the center of the coordinated model, finance was disbursed via main bank relationships, and preferential access to credit was afforded by the government. The keiretsu–main bank relations ensured that firms had access to finance to develop product lines internationally, as the banks extended credit lines even during hard times (Aoki and Dore 1994). The steady financing of the keiretsu encouraged *kaizen*, which amounted to steady process-based advances in production rather than disruptively new products. The public pension funds (*koteki nenkin*) were used by the government to "finance industrial development" (Park 2004, 549), and private pension funds (*shiteki nenkin*) were used by corporations "as patient capital for long-term investments" (Vogel 2006, 95).[3] The state-run predecessor to Japan Post Bank (which was privatized in 2007) also provided essential patient capital for postwar development by pooling together savings from post offices across the country (Calder 1990).

In the classic developmental state era, the innovation aim was one of catch-up technologies. Incremental innovation in the form of process-driven, manufacturing advances was central to the prowess of the keiretsu. These conglomerates were able to steadily advance technological capabilities due to other aspects of the model, notably the long-term employment of their staff and the availability of patient capital by way of the group's financial services component and forced pension savings (Jackson 2003). Already from the 1970s, though, the Japanese state was depicted as organizing consortia to move toward the technological frontier, including in personal computers, semiconductors, and supercomputing (Aoki et al. 1998; Callon 1995). The objective, by the end of the period, was increasingly to shape the technological frontier rather than compete in manufacturing established technologies. Japan's lead firms, working together and benefiting from the reinforcing finance and labor system, were expected to lead this upgrading.

Underpinning these reinforcing institutions, the social purpose was clear: the pursuit of equitable and stable economic growth (Garon 1997). Michael Lynskey and Seiichiro Yonekura (2001, 5) depict the role of the keiretsu in the mutually reinforcing social system as follows: "The keiretsu were at the center of a complex social contract between the government, banks, the corporate sector and the population. Government officials directed the banks to invest in certain sectors. The established companies provided lifetime employment for their staff, who then saved a proportion of their income in the banks." Forced savings provided a means of ensuring capital for the keiretsu and reinforced the system that strove for an "equal distribution of income and the minimization of risks to income and employment of wage earners" (Yamamura 2003, 139). Externally, the pursuit of competition in critical technologies was a measure of both high-tech development and national security (Kawashima 2005, 59). The state, particularly the MITI, underwrote the advance of technological catch-up toward the world frontier by encouraging R&D in the semiconductor industry from the 1960s and then supercomputers and machine learning/AI in the 1980s. As the economic miracle advanced, competing in these more radically innovative arenas became essential to the legitimacy of Japan Inc.

Thematic Analysis
Firm Size

In contrast to being hailed as essential motors of the postwar model, Japan's big businesses were named by some critics in the 1990s as inhibitors of innovation and the cause of unemployment. As part of the fallout, national and provincial governments made efforts to boost startup activities across Kobe, Kyoto, Osaka, Tokyo, and beyond (e.g., see Harris 2016; Fujisaki 2017; X-Hub TOKYO 2017; Osaka Innovation Hub 2020). In this context, efforts were implemented with the ambition of promoting new enterprises to revitalize national high-technology competitiveness. The Kobe City Government, for example, partnered with 500 Startups to establish an accelerator that would both boost local entrepreneurial activity and link the startups with large Japanese firms and banks as well as startup hubs around the world (author interview, Kobe, June 25, 2018).

In line with this litany of startup-themed plans, global media has increasingly covered Japanese startup efforts in positive terms. For instance, a June 2023 *TechCrunch* article asserted that "the Japanese government has also promised enthusiastic assistance to boost the startup ecosystem" (Park 2023). It was Kishida's December 2022 aim to increase annual startup investments by tenfold by 2027 that featured in the piece.

However, startup efforts have not come outside of the wishes of lead firms or main banks. Instead, the keiretsu have "lobbied the government for reforms that would expand their options" but not undermine their position (Vogel 2018, 87). To this end, Anis Uzzaman, founder and chief executive of Pegasus Tech Ventures, a VC fund active in Japan, noted that "large Japanese corporations have slowed down quite a bit" and that "the current government's initiative can help" as startups boost Japanese corporations' innovativeness (Park 2023).

Startups are often positioned in Japanese policy as a resource to fuel established firms' innovativeness. METI bureaucrats speak of the continued need to drive industrial revitalization, with an emphasis on encouraging startups alongside the keiretsu-led open innovation system (Kantei 2014). The innovation system was to shift from "one dominated by in-house R&D conducted at major corporations toward one based on networks among innovators by strengthening ties between university research laboratories and venture firms" (Vogel 2018, 107). In 2003, METI initiated a study to look at the potential for corporate spin-offs; finding that keiretsu spin-offs were more promising than independent new firms, METI wanted to encourage a venture movement that was embedded in the activities of the big companies (METI 2003). This finding helped substantiate initiatives that sought spin-offs that would have close engagement with the keiretsu rather than truly independent startups. Collectively, while attention on startups as innovation resources has proliferated in Japan, it continues to be embedded in existing interfirm relations. Said another way, startups serve oligopolistic competition (and thus Mark II prowess) rather than creative destruction dynamics.

In this open innovation spirit—but before the specific language of open innovation was coined in 2003—a series of cluster-building activities was implemented, as METI bureaucrats had closely studied Michael E. Porter's "Clusters and Competition" (Yamawaki 2002). Regional governments established incubation facilities that rented offices to startups and provided them with assistance in the form of financing, legal affairs, management, and technology development. The Innovative Cluster Plan and the Industrial Revitalization Corporation efforts epitomize METI's catchphrase of enabling "regional clustering" from 2000 (Vogel 2006, 86). The Cluster Plan and the Venture Laboratories initiative enable collaboration by providing research facilities located in universities with the aid of incumbents. Again, telling of the ambition of integrating with big businesses, once the METI's Organization for Small & Medium Enterprises and Regional Innovation (SMRJ) division, was set up in 2004, it launched the Business Startup Support Fund in which it invests alongside private (often corporate) VC funds (Seki 2008). Another illustration is the 2005 Program for Strengthening Functions of Organizations for Support of Local SMEs, which paired senior advisers to share their operational expertise with fledgling firms.

Since the concept of open innovation has proliferated, it has been used extensively in the Japanese approach. The Japan Open Innovation Council was established in 2015. In the years that followed, policy makers regularly named open innovation in their media engagements. For instance, at the Shibuya QWS Symposium in 2018, Tokyo Governor Yuriko Koike specified the aim of promoting open innovation, which constitutes linking together major corporations, financial institutions, foreign investors, investors, universities and venture companies.

In our own fieldwork, the open innovation lexicon was used in each interview. An example comes from an official at the Osaka City government, who explained that their aim is to: bring the innovation ecosystem together—that includes entrepreneurs, big companies, venture capitalists, angels, mentors, universities and government since we, the Osaka City government—*and the big companies*—believe in open innovation (authors' interview, Osaka, June 26, 2018).

White papers such as those on Open Innovation and the Venture Challenge 2020, published by the cabinet and several ministries, further reiterate the commitment of the Japanese government to fuel startups as part of the keiretsu-led open innovation system (METI 2020b). METI Minister Yoshiaki Ishii asserted that "rather than simply supporting startups," the aim is to incorporate "a mechanism to develop VCs and strengthen cooperation between large companies and startups to accelerate open innovation" (Newswitch 2018). Again, this points to the persistence of a big business–led paradigm and continued proximity to a Mark II paradigm.

METI's flagship startup program, the J-Startup Initiative, reiterated this approach when it was announced in June 2018 with the aim of helping to build twenty unicorns by 2023. The J-Startup Initiative is run in collaboration with the keiretsu leaders. METI and keiretsu representatives together select startups for the program (Ikeda 2018; Kuzina 2018).[4] What is more, METI's Takuya Fukumoto explained the long-term aim includes the keiretsu acquiring participating startups, since, "as an exit strategy for startups, there is the option of mergers and acquisitions by large corporations." Fukumoto added that "through the J-Startup initiative, I hope to increase collaboration between startups and large corporations" (*Forbes Japan* 2018). According to the *METI Journal*, the J-Startup Initiative collectively aimed to expand overseas, win government procurement bids and "create chances for them to establish relationships with executives of large companies" (*METI Journal* 2020).

METI partners with the Tokyo Stock Exchange to award Japanese companies for their startup collaborations to achieve digital transformation. For instance, Sumitomo was named one of METI's Noteworthy DX Transformation Companies in 2021 for its efforts to enhance its "global corporate venture capital (CVC) fields and by setting up an accelerator business in the hardware domain" (Sumitomo Corporation 2021). This all bodes for startups as firms operating within an industrial setting in which established firms continue to lead.

Another telling illustration of which size firm is the ultimate beneficiary comes from the 2022 "Startup Development Five-Year Plan." The plan explains that "it has become clear that even large, existing companies using older technologies can stay in business if they engage in open innovation, such as through M&A with startups and collaborations with startups to introduce new technologies" (Cabinet Secretariat 2022, 1). An open innovation tax credit was launched in 2021 to encourage corporations to invest in startups, as it offered a 20 percent credit on the money invested. This was extended in 2023 to incentivize startup acquisitions, as a METI-led set of government agencies launched an open innovation tax credit commensurate to the 25 percent of the money spent acquiring a startup.

As these policies show, startup largesse is not intending to disrupt the position of Japan Inc. In turn, efforts to encourage open innovation has been widely reflected by big business in Japan. Notably, Toyota has created the Toyota Open Labs to connect with innovative startups globally (Toyota 2023), and Nissan has a partnership with Plug and Play to collaborate with startups for "the benefit of our global customers" (Nissan 2018). To be sure, Japan's startup plan conceives of new entrants as resources to help Japan Inc. stay in business. In this way, while there has been a rise in the role of startups, Japan's startup capitalism retains large firms as its essential innovation engines. Startups are resources for incumbents, not disruptors that pose an existential threat to established firms.

Employment

The lifetime nature of Japan's employment system—which reinforced its big business-led model—has dissipated somewhat since the 1990s. It is worth beginning with the observation that, in the Showa era, the perceived risk associated with starting a new business enterprise was exceptionally high. Nobuyuki Hata and colleagues (2007, 173) explain that "accepting the challenge to create a new startup literally meant being prepared to die. This inevitably reduced the number of entrepreneurs in Japan." Thus, changes have, at least implicitly, sought to widen the pool of prospective entrepreneurs by updating cultural norms. This has been done by slowly dismantling the features that incentivized lifetime employment (e.g., the nonportable pension fund system), by encouraging a culture of risk-taking, and by working to attract foreign talent.

Change began in the pension fund system, as the problem of relatively persistent unemployment in the 1990s prompted policy makers to pass regulations that facilitated pension fund portability (Streeck and Yamamura 2003). The portability meant that employees could take their pension savings with them when they moved jobs.[5] This meant that midcareer moves could be made without incurring the significant loss of accumulated pension savings. This then enabled more movement in the labor market, as people could move across firms. Also, over the 1990s, the Japanese welfare state expanded, which notionally reduced the centrality of private pensions in life savings.[6] In the same period, there was also an unprecedented rise in unemployment rates—from just over 2 percent to nearly

5 percent by the end of the decade—as persistent poor performance for firms across industries led to widespread layoffs. Collectively, this all augured for a less permanent understanding of work; lifetime employment was less incentivized due to the pension portability, and a rise in layoffs meant that there was less certainty that one could spend their career with the same firm.

Along with the loosening of restrictions on the labor market, an important bedrock for employment in R&D-centric high-technology startups was laid in this period. Reticent to take on a permanent headcount, companies began using short-term contracts to hire R&D workers. These entailed higher wages and significant bonus elements. The result was that technical talent was being socialized into employment practices that favored greater short-term compensation over long-term job security and pensions.

Labor market fluidity was also boosted by the experience of young people entering the labor force. New hires were not made, which disproportionately affected young people (Ahmadjian and Robinson 2001; Chuma 2002). There were fewer permanent contracts at the keiretsu, so the prospect of working at a startup did not seem as risky to recent graduates as it would have in the previous era. Talented graduates now compared experience with a startup with unemployment rather than with a well-paid, long-term career.

Another boost for entrepreneurship came from changes to bankruptcy laws. The Japanese legislature (the Diet) reformed insolvency laws in 1999 (Levy 2000). Prior to the reforms, it had been difficult to declare bankruptcy, so if an entrepreneur started a business and failed, they would be stuck with their nonperforming company as an ongoing liability. This "zombie company" phenomenon scared potential entrepreneurs from taking the risk, which had an overall dampening effect on startup activity (Goto and Wilbur 2019).

More movement *toward* a Mark I employment setting has been seen in policy on stock options and taxes. Since the early 2000s, stock option treatment has slowly adapted toward encouraging employment at startups. First, issuing stock options to employees—a derivation of the Commercial Code's easing of stock option allowances (Itami 2005)—began in 2003, when SoftBank offered it to their employees, ushering in this LME practice.[7] Twenty years later, this was significantly expanded when the government acted to ameliorate tax liabilities for nonpermanent employees. In August 2023, the government adjusted the tax system such that startups could more easily offer stock options to external individuals—including "freelance programmers, designers, and management consultants—people doing side jobs" (*Nikkei* Staff Writers 2023b). Such tax reforms mark an advance toward fluid labor markets in which shares of ownership in a company can be offered to individuals without full employment contracts. This again suggests a move in the direction of a Mark I paradigm.

To help young members of the labor force gain experience without missing out on the opportunity of entering a lifetime employment track upon university graduation, policies have encouraged internships at startups. The METI's 2004 Challenge Community Creation Program worked to establish the mechanism of internships as a viable early career activity. Despite this initiative, it would be another decade before midcareer job markets advanced, with startups offering employment agency services and social norms about permanent employment slowly changing.

Collectively, Japan's employment environment has seen shifts away from its permanent character toward more fluidity and even some encouragement for entrepreneurship. Speaking to this trajectory, an entrepreneur based in Kobe asserted that the "lifetime employment idea is not real. So, startups seem less risky, because people know permanent employment is not secure" (authors' interview, Kobe, June 25, 2018). As his sentiment suggests, it is no longer considered uncouth to leave a job midcareer or to try to build a startup (Fahey 2018; Gagne 2018). In a similar vein regarding the changing norms around employment, Yoshiaki Ishii, of METI, commented that "more and more people who graduate from the University of Tokyo are not only aiming for large corporations and government offices as it used to be, but are also starting their own businesses" (Newswitch 2018).

However, this is not to say that the system has been revolutionized. Kenji Kushida (2023, 1) asserts that "Japan's lifetime employment system in large companies is alive and well" and that the rise of startup employment has grown "in parallel with corporate Japan's traditional employment system." Kushida's analysis aligns with other arenas in which the rise of startup activity and promotion has come within the existing keiretsu-led system. One of our interviewees at the Kobe City Government noted that "if you go out of a permanent contract, you can't easily go back in" (authors' interview, Kobe, June 25, 2018). In fact, startups in Japan are said to continually suffer from a lack of access to talent because of the relatively limited job switching.

There is mixed evidence that job mobility is growing and startup-centric employment is expanding. According to Ambi, a job placement website, the midcareer job market has grown, with midcareer switches growing to 21.1 percent of all job switches in 2018—an increase of 13 percent from 2017 (Suzuki and Nakai 2022). Yet, the overall duration of full-time jobs decreased by only 0.2 years between 2016 and 2020, with Japan's average job tenure of 12.5 years in 2020 still significantly longer than the United States (4.1 years) and the United Kingdom (8.6 years) (Suzuki and Nakai 2022).

In addition to efforts to boost flexibility in the Japanese labor market, several open innovation–labeled policies have been deployed to bolster the availability of talent. This has primarily been done in the context of attracting foreign talent. The launch of Cool Japan in 2013 epitomizes rising efforts to attract foreign entrepreneurs and to forge better bridges with global startups (Satoh 2023). The National Strategic Special Zones, also initiated in 2013, strive to accept entrepreneurs and diverse foreigners in a bid to further creativity and address Japan's demographic challenges by attracting foreign talent (*Nikkei* Staff Writers 2023a). In 2015, METI launched its Strengthening Global Venture Ecosystem initiative, which aims to build a bridge of innovation (*kakehashi*) between Silicon Valley and Japan. Also in 2015, the Immigration Bureau of Japan launched the Startup Visa in National Strategic Special Zones, which reduces the visa requirements in relation to funding and employees for foreign entrepreneurs. In addition, Startup Visa rules were further relaxed in 2023 as a means of attracting foreign talent to start a business in Japan (Nishino 2023).

Along with these attempts to increase the presence of foreign entrepreneurial talent, efforts have been made to encourage local entrepreneurial talent to be more globally minded. As part of the five-year startup plan, the government is "sending 1,000 entrepreneurs and businesspeople overseas to expand global networks and bases for Japanese startups" (Nagata 2023). This builds on the 2015 Japan External Trade Organization (JETRO) Sido program, which has been sending entrepreneurs to Silicon Valley for short stays. In a desire to expand beyond Silicon Valley (e.g., to Los Angeles, San Diego, and Austin), JETRO has expanded its foreign immersion programs for Japanese founders. It launched the Beyond Japan Zero to X program in 2023 to send "dozens of entrepreneurs and businesspeople" to "build relationships and skills" (Nagata 2023). The X-Hub Tokyo's Outbound Program also launched in 2023, which similarly strives "to support the overseas expansion of Tokyo startups in order to create globally active startups from Tokyo" (Tokyo Metropolitan Government 2023).

Undoubtedly, the various regulatory changes to enable career movements, the attraction of foreign talent, and concerted efforts to foster an international (Silicon Valley–styled) mindset among Japanese entrepreneurs point to *some* degree of a shift toward a more flexible labor market. However, this does not mean movement is entirely toward Mark I. Startup employment experience and the availability of foreign entrepreneurs are also framed as a means of big businesses accessing and developing talent. For instance, METI's Yoshiaki Ishii asserts that "young and mid-career workers at large companies [could] add a secondment to a venture-backed company to their career path" (Matsugae 2018). METI followed through on offering such a mechanism; employees at big companies, including Honda Motors and Fujitsu, were able gain experience in a startup by receiving a subsidy so that they do not have to "leav[e] the companies they work for" (METI 2022). Thus, the aim of some flexible employment provisions is about benefiting the staff of incumbent firms, improving their talent, and assisting startups.

Overall, while lifetime employment has become less common since the early 1990s in Japan, the labor market still serves established firms and lacks fluidity in key ways. In practice, leaving a well-paid corporate job remains risky, even though pensions are portable and midcareer movements are more common. Also, some of the fluid mechanisms involve de-risking experience in startups through internships and secondments so that talent can remain focused on careers with established firms. This increased flexibility serves a Mark II aim: because employees can gain startup experience, big businesses benefit from employees with new ideas, more creativity, and a willingness to take risks. So, while the face of the changes augurs for Mark I, it also leans toward an open innovation version of Mark II.

Finance

It was Japan's so-called financial keiretsu who first took the initiative of acting as investors in startups in the 1980s.[8] VC investments were made by main banks and insurance companies rather than independent asset managers as in Silicon Valley (Kenney et al. 2002). Japan's banks transformed the American VC model—which was based on equity investments in early-stage companies—and instead adapted the notion of VC as debt-based financing for later-stage firms (Hata et al. 2007).

By the mid-1990s, excitement about equity-based VC was rising. In 1995, the Venture Plaza was launched, providing opportunities for VCs to meet investors and management partners (Rowen and Toyoda 2002). Afterward, in 1999, the SMRJ Venture Fund was created to invest in startups within seven years of founding. As a boost to early-stage equity-based financing, in 1997, the National Tax Agency implemented Japan's first-ever tax incentive to encourage angel investors. The Angel Tax was implemented "to jump start high-risk/high-return investment" (Ibata-Arens 2005, 101). Regulatory changes also paved the way for early-stage equity investing. In 1997, the Limited Partnership Act for Venture Capital Investment was passed, enabling the use of the Silicon Valley–consistent LP structure, which helped VC managers slightly ameliorate the risk of their activities (Kenney et al. 2004).

The late 1990s saw more advances that augured for movement toward a Mark I variety of innovation financing. Significantly, the government helped launch startup-friendly stock markets, which gave high-growth startups the important initial public offering (IPO) exit pathway. The Market for High-Growth and Emerging Stocks (known as Mothers) on the Tokyo Stock Exchange and Centrex on the Nagoya Stock Exchange were initiated in 1999 (Japan Exchange Group 2020). Shortly thereafter, in March 2000, SoftBank helped push for the creation of Japan's version of NASDAQ—JASDAQ. Throughout the creation of these market institutions, SoftBank served as a role model, normalizing these activities in the Japanese context. In the late 1990s, SoftBank was increasingly "seen as the flagship of the 'new economy' in Japan, based on entrepreneurship, venture capital and internet startup companies" (Lynskey and Yonekura 2001, 1). It began a series of successful overseas technology investments, and in so doing, SoftBank helped to transplant the Silicon Valley VC approach to Japan.

In the early 2000s, various state entities ramped up their credit-based financing for startups, which encouraged a widening of the entrepreneurial pool, again suggesting more of a Mark I variety flavor. In 2001, the Japan Finance Corporation (JFC) launched the New Business Financing Program, which provided small firms with unsecured loans (Uesugi 2006). The offering of unsecured loans meant that startup founders could take a loan to help grow their business without using their personal assets, such as their home or car, as collateral. This helped to reduce the financial risk associated with starting a company. In a similar vein, the Small & Medium IT Startups Support program, launched by METI in 2003, provided financing for startups' development and commercialization. In the same year, METI also initiated the Program for Training Venture Capitalists to enhance the skills for the burgeoning Japanese VC market.

However, policies to advance equity markets were established in line with Japan's historical orientation toward a Mark II logic. For instance, in 2014, the National Tax Agency offered investors in venture funds the ability to accumulate 80 percent of loss reserves as a deduction from future tax liability (PKF 2015). In an effort to encourage corporations to invest in startups, the Open Innovation Tax Relief Program was adopted in December 2021.[9] Yoshiaki Ishii, speaking to the involvement of big business, emphasized the government's intention to boost exit opportunities by saying that it had been "taking measures to encourage M&A" such as the tax exemptions (Newswitch 2018). In a similar way, Hisaaki Terasaki, the director general of the Office for Strategic Policy and ICT Promotion for the Tokyo Metropolitan Government, described the strength of the Tokyo startup ecosystem as offering "the best opportunities for startups to access world-leading companies, talent and cutting-edge technologies" (Startup Genome 2020, 165).

In line with a Mark II logic, efforts have encouraged corporations such as Toyota, Fanuc, and Hitachi to actively take equity stakes in the startups. JETRO lists several corporate VC arms as "key players in the Japanese innovation ecosystem," including Mitsui, Nippon, NTT DOCOMO, and Sony (JETRO 2023). Their VC arms have, in some cases, been established for decades. For instance, Sumitomo established its first VC fund, Presidio Ventures, in Silicon Valley in 1998 (Sumitomo 2022). In describing their corporate VC aims, the company explains they strive to "deploy effective collaboration strategies to actively integrate cutting-edge technologies and innovation in order to increase the value of existing businesses and create new businesses for the next generation" (Sumitomo 2022).

In addition to their corporate VC funds, Japanese corporations even manage funds of VC funds. Honda, for instance, runs a "fund of funds that provides insights through several LP positions in VC funds in Europe and Asia" (Mind the Bridge 2020, 12). Explaining Sony's launch of their first VC fund in 2016, Sony Innovation Fund CIO Gen Tsuchikawa explained the venture would drive Sony's "next business" stage by investing in startups to acquire "new technologies and new markets, new business models, and talents familiar with new fields" (Tsuchikawa 2020).

Sometimes Japan's big businesses even collaborate in startup investing, which aligns more with an open innovation version of Mark II. For example, Alliance Ventures was created in 2018 by Renault and Nissan each providing 40 percent of the fund, with Mitsubishi contributing the remaining 20 percent (Welch et al. 2018). In publicizing the combined effort, the companies explained that "global automakers are seeking to marry their manufacturing prowess with the nimbleness of startups that are working on electrification, artificial intelligence and autonomous driving—technologies that are transforming the industry" (Welch et al. 2018). The marked proliferation of corporate VC funds suggests that Japan's conglomerates and banks are looking to startups for new areas of growth, with their cutting-edge technologies and entrepreneurial talent, in line with an open innovation variety of Mark II.

Speaking about the prevalence of VC investment by Japanese corporations, James Riney, a partner at 500 Startups Japan, remarked that "pretty much every corporate has a startup program" (Russell 2019). CB Insights (2021) shows that Japan's share of corporate VC, as a share of national VC activity, is greater than in other countries.[10] Industry analysts note that corporate investors speak of striving to obtain startups' technologies and talented staff (aka 'acqui-hiring') (Kaneko 2022). In this way, Japan's network economy has grown in the direction of policy makers and big business aiming for startups to benefit established national strengths.

In addition to the centrality of keiretsu, national and regional startup initiatives involve the main banks as core partners. Japan's main banks are essential backers for equity-based schemes such as accelerators and VC funds. The 500 Kobe program—which takes the form of a seven-week intensive accelerator—costs 120 million yen to run, with the Kobe City Government paying half and the remaining funding coming from sponsoring banks Sumitomo Mitsui Banking Corporation (platinum sponsor) and Nomura Securities (authors' interview, Kobe, June 25, 2018). Sumitomo Mitsui is a particularly active investor with its two funds: Japan Co-Invest and SMBC Venture Funds. This involvement of contemporary versions of Japan's main banks in startup-centric initiatives underscores the idea that these banks (along with keiretsu) remain key finance players that are to be central to this new capitalism.

Partially state-owned banks and money managers also allocate finance for equity investments in startups (Inagaki 2018). In June 2022, Kishida's cabinet announced that the mammoth Government Pension Investment Fund (GPIF), with its US$1.5 trillion under management and which provided crucial capital for the keiretsu in the postwar period, would become a key source of financing for the country's startups, as tens of millions would be allocated toward venture capital investments (*Nikkei* Staff Writers 2022; Slodkowski and Sugiura 2022). Once a stalwart of the patient capital provided by the developmental state, Japan's partially state-owned Post Bank has also been entrusted with investing in the country's growing unicorn cohort. In June 2023, the Post Bank's president explained that "there are too few unicorns in Japan," so the bank would leverage its network of 24,000 postal branches to identify high-potential startups, in which it would invest a total of US$7 billion (Kono 2023).

Despite efforts to encourage venture capital activity, some contend that Japan's initiatives have not delivered. Japan's startup and VC community have been vocal about their concerns that Kishida's new capitalism can deliver meaningful results (Suzuki 2022). Efforts are seemingly underway to attract more international investors in Japan's startup innovation. Notably, in a bid to strengthen Japanese VC funds' ability to raise money from international investors, 2023 regulatory changes removed the cap on foreign investors needing to allocate 50 percent of their fund to Japanese companies (Takeuchi 2023). The challenge of attracting international money to Japanese VC has perhaps been most incisively shown through the fact that Masayoshi Son's SoftBank Vision Fund, which launched with US$100 billion under management in 2017 as the world's largest-ever VC fund (Economist 2018c), invests almost exclusively outside of Japan.[11]

Collectively, conglomerates, main banks, and pension funds are major investors in Japanese VCs and startups, which points to relative continuity on the postwar Mark II financing mode. Movement toward boosting VC speaks to some shift toward a Silicon Valley model, but this has been done in tandem with big businesses as key investors and partners. Thus, Japan's financing for innovation has a hybrid nature in which equity financing is increasingly availed for startups but conglomerates and main banks play an outsized role (relative to corporate VC in other countries) as startup investors.

Innovation

By the 1990s, Japan had already advanced from catch-up to compete at the world's technological frontier. As such, policies strove to improve radical innovation via R&D, intellectual property rights, and technology transfer from universities. Efforts to promote startup innovation and creativity coincided with the 1993 election. In that year, the National Tax Agency amplified the generosity of the tax deduction for SMEs' special experimentation and research expenses from 6 percent up to 12 percent. The emphasis was on R&D and creativity, as the Diet passed the SME Creative Business Promotion Law in 1995. In 1999, there was a revision to the SME Basic Law that was aimed at encouraging small firms' innovation through state-provided credit (Seki 2008, 174).

In the late 1990s, there was a wave of policy adoptions inspired by Silicon Valley in spirit and name. The Industrial Revitalization Law in 1999 included the Japanese Bayh-Dole Act, named after the 1980 US law that dealt with IP from federally funded research (Vogel 2018, 104). The act aimed to encourage the patenting of research results from across the open innovation system (Committee on the History of Japan's Trade and Industry Policy 2020). Also, in ways more consistent with a Mark I orientation in the sense that it strove to widen the entrepreneurial pool, the Japanese version of the US Small Business Innovation Research (SBIR) program was launched in 1999 "to help SMEs enhance their technology-development capability and to support their creative business activities" (Goto 2009, 36).[12]

In the 2000s, Japanese firms were developing state-of-the-art technologies when a new problem came to the fore: the Galapagos Syndrome. This refers to Japan's technological leadership and innovation being limited to its domestic market, or "leading without followers" (Kushida 2011). For instance, in the early 2000s, Japan's cell phone industry was said to be world-leading, but the advances did not diffuse to international markets. Since the rest of the world did not take up the technologies, its innovations became an island (i.e., the Galapagos) rather than a global market leader. The salience of the Galapagos Syndrome was an important driver in the shift toward policies enabling a startup-fueled, internationally oriented open innovation system. Policy makers spoke of wanting to make a concerted effort to be globally relevant, so they pursued strategies to expand to numerous international markets (e.g., see Iwamoto 2017; Iwasaki 2016). So, Japan's innovation initiatives took a distinctly open, international character. In an interview, an Osaka City Government official responsible for industrial promotion explained that the "phrase [Galapagos Syndrome] triggered the open innovation movement by large companies" (authors' interview, Osaka, June 26, 2018).

In the spirit of open innovation systems that deliver incumbent-led advances, the early 2000s also saw an uptick in government efforts to promote new ventures in geographical clusters alongside universities and in partnership with government and big businesses. In 2001, METI launched a Regional Cluster Plan across nine regions. The plan had three intentions: to improve productivity, spur innovation, and foster new business creation. It targeted nineteen clusters across the country and was coordinated by national and regional METI bureaus (Ibata-Arens 2005, 92). The plan aimed to enhance the competitiveness of Japan through industrial clusters formed by local SMEs and venture businesses utilizing seeds from universities and other research institutions (Boyer 2003, 180).

Other programs took this startup-fueled cluster approach to open innovation forward. The Comprehensive Support Program for Creation of Regional Innovation, launched in 2006 by the Japan Agency of Science and Technology (JST), established an S&T incubation program in advanced regions. METI's Innovation Network Corporation of Japan launched in 2009 with a hybrid mission of investing in startups to help build unicorns *and* provide essential capital to established corporations struggling in the throes of the global financial crisis (Wells 2017). Commenting on this overall trajectory, Takuya Hirai, the former minister of state for Science and Technology Policy, noted that it is now known that "startups will be central players" and that "large firms are embracing open innovation in addition to their own R&D" (Rao 2020).

The rationale for striving to link established firms with startups has to do with the contemporary nature of frontier technologies and startups' speed and way of thinking being infused into large firms. In an interview, the chairman of the Japan Venture Capital Association, Soichi Kariyazono, explained that "the fourth industrial revolution, which creates innovation through the combination of technologies from different industries and different customer groups, is driving us to open-innovation through collaboration with startups" (Newswitch 2018). The director of METI's Startup and New Business Promotion Office, Hajime Furuya, similarly asserted that policies like the J-Startup Initiative can "create a significant impact on society by combining technologies and business models of startups with the business resources of large companies and help them develop as bases of larger growth" (*METI Journal* 2020). Startups are construed as resources that layer digital and technological prowess into established businesses. For this reason, Takuya Hirai noted their belief that "large firms are embracing open innovation in addition to their own R&D" (Rao 2020). In another demonstration of faith in the benefits that startups can bring to Japan's big firms, Takuya Fukumoto, the director of Industrial Finance within METI's New Business Policy Office, explained that "if fast-moving startups are linked with large companies and research institutions that have the technical and management resources, they will definitely be able to compete globally in the future" (*Forbes Japan* 2018).

As these statements illustrate, in Japan, policy makers strive for radical innovation by fostering mutual benefits for startups and incumbent firms. There is no expectation of the creative destruction of the big companies, but there is the assumption that startups will boost the innovation capacity of established firms and will simultaneously best achieve their own scaling-up by interacting with incumbents.

Social Purpose

Domestically focused social purpose, particularly the pursuit of equitable and stable economic growth, has underpinned the movements of these reinforcing institutions. Japan's startup capitalism began with the throes of the Heisei recession, which began in 1991. The recession was the result of the bubble bursting after the yen's sharp *endaka* (appreciation against the US dollar) due to the Plaza Agreement in September 1985.[13] Though the bubble burst was primarily a financially induced one (Grimes 2001; Koo 2009), the resulting malaise fueled a push for change to the socioeconomic system. It prompted calls for greater transparency in policy making and a crisis of legitimacy in the Japanese model vis-à-vis the US model (Jackson 2003). Even though the crisis was not caused by MITI's actions, it informed the sense that the bureaucracy, including the MITI, should change tack.

The pressure had to do with the merits of cross-shareholding, permanent employment, and the reliance on the keiretsu for export-led growth and technological upgrading systems, which all came under attack as the recession wore on in the 1990s. It spurred less confidence in the Japan Inc. model, including the state-business relations, lifetime employment, seniority-based pay, consensus decision-making, the main bank system, and corporate networks (Kato 2001). Marie Anchordoguy (2005, 64) asserts that it was acknowledged that the previous policies and institutions had become "much less effective in nurturing growth and technological advances," and as such, "state and business leaders increasingly contested the norms underlying these arrangements and tried to modify them." Collectively, there was a push for changes toward a Mark I model in terms of more fluid labor markets, a greater role for startups, and a boost for equity financing as the capital source for radical innovation (Pempel 1998).[14] However, this did not come completely or quickly; for instance, the Japanese corporate governance code only changed in 2015 to require the reporting of cross-shareholding. The transparency into crossholdings would apply downward pressure on the oligopolistic competition model.

So, while the big business–centered model did not unravel in the 1990s, startup promotion was incorporated as a means of addressing unemployment challenges. Several policies were initiated to encourage entrepreneurship as an alternative to lifetime employment by reducing the risk associated with working for high-stakes startups. A senior manager at the Kobe Enterprise Promotion Bureau explained that "in the early 2000s, the people who were doing entrepreneurship were [perceived as] arrogant and looking to make a quick buck" (authors' interview, Kobe, June 25, 2018).

Efforts were aimed at changing cultural norms around entrepreneurship to make it more acceptable and even desirable. One of the policies that sought to promote entrepreneurship is the Japan Venture Awards, initiated by the SMRJ in 2000, which promoted entrepreneurial role models. Other initiatives include METI-organized Silicon Valley study trips to popularize startup activity in Japan. Tohru Akaura, a partner at Incubate Fund in Tokyo, recalled that "in 2005 or 2006, the METI hosted a study group called the 'Virtual Silicon Valley Study Group' with the goal of revitalizing Japan" such that society embraced startups and VC (Incubate Fund 2020). In this way, METI was bringing together members of the Japanese innovation system with a view toward further encouraging an entrepreneurial culture.[15] As a related means of encouraging risk-taking related to startups, in 2008, the JFC began offering Re-Challenge Support Loans that target entrepreneurs who have tried to start a business and failed in an effort to ameliorate stigmas around failure.

In the contemporary era, social challenges, such as underrepresentation and exclusion, have been invoked as the purpose motivating startup initiatives. For instance, the Kishida cabinet's 2022 agenda that boosted use of government pension funding for startup investments asserted that "fostering start-ups is the key to promoting the dynamism and growth of the Japanese economy and solving social problems" (Slodkowski and Sugiura 2022). The METI's 2013 Micro Enterprise Revitalization Project strives, in collaboration with private financial institutions, to help micro enterprises led by women and young people. As another example, Carin Holroyd (2022) detailed the way that Japan's Society 5.0 coordinates academia, industry, and government to deliver its aims. And Tokyo Governor Yuriko Koike explained in a speech that the regional government created a system called APT Women to bring together talented women entrepreneurs to create new ventures based on new demands.[16] Such diversity efforts have been echoed by VC industry bodies. The Japan VC Association set a diversity target of 30 percent of senior leadership positions to be held by women, foreign nationals, and other underrepresented demographics (Chou and Suzuki 2024). Japan's startup capitalism, then, increasingly aims to drive innovation-led economic growth and social inclusion as it evolves.

While the social purpose portrayed in the launch of Japan's startup policies is often domestically oriented, startup promotion is also positioned as contributing to economic statecraft around critical technologies. Startups are construed as boosts to big businesses' capabilities in the context of Japan's plans to revive its status as a powerhouse in the global semiconductor industry. Semiconductor efforts centered on the creation of a new joint venture called Rapidus, which is "backed by the government and Japan's biggest corporations, and IBM" (Inagaki 2023). The aim is to have this new entity achieve mass production of two-nano-meter node chips by 2027—which would be a significant jump from the current forty-nanometer capability. Rapidus was formed by veteran Japanese semiconductor executives. Its partners are foreign research institutes (e.g., in Belgium), foreign firms (ASML in the Netherlands and IBM in the United States), and numerous Japanese firms and main banks—Toyota, Sony, NTT, NEC, Kioxia (Toshiba), Softbank, Denso, and Mitsubishi UFJ Bank (Shivakumar et al. 2023). The incumbents and main banks collaborate directly with startups globally as a means of bolstering their firms' capability to deliver. For instance, Sony Semiconductor Solutions has a lab in Silicon Valley (San Jose) that "provide[s] tools and working space to selected startups and enterprise companies" (Mendez 2023). Sony Semiconductor partnered with Silicon Catalyst in 2021 in order to "expand Sony's access to new innovations in sensing solutions development and facilitate Sony's ability to create strategic relationships with pioneering young companies that are developing technologies complementary to Sony's internal innovation" (Silicon Catalyst 2021). Sony is just one of the many Japanese partners leading the country's efforts to compete at the global frontier in semiconductors. Like the other big firms in the joint venture, it is leveraging startups around the world to fuel its abilities.

Continuity and Change in Japan

The extent to which there has been continuity and change in the firm size, employment, finance, innovation, and social purpose across Japan's antecedents period to the beginning of startup capitalism in 1991 is illustrated in figure 2.1. Overall, the big business–oriented institutional foundations have changed in step with one another, having an interlocking effect rather than a transformative one. Thus, there is continuity in how the Japanese developmental state has pursued startup capitalism. It has remained closer to a Mark II setting in which the keiretsu and main banks persist as partners for government efforts. The areas of greatest change are the moves toward more radical innovation (to a 3 on the fig. 2.1 scale), away from incremental innovation, and in finance, as equity-based financing has grown (and thus been represented with a score of 3).

Beginning with the size of firms central to innovation, we find that Japan's antecedent period closely approximated the oligopolistic competition variety, but it has modestly evolved toward small firms having a role. Depicting this evolution, the antecedent period is illustrated as a 1 in figure 2.1, while Japan's startup capitalism moves outward, but only to a 2 on the scale. This is because Japan

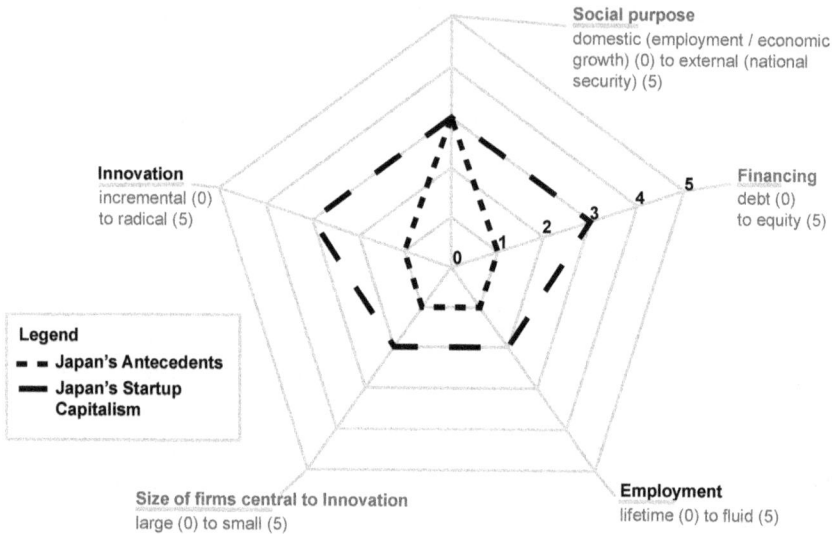

FIGURE 2.1. Analyzing Japan's institutional evolution: antecedents to startup capitalism

remains close to the Mark II type in which big companies are crucial innovation engines. There has been some outward shift toward the Mark I variety since policy has incorporated startups. Rather than (only) internal R&D and large firm consortia, incumbents actively leverage startups in open innovation systems. The big companies are selecting and investing in startups to boost their own capabilities. This is enabled by the government's approach, which involves established firms as investors and judges, and communicates the objective of having the big businesses benefit from access to entrepreneurial talent and ideas. Thus, the modest shift reflects the fact that Japan Inc. remain ultimate beneficiaries in even flagship startup plans like the J-Startup Initiative.

Employment has become more fluid with the availability of internships and secondments and the portability of pension savings. This all helps to usher in a culture more favorable to midcareer movements and entrepreneurial risk-taking. Yet, the shift toward Mark I is muted by our observation of two attributes of Japan's labor market. The first is that the movements into startups can often take the form of pre-keiretsu experience or secondments from the established firms. In this way, startup experience still fits within the lifetime employment apparatus. Work at a startup is conceived of as a mechanism for talent development for the keiretsu. The second is that Japan's labor market still favors long-term employment. While norms have updated in favor of entrepreneurial experience and midcareer movements, there is a persistent preference for stable employment with big companies. For these reasons, figure 2.1 shows a shift outward to 2, which is still closer to the Mark II ideal of lifetime employment, from the antecedent period, when permanent employment was dominant, which earned a score of 1.

Finance-wise, there has been an advance of equity funding for innovation, away from the decidedly debt-based character of the antecedent period. The starting point was again a score of 1 in Japan's antecedent period, as it was so heavily balanced toward credit provision. Figure 2.1 shows a greater shift than in the context of employment or firm size to a score of 3. The rationale for this move toward Mark I is the veracity of efforts to bolster equity-based venture capital and stock market activities. There is no question that capital markets have been significantly developed in the direction of equity-based investing in Japan since the 1990s. However, we did not assign a higher score, since the dominant players in Japan's burgeoning equity markets are the same as in the antecedent period. The main banks are active funders of startup spaces and investment programs. In addition, the same pension funding that enabled the keiretsu-led model is now being leveraged to encourage the Mark II open innovation system in Japan. Equity funding is, in many ways, another type of transaction from long-established financiers rather than from alternative investment managers.

Innovation has a similar movement, from an antecedent score of 1, reflecting the centrality of catch-up technology aims in the postwar period, to a score of 3 in the startup capitalism setting. Innovation aims clearly shifted outward, from incremental catch-up to radical innovation striving to compete at the world's technological frontier. This move to semiconductors and personal computing began, at METI's bidding, by the 1970s but moved toward innovation at the world's technological frontier in the twenty-first century. In this shift, startups are helping to fuel Japan's big businesses—and their combined efforts through consortia—to compete against American, European, Korean, and Taiwanese companies in key technologies.

Unlike the outward shifts in firm size, employment, finance, and innovation, in the context of social purposes, there is no movement in figure 2.1. Instead, in the antecedent and startup capitalism periods, there is a score of 3. This is because our analysis reveals that the underlying social purpose remains a combination of domestic issues, especially youth employment and an inclusive innovation system. However, while these domestic aims are named in policy rationale, innovation has been important to Japan Inc. and its competitiveness in critical technologies, including semiconductors. As such, we depict the social purpose as stable over time for this steady mix of domestic issues, with wider external competition motivations in the background.

Collectively, Japan's startup capitalism has not converged on a Mark I approach. Instead, startups are depicted as resources for open innovation systems in which the keiretsu remain essential partners for the state and main banks and pension funds, including those central to the postwar developmental state model, are essential equity investors. Creative destruction is not the aim underpinning initiatives that speak about creating unicorns; policy makers hope to bolster incumbents and foster volumes of startup activity simultaneously.

KOREA

"Open innovation projects serve as activities of conglomerates to induce new ideas and then bring in talent and tech," our interviewee at the Seoul Metropolitan Government explained when speaking about the embrace of open innovation in Korea. He added that "open innovation has been a slogan for us," but over time, there has been increasing awareness that "startups want to work with large firms, too" (authors' interview, Seoul, August 23, 2022). This vignette hints at the Mark II logic underpinning Korea's version of startup capitalism. In Korea, large firms remain central actors, but now startups are construed as important resources for the oligopoly-run open innovation logics. The chaebol envisage startups as a means of enhancing their own innovation capacity.[1]

Congruent with this logic, there has been a visible increase in startup promotion. In 2017, Korea became the first country in the world to establish a ministry for SMEs and startups, and like Japan, it has launched high-profile initiatives that strive to create unicorn cohorts. As this chapter shows, Korea's startup capitalism is consistent with its chaebol-led system. The chaebol act as corporate venture capitalists, and initiatives count chaebol licensing agreements and joint ventures as key performance indicators.

Korea is an interesting case because its antecedents are depicted as quintessential examples of a developmental state, which augurs for its starting point as one consistent with conventional Mark II logics. This is because the Korean developmental state depiction, like Japan's, centers on the role of its large firms—the chaebol—which were essential employers, innovators, and contributors to economic growth and stability (Amsden 1989).[2] As was done in Japan, the Korean developmental state rewarded its large incumbent firms with preferential access to credit and, in return, provided stable employment and technological upgrading. Closely aligned with Mark II, the chaebol had market knowledge and in-house R&D capacity (Kalinowski 2008).

The Korea chapter offers a nuanced insight into how startup capitalism can align with, rather than challenge, Mark II settings. In this sense, the antecedents of the Korean developmental state offer the opportunity to explore the extent to which startups have been positioned since the late 1990s as resources for incumbent firms. As an indication of the salience of this analysis, a policy maker at the Seoul Metropolitan Government shared with us that he worries that "every service is under chaebol control" and that perhaps startups *should* compete more with the long-established chaebol, like Lotte and Samsung, as well as new big firms such as Kakao and Naver (authors' interview, online, August 30, 2022). For now, the trajectory of Korea's startup capitalism mirrors that of an open innovation variety of Mark II as observed in the Japanese case.

Antecedents: Korea (1961–1997)

The depiction of the Korean developmental state centers on the chaebol as essential actors. From Park Chung-hee taking power in 1961 until the EAFC of 1997, its economic growth model had four main pillars: catch-up innovation; large, vertically, and/or horizontally integrated conglomerates; access to bank-based, long-term capital; and permanent employment (Amsden 1989). Korea followed an export-led growth model with ever-expanding chaebol favored by the government at the center (Cha and Pacheco Pardo 2023). Finance came from the mobilization of domestic and foreign savings disbursed to the export-oriented conglomerates through state-owned banks (Kim 1988). The literature depicts the Korean state and chaebol as having a largely symbiotic relationship (Woo-Cumings 1999). Taking a page out of Japan's playbook, the government encouraged savings that could be recycled to provide credit to the private sector, provided subsidies to companies operating in specific industries, enacted protectionist measures to weaken foreign competitors, and allowed chaebol to engage in oligopolistic behavior (Kim 1997).

For the most part, big conglomerates were the drivers behind Korea's growth and innovation as well as job creation and social stability. The chaebol's horizontal integration had the advantages of allowing diversification thanks to brand recognition, creating economies of scale and synergies across conglomerate units, facilitating long-term investment strategies, and reducing transaction costs (Jwa 2002). The chaebol also had relational power, meaning their size and centrality to the economy gave them access to the government, with all the benefits that come with it. Most notably, the Economic Planning Board (EPB) and other government agencies consulted industrial policy with the chaebol. The state prioritized the provision of financing to the chaebol that had a better chance at manufacturing the goods for export on which the economy relied. Furthermore, the chaebol provided high-quality, permanent employment that drove the improvement in the lives of Korean society while, crucially, during the years of dictatorship, dampening pressures stemming from job-related social unrest.

Long-term employment has been a key goal of the state dating back to the early post–Korean War years. Absent a strong welfare state, long-term employment and the associated corporate welfare were the preferred means for the government to promote social welfare indirectly. Both the chaebol and smaller firms offered corporate welfare packages, the former more generously (Fleckenstein and Lee 2017). These benefits were tied to seniority, as was pay; crucially, pensions were, too. Therefore, workers had an incentive to remain in their company throughout their career. In exchange for long-term employment, labor was expected to moderate its wage demands, refrain from challenging management decisions, and avoid industrial action (Kong 2013). Big conglomerates provided jobs and enterprise welfare, including pensions. In this context, entrepreneurship had limited appeal to the most qualified workers, especially top university graduates. The graduates from Korea's three top-ranked universities—Seoul National University, Korea University, and Yonsei University, collectively referred to as SKY—pursued well-renumerated roles at the chaebol. They were attracted to the job stability, higher pay, and welfare benefits of employment—and the social status that came with those roles (Heo and Roehrig 2014).

The state dominated the provision of financing, emphasizing the distribution of credit rather than equity investments during the Park and Chun eras. Commercial banks recycled savers' deposits to lend to corporations and invest in the economy. The government also monopolized foreign borrowing. Furthermore, the Korea Development Bank, set up in 1954, and the Export-Import Bank of Korea, established in 1976, became key providers of export financing and industry and infrastructure funding, respectively. The chaebol therefore became dependent on the state to finance their economic activities (Lee 2006). The bank-based financing model enabled the chaebol to access patient capital and, as a result, gave them the capacity for long-term planning in incremental innovation. Crucially, patient capital could be deployed by the government to foster the development of industries such as petrochemicals, shipbuilding, and steel in the 1970s, electronics and automobiles in the 1980s, and semiconductors from the mid-1980s (Yeung 2016). The chaebol often had no choice but to specialize in one or more of these and other industries according to governmental dictum (Woo 1991). In line with the state's central role in finance provision in this era, the government even offered direct and indirect subsidies to VC firms.[3]

From the beginning of the developmental state period, General Park had ambitions for Korea to eventually compete at the frontier of innovation. He was aware of the need to slowly move up the value-added chain until firms were ready to develop innovative products. Thus, throughout the 1960s and 1970s, his policies focused on catch-up growth with an eye toward making firms more innovative. The government set up the Korea Institute of Science and Technology (KIST) in 1966, a Ministry of Science and Technology (MoST) in 1969, and the Korea Advanced Institute of Science (KAIS) in 1971, today known as the Korea Advanced Institute of Science and Technology (KAIST) (Kim and Leslie 1998). This made Korea one of the few developing countries with a technology-focused ministry and university. Innovation at the technological frontier was limited throughout the 1960s and 1970s; the MoST was relatively weak, and technological developments were largely the result of imports (Hahm and Plein 1995, 20). For the most part, the economy was competing on good-quality manufacturing at lower costs (Wade 1990). The government and the chaebol only started to compete at the technological frontier by the 1990s. This helps to explain why R&D as a percentage of GDP remained below 1 percent until the mid-1980s but shot up to almost 2.5 percent by the mid-1990s, one of the highest figures worldwide (OECD 2020). Chun Doo-hwan's government (1980–1988) and the democratically elected governments of Roh Tae-woo (1988–1993) and Kim Young-sam (1993–1998) sought to promote capabilities at the technological frontier.

Korea's economic policy making during the classic developmental state epoch entailed a combination of external and domestically oriented social purposes. Domestically, the government offered guidance, finance capital, and a protectionist environment; in exchange, the chaebol provided permanent employment, and labor remained disciplined and accepted low wages in exchange for employment (Hwang 1996; Hundt 2008). High job growth came with low levels of inequality, which was another key domestic driver of industrial policy. The advent of democratization in 1988 brought a more organized labor force seeking a larger share of the Korean economic pie (Kong 2013; Lie 1998). The system did not change dramatically in terms of the purpose, but state-chaebol links weakened, and SMEs and labor started to demand change.

No explanation of the social purpose underpinning Korea's pursuit of catch-up economic growth and innovation policy would be complete without looking at the country's external environment. In particular, the geostrategic alliance with the United States and the very direct threat from North Korea allowed the government to pursue its preferred economic policy (Heo and Roehrig 2014). It also served the government to discipline labor (Brazinsky 2007). In addition,

Korea's normalization of relations with Japan in 1965 and the war reparations and investment by Japanese firms that followed also provided capital and technology transfers (Woo 1991). Economic growth and the advance of technological capabilities contributed to Korea's international stature and helped to address the North Korea threat.

Thematic Analysis

Firm Size

The EAFC served as a catalyst for the government to increase its backing for new entrants. To begin with, it resulted in some discrediting of the chaebol. This extended to their ability to innovate. There was a line of thought that posited that the chaebol were good at catch-up development, which had allowed them to thrive during the postwar years, but were unsuited for helping Korea compete at the cutting edge of innovation (Choung et al. 2014). As a result, on the eve of the EAFC, there was pressure for chaebol reform (Graham 2003). The chaebol were considered to be "at a crossroads," as they needed "to change the way they do business or risk extinction" (Beck 1998, 1018). The Kim government also sought to distance itself from "corrupt" chaebol, at least initially. During these years, the Kim administration came to power in the middle of the dot-com bubble. Daum, today Korea's second-largest search engine, had been launched in May 1997; Naver, Korea's first portal with its own search engine and today the country's leading internet firm, followed in June 1999. In other words, by the time the Kim government started to encourage startups in earnest and published Vision 2025 in September 1999, there were already examples of startups innovating in the new digital economy.

In this context, the Korean state established a policy of developing an entrepreneurial ecosystem embedded alongside the chaebol. Roh's Innovate Korea approach and the national innovation system concepts were designed to promote the creation of a chaebol-startup symbiotic setting (Seong and Song 2008, 33). The 2005 Act on the Promotion of Collaborative Cooperation between Large Enterprises and Small-Medium Enterprises symbolized this new approach. The Roh government sought to facilitate the integration of startups into the chaebol production and sales channels, which would inject the chaebol with renewed innovation capacity. This could be done by incorporating startups as suppliers or through acquisition, providing the chaebol with the startups' talent and technology. Without directly funding the chaebol, which would have attracted criticism, the government could ensure that large conglomerates continued to be competitive through cooperation with more innovative startups.

Like his predecessors, Myung-bak Lee assisted the chaebol. The chaebol could benefit from the work of startups and develop their own programs to nurture innovation by nonemployees. For example, SK Telecom, the largest mobile service carrier, launched programs to train IT experts and mobile app developers (SK Telecom 2011). And Samsung launched an in-house idea and startup incubator, C-Lab (Creative Lab), in 2012 (Samsung 2018). But these were not government-led or even underwritten programs. Rather, it was the chaebol seeking to promote innovation to increase their product range and talent pool.

Following from the approach pioneered in the aftermath of the EAFC, the state refrained from providing direct largesse to the chaebol. The distribution of government money to the chaebol was a nonstarter, considering the public's opposition to state-chaebol ties. This was the result of a string of scandals affecting the conglomerates, their leaders, and their family members. A consistent majority of Koreans came to see the chaebol as part of an elite group creating more inequality (whether perceived or real) and playing by a different set of rules. In this context, it would have been difficult for any Korean president to provide direct help to the chaebol.

Embracing the aims of engaging startups but avoiding publicly supporting the chaebol, the Park and Moon governments deployed efforts to develop startups as essential resources in chaebol-startup innovation systems.[4] They even did so using the language of open innovation that had been coined by Henry Chesbrough in 2003. Most notably, starting in 2014, the Park government launched nineteen CCEIs across the country's different provinces and main cities. Each had a specific sectoral focus related to the province or city and the partner chaebol; for example, automobiles in Gwangju Province (Hyundai), games and fintech in Gyeonggi Province (KT), and aviation and logistics in the city of Incheon (Hanjin) (CCEI 2019). At the CCEIs, startups receive direct assistance from the government, but the chaebol are essential to developing an entrepreneurial ecosystem around their industrial focus (authors' interview, Seoul, June 2017). As the quote that we opened the book with suggests, the aim of the CCEIs is not only to advance the capabilities of the startups that are receiving the mentorship and subsidized office space but also to help inject innovative DNA into the chaebol.

Another example of startup initiatives that embed the chaebol is the K-Startup Grand Challenge, which was launched in 2016 to bring foreign entrepreneurs to Korea. The K-Startup Grand Challenge offers foreign entrepreneurs funding, office space, and an accelerator program: 5,725 teams applied between 2016 and 2018, with 85 of them receiving the full set of services offered by the program (K-Startup 2018). An indication of its orientation toward involving and benefiting large incumbents, rather than purely focusing on startup capacity, is one of the program's objectives. The aim was for participating startups to secure licensing agreements or partnerships with a chaebol (authors' interview, Seoul, June 2017). So, K-Startup success was at least partially predicated on startups securing agreements with the chaebol.

In a similar vein, the MSS set up an SME Policy Deliberation Committee involving government officials, startups, and the chaebol (MSS 2019b). Chaebol were therefore directly involved in the design of startup initiatives. The incumbent aims are also reflected in the performance metrics of government divisions. For the Seoul Metropolitan Government's startup promotion division, for instance, key performance indicators include "joint ventures" between startups and large firms (authors' interview, Seoul, August 23, 2022).

Both the Park and Moon governments spoke of startup policies as aiming to deliver mutual benefit for the chaebol and startups. Therefore, startup efforts have the underlying goal of bolstering the innovation capacity of the chaebol. Otherwise, they could suffer the fate of big firms elsewhere that declined due to an inability to innovate and become stuck with outdated products. As the Seoul CCEI manager put it, "The government wants the conglomerates to gain innovative DNA by working with startups and the young generation. In the relationship, the chaebol get startups' DNA. Government wanted to involve the chaebol as they are dinosaurs. . . . It's a win-win for the chaebol and startups" (authors' interview, Seoul, June 20, 2017). Both the Park and Moon governments made a concerted effort to connect the chaebol and startups (Hsieh 2018). The logic was that the former could provide mentoring, funding, or even an exit strategy to the latter. Thus, the Park government launched nineteen CCEIs across the country to aid startups, with one of the chaebol serving as a corporate partner in each of them (CCEI 2019). Furthermore, the government involved the chaebol in the design of startup initiatives and the entrepreneurial ecosystem to facilitate the successful integration of startups into the Korean economy. And when Moon came to power, he included mutually beneficial cooperation in his five-year plan. The government was openly indicating that it wanted startups to work together with the chaebol.

The nature of the chaebol-startup relationship is not necessarily symbiotic. For instance, Park Jae-hyun, the CEO of Ant Institute in Seoul, noted that "because start-ups with a good item in the market have no choice but to accept big investments from major corporations, bigger companies take what they need from start-ups" and sell them (Lee 2019). Technologies and their emerging markets are said to be advanced by startups who are then gobbled up prematurely by the chaebol. Despite concerns about early acquisitions by Korea's dominant firms, startup policies continue to involve the chaebol in planning committees and implementation partners. For instance, in July 2023, the government announced that the Ministry of Trade, Industry, and Energy was leading "a corporate venture capital alliance consisting of 42 corporate venture investors including Posco Capital, CJ Investment, GS Ventures and Hyundai Venture Investment" that would "band together to create an 8 trillion won ($6.2 billion) venture fund for local startups by 2025" (Shin 2023).

Employment

"In Korea, to be an entrepreneur, you have to kill two women: your mother and future wife"—your mother by virtue of the shame you will bring the family by becoming an entrepreneur, and your future wife because of the lost income and shame your high-risk career threatens (authors' interview, Seoul, June 24, 2017). This was our interviewee's retort to questions about the aim of startup policies vis-à-vis shifting employment norms. Others made similar points. For instance, instead of entrepreneurial experience, the "aim is to work for Samsung, banks, or to get a government job" (authors' interview, Seoul, August 23, 2022). David Lee (2019) similarly quipped that "becoming a civil servant—such as a police officer or a town hall employee—is one of the most coveted jobs" in South Korea because, in addition to the honor, it "ensures a steady payroll, pension and social recognition." He noted that startups, "with their built-in risk and uncertain future," are the complete opposites. Policy makers work to overcome the entrenched expectations that the pursuit of an entrepreneurial career would cause such destruction socially and fatally harm one's family.

The labor market became more flexible as a result of the EAFC, which caused a spike in unemployment in Korea. Higher youth unemployment hovered around 10 percent throughout the early 2000s. Some chaebol had gone bankrupt. Those remaining sought to mitigate job losses among their existing workers by limiting firings and relying on natural attrition to reduce their headcounts (Lee 2006). At the same time, China's entry into the World Trade Organization (WTO) in 2001 resulted in the outsourcing of parts of the production process by Korean manufacturing firms, including the chaebol, to their lower-cost neighbor (Chang 2003, 261). The chaebol, therefore, could not sufficiently provide jobs for young Koreans joining the workforce.

In this context, the encouragement of more flexible employment, including as entrepreneurs and by joining startups, became a job creation tool. The decrease in the chaebol employment opportunities, the increase in governmental support for startups, and the availability of nonpermanent job contracts helped facilitate an increase in the number of high-tech startups. According to our interviews with entrepreneurship center managers and a Seoul government official responsible for startup policy, younger Koreans who in the past might have joined one of the chaebol or remained there throughout their career decided to launch their own firm instead (authors' interviews, Seoul, August 30, 2016 and August 23, 2017). A case in point is Lee Hae-jin, who left his job at Samsung in 1999 to launch Naver. This sort of career move became more common throughout the 2000s.

To make employment more fluid, the government introduced pension portability in December 2005 with the Individual Retirement Account (Korean Law Information Center 2008). This allowed employees to take (a portion of) their pensions to another firm and, if launching their own startups, to their newly established company. Together with defined contribution and defined benefits pension accounts, this became one of the three types of private pension funds available to workers (Ministry of Labor and Employment 2013). Importantly, the introduction of individual retirement accounts also allowed entrepreneurs to return to work for a chaebol or another private-sector firm if their startup failed without losing all the pension benefits accrued prior to launching the company.

Job creation was a top priority of the Lee government, particularly as the GFC threatened to result in huge layoffs, as had been the case during the EAFC. To begin with, KVIC and the Korea Finance Corporation launched a KRW120 billion Job Creation Fund in 2010, with a second KRW107 billion fund the next year. The specific goal of these funds was to invest in VC firms backing startups with high job-creation potential. The Korean state was therefore providing direct largesse to startups holding the promise to create jobs, including in so-called Next Generation Growth Engine industries (KVIC 2024f). By making explicit the goal of job creation, the government was also sending the message that funding would be forthcoming to firms helping to reduce youth unemployment.

In addition, and directly related to job creation for younger Koreans, the Young Entrepreneurs Startup Academy was set up in 2011 (KOSME 2017). This agency was launched not only to provide funds to would-be young entrepreneurs—meaning those under thirty-nine years old—but also to offer office space, training, and mentoring. The largest barrier to prospective entrepreneurs is a lack of managerial, legal, and other skills necessary for people who essentially become CEOs and, oftentimes, CFOs once they launch their business (Schoof 2006). The academy was designed to address this issue.

More fluid labor markets were also fostered in 2011, as the Act on the Fostering of Self-Employed Creative Enterprises was passed. Self-employed individuals or business entities comprising fewer than five nonregular workers were allowed to continue to operate self-employed firms for three years after they had expanded beyond five workers. This gave them tax and other advantages, thus reducing labor costs. Furthermore, these firms received assistance from the government, including, potentially, funding. The act addressed the concern that the creative industries, a potential source of new jobs, were hindered by employment costs being higher than they could absorb.

The Park and Moon governments saw startups as job creation tools. As an interviewee at the Seoul CCEI put it: "It's all about job creation. Startups are about jobs, not exits or changing the world like in Silicon Valley" (authors' interview Seoul, June 20, 2017). As the MSS pointed out, one of the key metrics to determine the success of its fund-of-fund program was the number of jobs it had created (MSS 2019a). To this end, both governments actively pursued startup job creation programs. They continued Lee's Young Entrepreneurs Startup Academy, rebranded as the Youth Startup Academy, to ensure that poor managerial skills did not prevent the continuing operation of successful startups (KOSME 2018). The theme of good jobs was important for the Moon government, which stressed the need for startups to create high-quality jobs.

Focusing on the education system, initiatives strove to increase the entrepreneurial talent available within the Korean ecosystem. The Park government continued the BK21 program first established by Kim. Rebranded as BrainKorea21[Plus], this education program again provided financing for universities and students, with a focus on funding for students and infrastructure. The Moon government continued the program (National Research Foundation of Korea 2017). This orientation toward upskilling entrepreneurial talent also manifested at the regional government level. Notably, in April 2019, the Seoul Metropolitan Government announced its Global TOP 5 Start-up City Seoul initiative, which included its aim of nurturing "10,000 innovative talents who lead the technology startup" as well as increasing the stock of startup office space and enabling infrastructure (Seoul Metropolitan Government 2019).

The Park and Moon governments have also worked to attract foreign talent, underpinned by the belief that highly skilled foreigners could be attracted to Korea. Seoul launched an entrepreneur visa for foreigners willing to launch a startup in Korea. These policies continued under the Yoon government, with his team vowing to encourage startups in an effort to create jobs (Choi 2022) and the president drawing a direct link between startups and job creation in his 2023 New Year address.[5]

While more flexible labor markets could indicate a shift toward Mark I, we note that attention has been given to how Korea's more creative, risk-taking labor can serve the chaebol. For instance, an interviewee remarked that "the chaebol now hire experienced employees rather than rookies or fresh [straight out of university] graduates. As a result, graduates do startups as a means of getting experience" (authors' interview, Seoul, August 23, 2022). While this sparks new questions about the intensity or value of the startup activities that young Koreans engage in, it suggests some reduction in the linear career path in which graduates of top universities join chaebol straight out of their degree program. The chaebol have come to value the experience that their employees gained at startups.

Finance

The EAFC served as a critical juncture to the financing of innovation in the economy. Korea's domestic banking sector suffered heavily from the EAFC and was in a very different shape once the effects of the crisis were over (Jeon and Miller 2005, 149). In this context, policy makers moved in two directions. To begin with, the state sought to further develop domestic capital markets, including VC markets. The government launched its own VC funds and created a program to provide matching funds for VC LPs. Particularly significant was the launch of KVIC by the Roh government in 2005. KVIC underwrites the VC market through the thirty-year Korea Fund of Funds (FoF), an investment vehicle in private VC funds. The FoF was not directly picking winning firms (or sectors). Instead, it was investing in private VC firms that then made their own investments into high-growth startups (Thurbon 2016). KVIC fostered private investment by promoting participation by institutional investors and pension funds while working to boost the number of angel investors (KVIC 2024d).

The Korean government used financing to address one of the perceived weaknesses of startups: their failure to commercialize innovative products. The Ministry of Information and Communication established business incubators, called iParks, in eight locations across the world, including Silicon Valley and other innovation centers. These incubators provided startups with free office space and mentoring and enabled the establishment of partnerships with local commercial entities (Thurbon and Weiss 2006). In a similar vein, the Kim government launched Korea BioValley in San Diego, California, in 2002. The focus was on biotech innovation, with the government building the infrastructure and providing below market rate or free leases to companies in this sector (Niiler 2002).

In addition, in 2012, the National Assembly passed an amendment to the Korea Technology Finance Corporation Act. The amendment allowed the Korea Technology Finance Corporation—founded in 1989 as the Korea Technology Credit Guarantee Fund—to provide equity investment to early-stage venture businesses. This was a significant change insofar as the government had previously provided loans or credit guarantees to startups or to firms financing them, such as VC firms. But the government could now have a direct equity stake in startups.

Equity funding for startups substantially increased under the Park and Moon governments. KVIC continued to be a main source. It took a more nuanced approach, with the launch of three new funds to provide more targeted largesse.[6] Seeking to tap into private funding, KVIC also launched two joint funds under the Park and Moon governments, respectively. The KEPCO FoF was launched in 2015. With a fund size of KRW52.5 billion by the end of 2018, its focus was to boost the power and energy sectors as well as ICT startups in both Gwangju and South Jeolla Province. Meanwhile, the KRW110 billion KEBHana-KVIC Unicorns Fund of Funds was formed in 2018 to foster startups in the innovation ecosystem and, relatedly, to nurture unicorns through indirect investments (KVIC 2019, 8). In addition, the Korean government's long-standing financial institutions ramped up their investments in startup. The Financial Services Commission pledged KRW7 trillion (US$5.9 billion) for startup investments, and the Korea Development Bank and K-Growth committed allocations of KRW8 trillion between 2018 and 2020 (Lee 2019).

In the spirit of encouraging Silicon Valley–styled financing for innovation, the Park government set up several equity-based investment mechanisms. Managed by K-Growth from 2016, the Ladder Growth Fund was divided into separate funds specializing in the seed, growth, and later stages of a startup's life cycle (K-Growth 2020). KONEX was created as a stock exchange for startups prior to them being capable of listing on KOSDAQ. In other words, it was created as a vehicle to provide an exit strategy to startups not yet ready to be accepted for listing on KOSDAQ (KONEX 2020). To further foster financing of Korea's growing startup ecosystem, Moon announced a so-called Second Venture Boom in March 2019.[7] The focus was to help startups to scale up as well as to prevent them from going bust due to a lack of funding at the crucial point of working to achieve product-market fit. Building on this commitment to boost the availability of early-stage VC, the National Pension Service (NPS) committed US$127.2 million to four Seoul-headquartered venture capital funds: SL Investment Co., DSC Investment Inc., Stonebridge Ventures Inc., and Mirae Asset Venture Investment Co. (Kim 2021).

The Moon government also launched the K-Unicorn program in 2020 to attract private capital—including foreign capital—to select startups with the potential to become unicorns. Korea Institute of Startup & Entrepreneurship Development (KISED) identified innovative "baby unicorns" (defined as having a corporate value less than KRW100 billion) that could graduate to "preliminary unicorns" (value over KRW100 billion but less than KRW1 trillion) and then become "unicorns" (value more than KRW1 trillion) in their own right (KISED 2021). As of 2023, fifty South Korean open innovation ecosystem players, including accelerators, banks, chaebol, government agencies, VC funds, and unicorns themselves, had provided funding, mentoring, training, and internationalization assistance for these growing startups (KVIC 2023).

While the chaebol had been involved in startup financing in tangential ways, Korea's big businesses explicitly entered the country's growing startup-oriented equity markets, as a regulatory change in 2020 allowed them to run corporate VC funds in Korea. The corporate VC regulatory change enabled their equity-based investments, as "it strictly prohibits expanding into lending among other financial service businesses" (Lee 2020). Speaking to the open innovation orientation, an interviewee remarked that the change means that "startups have a good opportunity to network with the chaebol as investors" (authors' interview, Seoul, August 23, 2022). The government announcement emphasized the mutual benefit for startups and chaebol, with the assertion that "large conglomerates will be able to seek greater business opportunities and startups will be able to share corporate growth strategies including technological development and overall management from the capital provider" (Lee 2020). In addition to domestic regulations allowing Korean corporate VC, the chaebol continued to operate as VCs internationally. For instance, Lotte, a large chaebol, announced its plan to open a Silicon Valley VC unit in May 2023. A press release noted that "the group established Lotte Ventures Japan Co. last year [2022] with an aim to invest in local startups in cooperation with Mizuho Bank, one of the country's three mega-banks" (Bae 2023). This is a telling example of the involvement of the chaebol in Korea's VC industry.

The Yoon government furthered this trend toward the chaebol providing financial assistance for startups. The minister of Trade, Industry, and Energy, Lee Chang-yang, announced in July 2023 an initiative to fund a corporate venture capital alliance with several chaebol to invest more than US$6 billion in Korea startups by 2025 (Shin 2023). Also in 2023, the government announced a KRW10.5 trillion investment plan to mitigate the global startup investment crunch (Pulse News 2023). Part of this decisive action has been in close collaboration with the chaebol, which, in the case of the corporate venture alliance, provided most of the money (KRW8 trillion), while the government itself commits to a more modest amount (KRW1 trillion).

Innovation

As Korea sought to find new sources of growth in the aftermath of the crisis, startup-fueled innovation became one of the areas prioritized by the government (Choung et al. 2014). Nimbler, in need of new products, and unhindered by internal bureaucratic hurdles, startups were considered to have a competitive advantage over their larger peers when it came to the R&D of new technologies (authors' interview, Seoul, June 20, 2017). For the first time, Korea conducted technology assessments of nano-bio-info and radio-frequency identification technologies (Seong and Song 2008, 38–39). The goal was to harness the expertise of groups with different knowledge and skills, which could boost frontier innovation. Thus, as Korean startups moved into internet technologies, Korea Trade-Investment Promotion Agency (KOTRA) began launching themed programs in Silicon Valley, including Invest KOREA Online in 2003. The iPark Silicon Valley, established with government funding in 2000, was the first of the government's incubators to open globally, which underscored the primacy of efforts to develop close relations with Silicon Valley and thus advance national capacity toward the technological frontier (Thurbon and Weiss 2006, 12).

The Korean state felt that the national education system might be inadequate to develop the necessary human resources to promote innovation at the technological frontier. In 1999, the Ministry of Education and Human Resources Development launched Brain Korea 21. This was a US$21 billion, seven-year education project aimed at supporting and developing graduate schools that could produce creative knowledge. All areas of knowledge received funding, but the emphasis was on natural and applied sciences. Most of the funding went to students and infrastructure to ensure that it reached its intended beneficiaries (Moon and Kim 2001, 99). Brain Korea 21 was subsequently renewed by the Roh government and survived until 2012.

Dating back to the 1980s and especially in the 1990s, Korea feared that it would be sandwiched between "high-tech" Japan and "low-cost" China, leading to both a lack of competitiveness and the hollowing out of its industry. This was the economic iteration of the centuries-old "shrimp among whales" syndrome (Pacheco Pardo 2022), whereby Koreans feel that their well-being is not in their hands but instead depends on the actions of bigger countries in the region. In the aftermath of the GFC, and with China attracting an ever-growing number of manufacturing jobs and moving up the value-added chain, this fear intensified. The feeling was that Korea was in dire need of upgrading its innovation capacity, and entrepreneurial thinking was construed as an important element for making this shift.

From the Lee government's perspective, boosting Korea's basic research capabilities was necessary if it was going to compete at the technological frontier. The Ministry of Education, Science, and Technology (MEST) was entrusted with this task. Already from the 1980s onward, it was clear that the chaebol were leading Korea's innovation through their internal R&D units rather than in cooperation with public bodies (Mok 2013). By bringing together education and S&T under the same ministry, the government was seeking to strengthen the links among the country's school education policy, basic research conducted by universities, and competitiveness in new technologies fostered by the chaebol and startups. This included an education policy fostering basic skills and creativity. This was coupled with an S&T approach based on greater funding for such high-risk, high-return areas as biotechnology, brain research, and nanotechnology.

The ongoing need to compete at the frontier stage continued to be a driver of the Park and Moon administrations' startup policies. Park established the Ministry of Science, ICT, and Future Planning upon starting her term in office. This so called super-ministry had control over all government R&D funding as well as all S&T policies (Larson and Park 2014). When Moon took office in 2017, it was succeeded by the Ministry of Science and ICT, which retained broadly the same competencies, as his government focused on the Fourth Industrial Revolution. Within this wider setting, the Park and Moon governments targeted startups for the purpose of boosting national innovation capacity, especially those in the services sector (OECD 2014, 36). A key reason behind the focus on startups was the belief that the chaebol might find it more difficult to innovate in new areas due to their strength in existing sectors. Since the chaebol were stronger in manufacturing, the government could see startup-centric innovation in services to compensate for the chaebol weaknesses.

The Yoon government then introduced a regulatory change to spark innovation new to Korea and still relatively rare across Asia: negative regulation. For the first time, startups establishing operations in ten innovation special zones across the country would be allowed to innovate in an environment in which almost everything (except what was explicitly prohibited by law) was permitted (Im 2023). The aim was to promote radical innovation by removing regulatory constraints on new ideas, products, and services. In addition, the Yoon government formally announced in March 2023 that it would launch K-BIO Lab Hub. Modeled on Boston's LabCentral, this was to become a hub for the government, chaebol, and startups to collaborate in the biotech sector (Hwang 2023). Plus, the Seoul Metropolitan Government announced the establishment of the Seoul Unicorn Startup Hub, which it claimed would be one of the biggest such hubs across Asia once opened (Lee 2023).

In sum, the aim of startup capitalism in Korea has been to foster the country's ability to achieve its increasingly radical innovation aims. Initiatives have often striven to leverage the relative strengths of the chaebol and startups by fostering chaebol-startup collaboration in an increasingly open innovation context. An interviewee who mentors startups at the CCEI in Seoul explained that the expectation today is increasingly that "ideas need to be globally innovative; not just copying what is happening elsewhere, and translating it to the Korea context" (authors' interview, Seoul, August 24, 2022). Fomenting Korea's collective ability to innovate at the frontier has involved the incorporation of Mark I radical innovation aims, but this has been done in the context of the chaebol delivering these evolutionary (manufacturing-based) advances with input from startups and an increasingly entrepreneurial society.

Social Purpose

Domestic issues—particularly job creation—have been central to the social purpose motivating Korea's startup capitalism. To begin with, the EAFC was blamed for the developmental state model itself (Chang 2003; Hundt 2005). In particular, close links between government and the chaebol, and between the chaebol themselves, were said to have entrenched corrupt practices that were preventing the Korean economy from competing with other developed countries.[8] Several chaebol had gone bankrupt, and many others laid off staff. This served to further erode trust in the chaebol, which were seen as not keeping their side of the bargain by providing stable employment. The social contract underpinning socioeconomic relations for decades was thus undermined (Wang 2007). At the same time, democracy was in the process of consolidation, and 1997 brought the peaceful transition of power to a liberal president—Kim Dae-jung—for the first time in Korean history. A growing number of Koreans expected the welfare state to become stronger and the government to become more interventionist in support of the general population.

The Kim government therefore came to power with the need to look for a new economic model. Given Kim's own life trajectory—namely, his decades-old position as a prominent liberal opposed to previous dictatorial governments—he was already predisposed to reduce dependence on the chaebol as a source of economic growth (Kim 2019). Elected in the middle of the dot-com bubble, Kim saw entrepreneurship as a means to spark economic growth, create jobs, promote innovation, and diversify the economy. The Kim government thus launched an array of plans, regulatory changes, and other initiatives designed to make startups more central to innovation and economic growth in Korea. Roh Moo-hyun, his liberal successor, would follow suit, seeing startups as unhindered by the bureaucratic impediments that rendered innovation more difficult for the chaebol (authors' interview, Seoul, June 20, 2017). Therefore, the Kim and Roh governments believed that startups could become a source of high-quality jobs along with the chaebol (Klingler-Vidra and Pacheco Pardo 2019).

Lee Myung-bak became the first conservative president in ten years when he took office in 2008. The former CEO of a Hyundai unit, he campaigned on a platform calling for deregulation and less state interventionism.[9] The Lee government continued to support innovative startups. The main social purpose of Lee's startup policy was job creation (Klingler-Vidra and Pacheco Pardo 2020). This was a continuation of his liberal predecessors' aim of boosting high-quality employment through innovative startups. In particular, the government wanted to increase the number of jobs available to younger Koreans who otherwise might find it difficult to find high-quality positions. Thus, in March 2010, the Ministry of Knowledge Economy announced plans to help talented Koreans become "the next Steve Jobs or Bill Gates in the software industry" by backing ten would-be entrepreneurs to set up their own company (Bae 2011). Indeed, in his 2012 New Year address, Lee mentioned the case of a young Korean entrepreneur who had launched a startup and "hired 20 young workers in just one year."[10] This epitomized the emphasis on startup capitalism's ability to deliver job creation.

The social purpose of encouraging a more creative, risk-taking society came to the fore when Park Geun-hye made the "creative economy" one of the centerpieces of her inaugural address in February 2013, after mentioning the topic during her campaign.[11] Her government unveiled a Creative Economy Action Plan shortly after, in June.[12] Continuing along the same lines, Moon put the Fourth Industrial Revolution at the center of his economic policy in one of his first major economic speeches in June 2018;[13] this was barely a month after his inauguration and followed repeated discussion of the issue during his campaign. In October, the Moon government launched the Presidential Committee on the Fourth Industrial Revolution, tasked with making Korea a world leader in areas such as ICT and AI (Sohn 2017). This signaled that the Korean state thought that innovation and startups were not optional but rather major elements of the present and future of the Korean economy, as both Park and Moon sought to develop sustainable entrepreneurial ecosystems.

As an official working for the MSS put it, startups are seen as an engine for quality employment, especially in acknowledgment that the chaebol cannot always provide the number of high-quality jobs that the market demands (authors' interview, Daejeon, August 25, 2017). Park and Moon encouraged entrepreneurship through media appearances and visits to startups. They sought to change the mentality of the population so that failure in one startup did not result in loss of respect or financial ostracism.

From the beginning of the Moon administration, social inclusion has been named as a driver of startup largesse. To this end, the government launched the 2019 Master Plan for Promoting Women's Entrepreneurship Activities. The master plan included several funding lines and guarantee programs to bolster female entrepreneurship (MSS 2019b). Considering that the female labor force participation rate historically lagged the male rate and stood at 53 percent in 2018 (World Bank 2020c), the master plan was a means to create jobs for an underrepresented segment of the population. According to entrepreneurs we interviewed, women feel that startups provide more flexibility and a better work-life balance compared to the chaebol (authors' interview, Seoul,

August 30, 2016). It therefore made sense to boost job creation through efforts to encourage female entrepreneurs. As a reflection of this, already in 2016, the country's startup ecosystem had a higher ratio of female employees compared to Silicon Valley and other ecosystems (Korean Startup Ecosystem Forum 2016).

In line with the aim of boosting female inclusion in employment, the MSS announced a US$465 million package as part of the 2019 Master Plan for Promoting Women's Entrepreneurship Activities, along with a US$7.85 billion public procurement program to purchase products from women-led startups. The objective was to promote women-led startups through the provision of special guarantees, R&D assistance, and purchases (MSS 2019c). The explicit encouragement for female entrepreneurship also continued during the Yoon government via the MSS (Kim 2023). In March 2023, for instance, the MSS launched a new women's venture-fostering project that targets "female startups with less than 7 years of entrepreneurship" and provides "a comprehensive support system such as customized education and mentoring, commercialization fund support, and cooperative networks" (Dave 2023).

Thus, despite the wider imperative of technological innovation as a means of bolstering national security vis-à-vis North Korea, much of the social purpose underpinning Korea's startup capitalism is domestic-oriented. Job creation and social inclusion are the rationales often given when startup policies are launched.

Continuity and Change in Korea

Korea's first big wave of help for startups took place following the EAFC. With the chaebol criticized for their alleged role before and during the crisis, and inspired by the ongoing dot-com bubble, the government championed startups as the center of its economic policy. There was a degree of continuity with the approach taken prior to the crisis, but there was a rapid increase in the provision of equity investment, a move toward radical innovation and more fluidity in the labor market. However, these shifts have happened in the context of a continued focus on large firms, with startups contributing to their open innovation systems. Figure 3.1 summarizes the evolution of firm size, employment, finance, innovation, and social purpose in Korea's startup capitalism.

Throughout its different phases, the institutional foundations of the Korean developmental state have evolved, though the chaebol remain central to the innovation system. The social purpose has not changed significantly and remains centered on job creation, though the external security threat is an important motivator for economic and technological performance. Employment, financ-

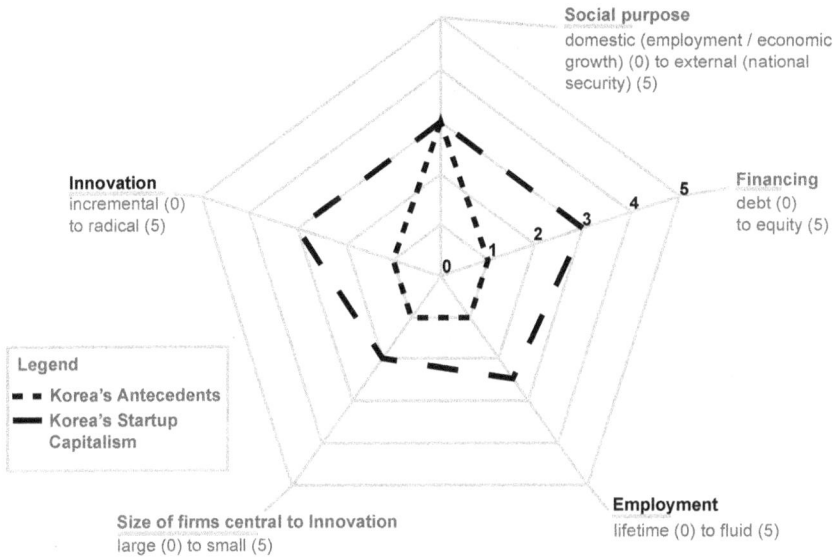

FIGURE 3.1. Analyzing Korea's institutional evolution: antecedents to startup capitalism

ing, and innovation have all moved in the direction of Mark I logics, becoming more fluid, equity-based, and radical, respectively. While those three institutional areas move toward scores of 3, the size of firm central to innovation remains, on balance, closer to the Mark II end of the continuum (with a score of 2 in fig. 3.1). This reflects the fact that while direct state support for the chaebol has become less politically salable, startup capitalism is oriented toward indirect help for the chaebol and encouraging cooperation between startups and the conglomerates.

Thus, figure 3.1 portrays the relatively modest movement, over time, toward startups as important contributors to innovation. The starting point for firm size in figure 3.1 illustrates that the chaebol were the main beneficiaries of government efforts to drive innovation up to the 1997 EAFC. Korean governments throughout the catch-up growth state involved the chaebol leaders in the decision-making and implementation processes. The situation has evolved slightly post-EAFC, as largesse for innovation has often been directly linked to support for startups. However, startups have been portrayed as fueling chaebol-led open innovation systems. The chaebol are involved in initiatives that intend for them to achieve mutual benefit through their interaction with startups. In this sense, startups have not been construed as disruptors. While startups now play more of a role, the center of gravity of Korea's startup capitalism with respect to firm size remains focused on oligopolistic competition, and thus the illustration of firm size in figure 3.1 remains closer to the Mark II variety of startup capitalism.

Korea's labor market has become more fluid over time, moving close to—but not achieving—a score of 3 in figure 3.1. The antecedent period is illustrated as close to a permanent employment ideal, consistent with Mark II. This is because, throughout the catch-up growth period, employment in Korea was defined by the chaebol-based permanent employment model, whereby workers could expect steady income and benefits as they climbed up the corporate ladder. Certainly, the benefits associated with employment in the chaebol have continued, including higher salaries and generous pensions. But at the same time, this implicit social contract broke down. This began with the EAFC and the relatively high youth unemployment it brought. Startups were increasingly seen as a socially acceptable source of employment. This was reinforced through policies that encouraged fluidity, including pension portability, education programs, and funding for entrepreneurial ventures. While flexibility has advanced and many graduates now seek startup experience, such undertakings are often assumed to lead to the procurement of long-term employment with a chaebol.

The financing for innovation has also seen a shift in the direction of a Mark I setting but, again, not convergence on this Silicon Valley type. Figure 3.1 shows a score of 3, reflecting the proliferation of equity-based financing, especially in the post-EAFC context. In the classic developmental state setting, state provision of credit to (large) firms was core, and as such, Korea's antecedent score for financing was 1. Korea's financing has evolved from that bank-based characteristic, as equity-based financing activities have proliferated. Successive governments have launched VC funds, startup-friendly stock exchanges, and more. In line with the persistence of the chaebol as central to Korea's innovation system, since 2020, the government has enabled the oligopolistic firms—including long-established chaebol like Samsung and new ones like Naver—to operate as important equity investors in Korea's startups.

In a similar way, there has been a shift—like the one seen in Japan, but about a decade later—from catch-up toward the technological frontier. As a result, Korea's antecedent period's innovation was scored as 1 in figure 3.1, reflecting the incremental nature of its innovation. Innovation from the 1960s to the 1990s was based on a catch-up approach. Korea was trying to climb up the innovation ladder by making use of government investment and cheap labor to compete with more advanced countries. A shift started in the 1980s, with the government and several of the chaebol seeking to compete at the frontier. Since Korea achieved developed country status in the 1990s, there has been a concerted shift toward innovation at the technological frontier. In this context, the Korean government has seen startups as the solution to the potential problem of the chaebol not being able to compete at the frontier stage. Startups could be partnered with the chaebol to complement and boost their ability to deliver novel technological innovation. Thus, Korea's startup capitalism's innovation orientation is scored as a 3, reflecting this movement toward radical innovation.

There has been persistence in the social purposes motivating startup efforts. Job creation and an injection of innovative ideas and talent into the chaebol underpin initiatives. In line with other East Asian cases, these domestic social purposes and the desire to compete at the technological frontier as a means of engendering economic competitiveness and national security have been consistent. As a result, figure 3.1 illustrates this with both the antecedent and startup capitalism epochs having the same score of 3, a combination of domestic and external social purposes.

TAIWAN

"The government does not intend to tell businesses what to do or what not to do," President Tsai Ing-wen explained in response to criticism by TSMC Chairman Morris Chang in October 2017 (*Taipei Times* 2017). Chang had lashed out after the announcement about industrial policies that would focus on building new sectors, like biotechnology, green energy, and smart machinery, rather than champion the all-important semiconductor sector. Chang's reasoning centered on how important semiconductors were to the Taiwanese economy and society. According to Chang, the country faced an existential crisis in which the "Silicon Shield" supplied by the global position of semiconductor manufacturing firms (Klingler-Vidra 2023; Cheng and Li 2021), especially TSMC, was being threatened. Tsai's response that she did not intend to help Taiwan's semiconductor giants was consistent with Taiwan's policy approach since the onset of the twenty-first century to widen the pool of entrepreneurs in new industries rather than to shore up the competitive positioning of its dominant firms and technologies. It was also in line with Taiwan's long-established orientation toward encouraging technology-centric startups rather than coordinating capacity-building among large leading firms.

As this semiconductor vignette suggests, Taiwan offers a different starting point, and thus a distinct continuity-change trajectory, in comparison to the two previous cases. The key difference is that the Taiwanese developmental state is characterized as being oriented toward small high-technology firms in select (critical) technologies. Volumes of research assert that Taiwanese industrial policies favored small firms (see Amsden 1985, 2001; Simon and Kau 1992; Yu

2012).[1] For instance, Karl Fields (1997, 125) notes that the Taiwanese state's ties with its "less concentrated private-business sector" were "decidedly more particularistic, diffuse and distant than those in Korea." In placing Taiwan in East Asian business systems scholarship, Richard Whitley (1992, 53) similarly asserts that the "dominant feature" is the "small size of most firms."

Thus, the Taiwanese case offers the opportunity to analyze continuity and change for the developmental state characterized as closest to the Mark I mode in its antecedent period. As this chapter shows, though its lead firms, notably TSMC, have adopted open innovation tactics, the Taiwanese state has largely exhibited continuity in its aim of widening entrepreneurial markets rather than fostering oligopolistic competition.

Antecedents: Taiwan (1949–1970)

Taiwan's economy has long been depicted as small-firm dominant, relative to the other East Asian developmental states of Japan and Korea. The small-firm orientation was fostered by public policies as the state drew on a variety of "financial regulations, tax and labor laws" to provide "strong incentives to limit firm size" (Fields 1997, 130). The early focus on small firms is explained, by Robert Wade (1990) and others, as being due to the Kuomintang (KMT)'s desire to ensure that indigenous Taiwanese entrepreneurs would not pose a rival center of power to the martial law–era government.[2] Analysts have observed that the Taiwanese state, from the martial law era, pursued technology- and small-firm-led "economic growth as congruent with, if not central to, enhanced national security" (Pempel 2021, 15).[3]

The regime's interests in encouraging a flexible labor market focused on encouraging entrepreneurs leading export-competing firms. There's a well-known saying in Taiwan that it is "better to be the head of a cock than the tail of a cow" (Kung and Yen 2018, 59). Said another way, it is better to be an entrepreneur and lead your own small company than it is to be an employee of a large company. Analysts note that in Taiwan, "workers generally did not picture themselves as lifetime industrial laborers; rather, a sizeable number were using their job to accumulate enough capital to start their own enterprise" (Gold 1986, 89). Despite the cultural values favoring entrepreneurship as a form of employment, in Taiwan's early years, the talent pools, especially for science and technology-based entrepreneurship, were limited. J. Megan Greene (2008, 41) notes that "relatively few highly trained scientists and technicians had fled to Taiwan with the KMT"; they instead moved to the United States and Europe.

Rather than focusing on catch-up aims, policy sought to boost innovation capacity toward the world's technological frontier. Analysts observed that they could see the gradual emergence of an overarching science policy from when the father of Taiwan's economic miracle, Kwoh-ting (K. T.) Li, pursued strategic efforts to boost the talent pool for technologically oriented entrepreneurship (Kuo 1983). Li's perspective was that the success of policies to incentivize small firms' science and technology prowess were "vital to Taiwan's future economic prosperity, and perhaps, political survival" (Winckler and Greenhalgh 1988, 219). Technology-centric economic competitiveness would help Taiwan to survive as a state and demonstrate the performance of the non-Communist approach (Amsden 2001). Yet Taiwan's small firms were said to not naturally invest in significant R&D or upgrading. Instead, Whitley (1992, 55) characterizes the tendency for Taiwan's small firms' "technology investments" to be "short term so that they can be written off after a few years."

In this spirit, the state encouraged small firms to export in particular industries through the Nineteen-Point Economic and Fiscal Reform Program (Nineteen-Point Program) and the Statute for the Encouragement of Investment (SEI) in 1960.[4] Crucially, the lists of industries eligible for these tax relief initiatives reflected policy makers' assessment of which technologies and industries were at the technological frontier at given points in time and central to national capacity upgrading (Wade 1990). The SEI was updated more "than a dozen times by 1980" and specified "categories and criteria of strategic productive enterprises singled out for special encouragement" (Gold 1986, 78). To further encourage Taiwan's small firms to invest in R&D, the government offered a series of tax incentives, including an R&D tax rebate, a five-year tax holiday for new industries, the accelerated depreciation of investments, and special tax credits for new strategic industries (World Bank 1993, 229). In addition, part of efforts for improving small firms' technological capacity was to secure technologies from abroad, attracting multinational companies to Taiwan and state firms and institutes transferring technology (see the China Data Processing Center, which was the country's first data-processing and software company, for instance; Breznitz 2007, 102).[5]

Unlike the Japanese and Korean cases in which significant lines of credit were made available to (large) firms, the little money provided to Taiwan's (small) firms came as a mix of equity and debt. The Chiang Kai-shek regime was careful to not allocate too much to any company, as the authoritarian leadership was worried that a concentration of capital could be used to mobilize support against the KMT. Finance for industry was "tightly controlled" (World Bank 1993, 20), allocated in small increments and through state-run banks. Small firms instead sought equity-based financing and loans from friends, family, revolving credit associations, and the unrelated "curb" loan clubs (Fields 1995). Another alternative to domestic banks as sources of financing in the 1960s was the US Agency for International Development Small Industry Loan Fund and Model Factory Program (Gold 1986, 71). With this funding came influence on policy in terms of American demands that "pushed for start-up companies," given the capital and individuals available on account of land reforms (Rubinstein 2013, 30). This again augured for the early fostering of equity-based, Silicon Valley–styled financing.

Thematic Analysis

Firm Size

By the 1970s, the Taiwanese electronics industry—and local firms that were competing in this global market—was booming. Thomas Gold (1986, 88) remarked that a motivating credo for the era was that "everyone wants to be chairman of his own company." Policy continued to encourage startups' upgrading capacity by helping them "to locate, purchase, diffuse and adapt new foreign technologies" (Lall 1996, 208). Policy leaders like Sun Chen noted that there was a need for the state, through Industrial Technology Research Institute (ITRI), to provide R&D services, as the SMEs did not "enjoy sufficient economies of scale to justify extensive spending on R&D" (Greene 2008, 121). With the establishment and take-up of the Hsinchu Park by returning overseas Chinese, the government's startup-centric innovation efforts were crystalizing. Gold (1986, 104) explains that the state hoped that "small, innovative companies headed by dynamic Chinese with experience abroad, buttressed by government technical and financial support," offered an important niche for Taiwan in global computer and consumer electronics markets.

In line with its wider Mark I character, small firms remained essential to the technological upgrading effort. The tax rate for profits on high-technology investments was set at zero from the 1980s, as small high-tech firms were categorized as "strategic industry enterprises" that received a tax holiday (Wang 1995, 5–6). Policy makers, particularly those on the Council for Economic Planning and Development (CEPD), encouraged growing Taiwanese companies such as Formosa Plastics and Acer to invest in local startups as venture capitalists. One aim was to foster integration between growing firms and fledgling firms and entrepreneurs.

The term *startup*, rather than SMEs or small firms, began being used by science and technology policy makers in the early 2000s. In 2002, Taiwan's SME Administration launched the Business Startup Award, stating that the "purpose of the award is to create more Startup companies" (MoEA SME Administration 2019a). Efforts were taken to boost available talent and financing for startups and to position startups as the organizational means for competing in innovative sectors in the knowledge economy. Already by the mid-2000s, the SME Administration had financially and administratively assisted seventy-nine startup incubation centers, sixty-five of which were within, or attached to, colleges and universities (Lee and Lai 2005, 2). The 2005–2008 Science and Technology Development Plan expanded on these efforts, with the Executive Yuan specifying the promotion of startups through the support of: (1) spinouts from R&D undertaken at universities; and (2) incubation services for technology-based startups (Executive Yuan 2005). The 2009–2012 S&T Development Plan took a similar tack, noting that encouraging "young people to establish their own businesses, and thereby transforming R&D capabilities into spin-off companies, will be a key method of fostering entrepreneurial innovation" (Executive Yuan 2009, 37). In a similar vein, efforts by the Ministry of Education to incentivize entrepreneurship included instruction, teaching, and competitions at universities (Executive Yuan 2009, 30).

Contemporary policy for startups has increasingly centered on fostering links with global ecosystems. For instance, in 2015, the National Development Council established Taiwan Startup Stadium (TSS) as an ecosystem builder; it aims to "cultivate globally-minded entrepreneurs and showcase the most innovative Taiwanese startups to the world."[6] Another example of a bridge-building initiative is the Taiwan Innovation and Tech Arena (TITAN), which was launched by the Ministry of Science and Technology (MoST) as a "tech startup ecosystem building program" in 2018 and partners with overseas innovation organizations in order to provide training and exposure for Taiwanese entrepreneurs (MoST 2021). Mentorship in the TITAN program is provided by foreign experts, especially in Silicon Valley, as a means of helping Taiwan's startups to go global, and access is equally given to foreign talent looking to establish or grow their startup in Taiwan. TITAN, for its inbound efforts, is described by FutureWard as aiming "to boost the diversity of Taiwan's innovation ecosystem by inviting talents from all over the world to create the next big thing with Taiwan's startups" (FutureWard 2019). In 2022, TTA ran the first iteration of an accelerator program with 500 Startups in which twenty startups (or those planning to enter the market) from Taiwan participated (Kong 2022).

While startups persist as key beneficiaries, policy efforts increasingly include attempts to foster an open innovation approach alongside large firms. This has often been via partnerships with foreign companies rather than big domestically based businesses like TSMC. In 2019, the Executive Yuan partnered with AWS to create a Joint Innovation Center at the Startup Terrace innovation park (Executive Yuan 2019a). The rationale for the collaboration is that with AWS's "discerning vision, technology services and capable guidance," Taiwan's startups "will be able to grow more quickly and connect to the global market to hone their competitive advantages" (Executive Yuan 2019b). In 2021, ITRI partnered with Arm, a British integrated circuit design firm bought by SoftBank in 2016, to run the "IC Design Platform for Startups" to "assist startups in accessing critical IP and accelerating the launch of competitive products for the global market" (ITRI 2021).

The contemporary open innovation setting is more software- and internet-based than the strategy of attracting multinational companies for hardware-focused technology transfer, initiated in the 1960s, but it does offer similarities. It also echoes some of the tech transfer aims of ITRI; rather than Taiwan's government entities playing this role, collaboration with leading international firms is expected to enable technology upgrading opportunities for Taiwan's startups. The beneficiaries remain local startups, not large firms. In this sense, there is not a shift toward Mark II, as Taiwan's small firms, not its leading oligopolistic firms, remain an essential engine for innovation in new cutting-edge technologies.

Separate from government policy, large Taiwanese incumbents, including TSMC, have embraced open innovation approaches. In 2009, TSMC made headlines when it announced the Open Innovation Platform, in which the company moved to share "R&D efforts with clients" (Kwong 2009). While using the language of open innovation, however, the platform did not specifically target startups but rather their clients in a bid to share R&D costs. On its corporate blog, TSMC's director of market development and emerging business management, Lucas Tsai, explained that "since its founding 35 years ago, TSMC has been working with startups across the industry, providing access to its technologies and manufacturing capacity to help them grow and thrive" (Tsai 2022). Tsai added that at the TSMC Open Innovation Summit, they brought together "startups, investors, and other chip innovators to discuss transformational silicon designs" and would work in partnership with Silicon Catalyst to run a semiconductor-focused incubator program (Tsai 2022). TSMC, as part of these activities, made headlines in 2023, when a former Kleiner Perkins partner, Wen Hseih, announced he was leaving to launch a Silicon Valley–based VC fund, Matter Venture Partners, backed by TSMC (Hu and Lee 2023). Thus, while Taiwan's startup policy continues to operate largely in line with its antecedent period in terms of targeting and striving to benefit a widening pool of startups, some of its lead firms have embraced startups as a resource for their open innovation systems.

Employment

Taiwan's labor market was more fluid and oriented toward entrepreneurship in its antecedent period. Over time, though, this propensity has been encouraged by policies that further promote startup activity. As such, Taiwan's focus on upskilling and incentivizing technology-centric entrepreneurs has only grown.

Already in the 1970s, Taiwan's emphasis was on skill development. To increase the availability of high-tech talent, Taiwan trained 50 per cent more engineers per 1,000 population than the United States (Wade 1990). In addition to domestically trained talent, overseas talent was also regarded as a bank in a brain circulation process, with policies trying to bring computer science PhDs back to Taiwan. This was possible, as Taiwanese students had begun moving to the United States to study (primarily PhDs in engineering) by way of American-Taiwanese funding programs, such as the US AID, in the 1950s (Greene 2008, 55). From the early 1980s, policies saw this overseas-trained talent as a resource that should be recruited back to Taiwan.

A concerted effort was made to foster an environment that would attract such talent with highly paid and intellectually interesting roles at high-growth firms. In December 1980, Hsinchu Park was established near ITRI and two elite engineering and science-focused universities in a bid to consolidate a hub of high-technology startup activity in Taiwan.[7] To attract entrepreneurs to set up in Hsinchu Park, the state offered "preferential tax and other treatment, including low-interest loans and tax-free privileges" as well as subsidies for up to 50 percent of R&D costs (Wen and Chen 2014, 229). The state also offered financial assistance to entrepreneurs in the form of equity investment in ventures operating in the Park. Given these advantages, Hsinchu Park was a crucial means of attracting overseas talent (back) to Taiwan's growing startups, as it quickly came to be "a beacon seen by Taiwanese engineers and scientists" working in the United States at firms such as IBM, RCA, and Texas Instruments (Rubinstein 2013, 41). Working at public research institutes in Taiwan, particularly ITRI, also proved a boon for technology-oriented entrepreneurial talent and inclination (Wen and Chen 2014, 228). Once engineers gained experience at ITRI, they were open to starting and scaling innovation-centric technology businesses. AnnaLee Saxenian (2006, 190) notes that between its founding in 1973 and 1998, "approximately 10,000 ITRI researchers left the agency to join the private sector."

Encouragement for fluidity in labor markets came from the productive movements between Hsinchu and California, coined the Silicon Valley–Hsinchu Connection in reference to the interactions between the two startup clusters (Saxenian and Hsu 2001). The semiconductor connection was initially boosted by six Taiwanese engineers quitting their jobs at Silicon Valley's leading semiconductor firm at the time, Fairchild Semiconductor, to return to Taiwan to set up their own firms. The connections played a role in UMC's success, as it "was able to conclude agreements with three Chinese-owned startups in Silicon Valley" to develop chip design (Lall 1996, 73).[8] Pioneer returnees "became role models for hundreds of subsequent returnees" (Saxenian 2006, 2). Through these efforts, by the late 1980s, 180,000 Taiwanese engineers had returned, many from Silicon Valley (Fuller 2002, 16). The scale of returnees was so immense that there were even associations of former employees of American tech companies, like Bell Systems. In 1992, for instance, the "Taiwanese Bell Systems Alumni Association had some 120 members" (Yeung 2016, 45). At the peak of the impact of this connection, in late 1998, 109 companies in Hsinchu Park were founded by returnees from the United States (Wen and Chen 2014, 234–235).

Despite the positive trend, and because of the phenomenal growth of Taiwanese firms in the critical technology of semiconductors, concerns about a talent shortage were a common refrain at the beginning of the twenty-first century. Growing opportunities in mainland China, among other overseas destinations, had meant that the engineering graduates coming from Taiwan's universities would not satisfy hiring demands (Miller 2022). For instance, "a 2005 ITRI study found that the country's semiconductor industry would need 37,500 new skilled workers over the next three years," but the country's university system could only supply 21,800 such graduates (National Research Council 2013). This shortfall was worrying, as analysts remarked that Taiwan's universities, including those around which Hsinchu Park was based, had been "viewed mainly as skilled labor–creating mechanisms" (Breznitz 2007, 137). Also, while ITRI had acted as a crucial training ground for would-be tech-centric entrepreneurs, in the 2000s, it was increasingly seeing its staff leave to embark on opportunities in mainland China rather than stay to start a company in Taiwan.

To retain talent in Taiwan, the government launched education and training efforts around startups. In 2003, the SME Online University was created with a startup-focused segment as one of six core areas, with others including IT, marketing, finance, human resources, and comprehensive knowledge (MoEA SME Administration 2019a). Toward the end of the period, the Science and Technology Development Plan (2009–2012) specified universities for their role in boosting entrepreneurship. The plan presented the observation that European and North American countries had promoted entrepreneurship in universities, so "Taiwan should keep up with this global trend by strongly promoting entrepreneurship education and related entrepreneurial activities at universities" (Executive Yuan 2009, 38).

In addition to promoting Taiwan-based entrepreneurship, efforts to encourage global connections and international exposure were made.[9] The Ministry of Economic Affairs (MoEA)'s SME Administration cited the Global Entrepreneurship Monitor (2019) report, which found that Taiwanese entrepreneurs lack awareness of opportunities. To remedy this, the agency aimed to deliver internationally linked programs to help ensure that "by taking part in international activities as well as making visits to multinational incubators and accelerators, the ecosystems will be filled with diverse possibilities and connecting with world-wide resources" (MoEA SME Administration 2019b). This aim was reflected in the From IP to IPO program launch in 2013, "which includes mentoring on venture capital negotiations by entrepreneurs and venture capitalists in Taiwan and Silicon Valley, to 40 selected start-up teams each year" (Klingler-Vidra 2018, 90).

Labor market fluidity has advanced through a concerted push to increase the availability of foreign talent for the startup ecosystem. One step toward this aim was the creation of the Contact Taiwan Program by the National Development Council in 2015. The program is an "all-out campaign to attract talent globally" to Taiwan (NDC 2015). With the program in place, the government passed the Act for the Recruitment and Employment of Foreign Professionals, which created an Entrepreneur Visa (Contact Taiwan 2018). Since its passage in 2015, the Entrepreneur Visa encourages foreigners to establish a startup in Taiwan that is focused on either serving the local market or having Taiwan as its headquarters (MoEA SME Administration 2023). Qualifications include the foreign national's ability to secure VC funding or obtain a recommendation from an incubator or science park. Also, in 2020, the MoEA established Taiwan Accelerator Plus, which includes an international program that offers help to international start-ups interested in expanding to Asia using Taiwan as their point of entry.[10]

Startup policies encourage this widening pool of domestic and international entrepreneurs to focus on *specific* emerging industries and technologies, like biotechnology and financial technology (fintech). In 2018, for example, the Financial Supervisory Commission, in partnership with its private-sector partner, the Taiwan Financial Service Roundtable, launched FinTechSpace, the country's first fintech-focused coworking space. Speaking at the launch event, the Financial Supervisory Commission Chairman Wellington Koo said that "the authorities will continue to seek more workspaces across the country for startups at affordable prices to enable them and Taiwan's economy to flourish" (Yang 2018). Fin-TechSpace opened with startups founded by foreigners constituting more than half of the accepted tenants.

To be sure, Taiwan's employment setting has remained largely aligned with the Mark I variety, with policies striving to widen the pool of highly skilled entrepreneurial talent by encouraging internationally minded entrepreneurship among Taiwanese citizens and attracting foreigners to the ecosystem. It remains fluid rather than striving for lifetime employment with large firms. Unlike Japan and Korea, incumbent Taiwanese firms are not included in the judging process or named as intended partners for the startup talent development, nor are government programs encouraging secondments. Instead, the flexible labor market initiatives continue to motivate high-technology startup employment and moves across geographies and firms.

Finance

In the antecedent period, Taiwan's state-owned banks directed little credit to small firms. These state-owned banks, especially before financial liberalization in the 1980s, had significant control over the provision of credit. As a result, start-ups had to seek alternative means of financing, including unregulated and unofficial sources (the grey market) (Chu 1999). Policy also provided other forms of help for startups, including R&D infrastructure and tax incentives (Fields 2012). The state, continuing the SEI practice, offered tax credits of 20 percent for high-technology sector R&D in the 1970s as well as a five-year corporate income tax holiday for "newly established capital or technology-intensive projects" (GIO 1986, 237).

Unlike policy makers in Japan and Korea, those in Taiwan worked to ensure that equity-based venture capital in the early 1980s was available to technology startups. They aimed to foster a local VC market, like that in Silicon Valley, to encourage Taiwan's growing technology firms (Yeh 2006). For K. T. Li, the expectation was that a VC market could expand Taiwan's incomplete financial services sector, promote its technology startups, and advance the local use of modern management techniques (Saxenian and Li 2002, 140). In 1981, Li organized for a group of senior policy makers and select industry leaders to take a study trip to the United States and Japan to learn more about VC.[11] By the end of the trip, Li and his colleagues concluded that venture capital would "integrate capital, technology, talent, and management for the purpose of upgrading Taiwan's technological developments" (Klingler-Vidra 2018, 81). Two years after their study trip, Taiwan's CEPD passed a Ministry of Finance bill—the Regulations for the Administration of Venture Capital Enterprises—that gave a 20 percent tax credit for first-time VC investors (Wang 1995, 2). The 20 percent tax credit was offered to local first-time VC investors if they maintained their high-technology VC investment for a minimum of two years.

In the years that followed, additional efforts sought to boost the availability of equity-based VC for Taiwanese startups. In 1985, the Chiao Tung Bank formed a VC fund by providing capital along with the Development Fund and the Sino-American Foundation, with the remaining half of capital coming from the American investment bank H&Q. To bring local incumbents into the growing VC market, tax credits were expanded to incentivize local corporations to invest as VCs in 1991 (Kenney et al. 2002). VC reinvestment was encouraged, as tax exemptions were then offered on the capital gains earned by venture capitalists exiting from their investments in high-technology startups (Koh and Wong 2005, 26).

With the Democratic Progressive Party government coming into office in 2000, after having run on a platform that promised to lessen the allocation of state resources to established industries, except the R&D tax credits for breakthrough technologies, the state discontinued the 20 percent venture capital tax credit. The rationale was that Taiwan's VC industry no longer needed such help, as it had become the fourth largest VC market in Asia (behind Japan, Hong Kong, and Singapore) and the world's third most active, in terms of deal volume, behind only the United States and Israel (AVCJ 2005). It was also said to be the Asian venture capital market that was "most Silicon Valley–like" (Gulinello 2005, 845).[12] While tax credits were ceased, additional government funding for this early-stage equity market came in October 2001, as the Development Fund participated in the National Development Plan. The fund raised the remaining 70 percent of the money from private-sector investors (Klingler-Vidra et al. 2016).

Despite its vibrant venture capital market, the MoEA oversaw several regulatory changes as a means of trying to encourage even more private capital in the VC market. For instance, in 2004, the Amendment of Regulations on the Scope and Guidance of Venture Capital Enterprises effectively expanded funding channels and eased restrictions on investment scope and fund utilization. Then, in 2006, a Relaxed Scope was passed, which made it easier for investors to exit their positions by decreasing the required holding time of company securities and lifting the limit on share sales. Collectively, the VC and stock market policy changes helped to improve the exit environment for equity investors in Taiwanese startups.

Policy makers have worked to expand stock market access for Taiwan's high-growth startups and even for foreign startups. The Emerging Stock Board was created within the Taipei Exchange in 2002 to help startups access the capital market as a "pre-IPO" platform. The ESB was created in response to specific concerns about the stringency of rules around listing on the Taiwan Stock Exchange and the requirements for several years of revenue, which high-growth startups struggled to meet. With this, stock market access was expanded such that the number of companies listed on exchange grew to five hundred by 2005, and in 2009, the first foreign company listed on the Emerging Stock Board (Taipei Exchange 2022).

The launch of the InvesTaiwan Service Center in 2010 would further attract equity financing—from foreign sources—for the country's growing technology startups. The InvesTaiwan Center had ITRI representatives, as the MoEA was targeting foreign investment into growing companies in the information technology and biotechnology sectors. Given the contemporaneous signing of the Economic Cooperation Framework Agreement with China, the InvesTaiwan Center was expected to help address the "many foreign investors [who] have expressed interest in investing in Taiwan" (Lin and Huang 2010). As part of the HeadStart Taiwan initiative, the National Development Fund offered US$400 million in matching funds for venture capitalists investing in Taiwanese startups (NDC 2014). The HeadStart funding included a 40 percent match funding provision, as had previous National Development Fund initiatives, to entice international VCs to invest in Taiwanese startups. Also, in a bid to attract foreign VC, in 2015, the NDC announced further efforts to boost local startups, with plans to co-invest alongside four international funds, including 500 Startups and AppWorks (Fulco 2015). Policy makers also created a bilateral VC fund, run in partnership with New Zealand, in March 2012, and in 2017, the National Development Fund established the NT$2 billion Business Angel Investment Program (NDC 2019).

Continuing with the thrust of equity investment as a primary means of boosting innovation in new industries and firms, a major funding development came in 2017 with the launch of Taiwania Capital by the National Development Fund and private investors (NDC 2017). Taiwania describes itself as the government's venture capital arm; it aims to "boost Taiwan's economic growth by partnering cutting-edge startups in sectors including information and communication technology (ICT), biotech, material, energy and new agriculture."[13] At the other end of the equity investment cycle, the Taipei Exchange created the Pioneer Stock Board to help companies operating in priority industries access the public equities market.

Collectively, since the deliberate growth of venture capital markets since the 1980s as a means of providing smart money for technology-oriented startups, policies have remained equity focused and have sought to expand the set of equity investors geographically (by eliciting international investors) and across the early stage (e.g., angels and VCs) and to advance exit venues available for selling equity stakes (e.g., startup-friendly stock markets). Thus, Taiwan remains closest to the Mark I variety in its equity-based financial system.

Innovation

Already in its antecedent period, Taiwanese policy aimed for the technological frontier rather than catch-up technologies. It established technology-specific labs, notably the crucial Industrial Technology Research Institute (ITRI) in 1973, as a key lab for technological advances. ITRI "received government contracts to conduct research programs, develop key technologies and transfer the results to industry in a non-exclusive manner" (Tsai 1999, 73). ITRI's aim was to advance cutting-edge innovation capacity, particularly for integrated circuits via the 1974 creation of the Electronic Research Service Organization (ERSO). Taiwanese engineers called the ERSO mode of technology transfer "R&D: reverse and duplicate," given the emphasis on reverse engineering rather than exploratory research (Saxenian 2006, 189).

As high-profile initiatives like ITRI and the Hsinchu Park signify, Taiwanese policy has long striven to achieve high-tech industrial development. Complementing the concerted push in Hsinchu Park, strategies such as the Four-Year Plan for 1982–1986 and the Ten-Year Plan for 1980–1989 constituted a continuing shying away from capital-intensive activities and toward technology-intensive industries, especially computers, telecommunications, and robotics, in which small firms could compete. Competing at the technological frontier was already essential from the 1980s, given the rise of quotas or tariffs in foreign markets. Owing to Taiwan's early success, its firms were already facing protectionism in key international markets, so new technologies that would not yet be subject to trade barriers were backed. Industrial policy demonstrated the push for R&D so that Taiwanese firms were competing at the international technological frontier. In particular, the Statute for Encouragement of Investment was revised (again) in January 1981 by K. T. Li, such that "industries receiving benefits under the statute" had to "spend a standard amount of money on R&D" (Gold 1986, 103).

The focus on radical innovation, though, was not entirely smooth, as it still relied on the acquisition of foreign technology or on the manufacturing end of technologies designed elsewhere (e.g., in semiconductor manufacturing). While the acquisition of technology was often done on the backs of key geopolitical connections, there were cases, especially around the personal computer (PC) industry, where it received growing scrutiny. For instance, in 1982, Apple "clamped down on the thriving Taiwanese Apple II cloning industry" (Breznitz 2007, 114). There were challenges around the use of intellectual property from US companies, as in "1984, US Customs agents seized Taiwan-made, ERSO-designed IBM-compatible personal computers as fake IBM" personal computers (Gold 1986, 104). Despite the issues with IP infringement in the development of Taiwan's PC industry, these early imitation experiences helped to establish technical abilities. Acer, in particular, had gleaned competitive capabilities in the PC market by the mid-1980s (Wen and Chen 2014, 231).

Competition at the technological frontier was fostered by the state's help in creating and scaling new firms—or, in Mark I terms, in creating new entrepreneurial pools. Arguably the most successful illustration of this approach is TSMC, which was founded in 1986 as a pureplay semiconductor chip fabrication foundry spun out of ITRI's ERSO.[14] TSMC's approach—which separated semiconductor chip design from fabrication, enabling it to produce chips for a wide range of companies, as it did not pose a competitive threat—aimed to super charge the centrality of Taiwan in the global semiconductor industry, *the critical frontier technology of the time*. Though the state helped create TSMC initially, it also restricted its strategy, as TSMC was "forbidden to design products of its own" so that it would "not rival smaller, private firms" (Fields 1997, 146). Furthermore, the "foundry model suited small firms, such as TSMC, trying to advance technologically because these firms could learn through serving their customers" (Fuller 2013a, 52). TSMC's focus on foundries—and not integrated chip design—suited its international customers and made space for would-be Taiwanese startups competing in the space.[15]

The state continued to focus on the technological frontier. Owing to the success of its semiconductor industry, the state availed largesse for startups competing at the frontier of emerging technological areas, including biotechnology, optoelectronics, and green technologies, and not semiconductors (Wong 2005). For instance, biotechnology and digital content were named as "twin stars" in the 2002 launch of the Challenge 2008 project (Lee and Lai 2005).[16] In 2006, ITRI established a science park in Tainan to boost one of the new priority industries. Rather than serving as an extension of Hsinchu and its focus on semiconductors, startups in Tainan were encouraged to focus on displays and optoelectronics, particularly liquid crystal displays (LCDs) (Kung and Yen 2018, 61). The Tsai administration, upon taking office in 2016, offered tax breaks aimed at specific emerging technologies (Kuo and Han 2017). It prioritized five industries: green energy technology, smart machinery, internet of things, biotechnology, and defense industry. As mentioned at the beginning of this chapter, Morris Chang, founder of TSMC, expressed his disappointment that the semiconductor industry, a critical technology and significant contributor to the Taiwanese economy, was to receive little assistance from the government's plan (Chang 2017; Klingler-Vidra and Kuo 2021). As the Tsai administration entered its second year (in 2017), this priority list developed into the so-called 5+2 Industrial Innovation Plan, adding Asia Silicon Valley and the circular economy. The policies focused on new technologies and emerging industries rather than semiconductors and Taiwan's oligopolistic firms further leading the market.

Social Purpose

Compared to the cases of Japan and Korea, the Taiwanese case has a more explicit focus on external motivators, relative to domestic social purposes. This stems from the centrality of economic competitiveness to national security—even its very survival as a state—from the 1970s. Taiwan's economic statecraft was piqued when the United Nations voted to recognize the People's Republic of China (PRC) in October 1971 and simultaneously expel Taiwan. Taiwanese policy makers feared the implications of the "vulnerability of Taiwan's de facto sovereignty" (Pempel and Tsunekawa 2015, 6) and prioritized strategies for helping ensure trade continued. Reflecting this reality, the "regime increasingly based its legitimacy on its ability to promote economic growth" (Gold 1986, 90). Economic competitiveness based on high-technology prowess was seen as essential to the survival of the (autonomous but little recognized) Taiwanese state.[17] At the same time, innovation performance had domestic imperatives, as newly imposed tariffs and the increasing cost of Taiwanese labor was causing an increase in the costs of made in Taiwan products. This expedited the need to move up the value chain rather than compete on catch-up technologies on a cost basis.

Faced with what we would now call a middle-income trap, in the 1980s, Taiwanese policy makers, in consult with domestic and foreign advisers, focused "on high-technology industries: information, biotechnology, electro-optics, machinery and precision instruments, and environmental technology industries" (World Bank 1993, 133). The "authorities had made it clear that they were completely behind the policy of rapid industrialization and trade" and intervened to develop, and transfer, technologies (Gold 1986, 90).

By the dawn of the twenty-first century, the social purpose underpinning its startup capitalism remained a mix of domestic and external drivers. Rather than being too reliant on the Silicon Shield afforded by its position in the global semiconductor industry, the state was keen to diversify to emerging technologies. This included biotechnology, the green economy, and fintech (Executive Yuan 2001; Williams and Chang 2008). The aim was to build global links in these ascending technologies. This was evidenced in September 2016, when the NDC announced the Asia Silicon Valley Development Plan, which would promote Taiwan's innovation and R&D activities and upgrade its startup ecosystem. The goal of the plan is to promote "innovation and R&D for devices and applications of Internet of Things (IoT)" and globally integrate "Taiwan's startup and entrepreneurship ecosystem" (Asia Silicon Valley Development Agency 2024). The government has been promoting Startup Island Taiwan as a global brand. As part of these efforts, in October 2021, President Tsai announced the selection of nine startups as the country's "Next Big" representatives, in a bid to both showcase startups and help these companies "expand to global markets" (Yen 2021).

The externally oriented social purpose of fostering global links revealed inherent tensions regarding how to reap opportunities in mainland China while not exposing the Taiwanese economy to too much of a national security risk. Especially considering the Economic Cooperation Framework Agreement's 2010 furthering of ties, concerns were heightened. Perhaps the most visible tension came from the "the student-led Sunflower Movement" in 2014, which "successfully blocked the ratification of an agreement that would have allowed greater Chinese investment in Taiwan" (Lin 2021, 143). The aim was to navigate global opportunity, including that in mainland China, while working to retain talent and the technological edge in Taiwan.

Domestically, startup capitalism has been motivated as a mechanism to assuage rising living costs and slower growth. For instance, in 2008, the KMT candidate, Ma Ying-jeou, won and sought to enable closer cross-strait economic relations in order to address "slower growth, stagnating wages, demographic decline, a high youth unemployment rate, and the inequalities and risks produced by financial-ization" (Lin 2021, 142). Efforts were formalized in the Economic Cooperation Framework Agreement, which was signed in June 2010, to boost trade with main-land China. This opportunity to boost operations in China and receive invest-ment from Chinese companies and VCs brought risks, too; Taiwan was ushering in unification, so the social purpose of subsequent policies was to achieve the delicate balance of benefiting from enhanced access to the mainland while not giving away Taiwan's independence and unique competitive advantages.

As in Japan and Korea, greater diversity and inclusion also increasingly inform the rationales given when startup policies are launched. For instance, the MoEA SME Administration launched the Women Entrepreneurship Awards in 2018 and the Women Entrepreneurship Program in 2021. The program offers a range of services to bolster the presence and ability of women in the Taiwanese startup ecosystem, including "training courses, group counselling, accelerators for women, women entrepreneurship competition, financing, and networking, to emphasize enhancing the technological and international power of the female enterprises" (MoEA SME Administration 2021).

Taiwan's motivating social purpose has remained more explicitly at the nexus of technological competitiveness and national security. The aim of fostering national security through its competitive position in critical and emerging tech-nologies has adorned Taiwan's policy making for decades. While startup policies are also construed as a means of job creation and social inclusion, the centrality of national security as a motivator tips the balance toward the external end of the continuum.

Continuity and Change in Taiwan

Taiwan's policy orientation was firmly established toward small firms already in the antecedents era. In this sense, Taiwan offers a different trajectory from Japan and Korea, which were large firm–centric at the outset. Taiwan was the East Asian state most like a stylized startup nation, given the early encourage-

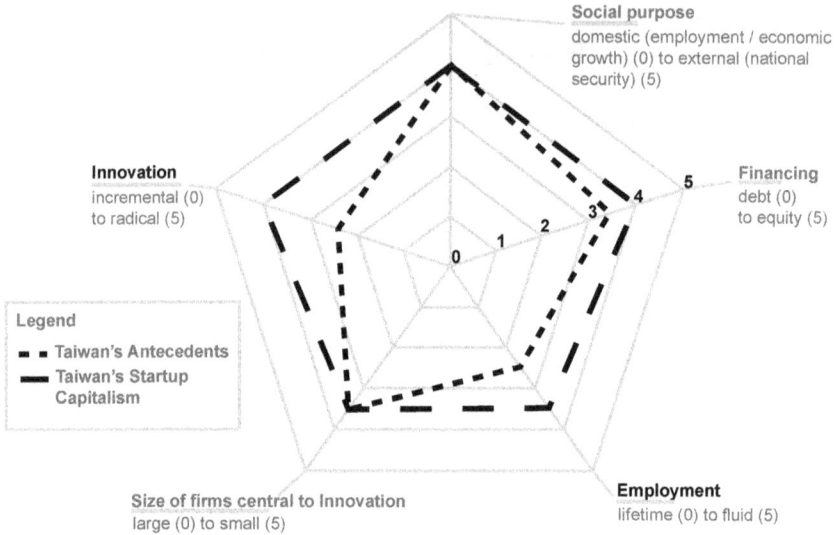

Social purpose
domestic (employment / economic
growth) (0) to external (national
security) (5)

Innovation
incremental (0)
to radical (5)

Financing
debt (0)
to equity (5)

Legend

■ ■ Taiwan's Antecedents
■— Taiwan's Startup
Capitalism

Size of firms central to Innovation
large (0) to small (5)

Employment
lifetime (0) to fluid (5)

FIGURE 4.1. Analyzing Taiwan's institutional evolution: antecedents to startup capitalism

ment of startups rather than conglomerates and the corresponding availability of early-stage equity investment. Figure 4.1 offers an illustration of Taiwan's change and continuity examined in this chapter and shows it has largely remained closer to the Mark I mode.

Figure 4.1 illustrates Taiwan's different trajectory as it begins, and remains, at 3.5 in the size of firms central to innovation arena. This is owing to small firms having long been integral to the Taiwanese state's growing export-led growth competitiveness.[18] Policy in even the antecedent period emphasized the boosting the capabilities of small firms by incentivizing R&D and export activity. Taiwan's innovation economy includes giants, like Acer and TSMC. Unlike in the previous cases of Japan and Korea, however, startup policy has not aimed to boost the competitiveness of its leading firms and established industries. Open innovation efforts have been undertaken by oligopolistic firms independently, and the state has invited established firms to serve as investors in VC vehicles. But the thrust of Taiwan's startup capitalism is around widening the entrepreneurial pool by inviting foreign talent and directing attention to emerging technologies. Thus, small firms—not oligopolies—remain central to its approach.

Employment has seen a shift toward Mark I's fluidity (to 3.5), even though it began with a score of 2.5 in the antecedent period. The relatively high, and outward, movement of the Taiwanese case's employment context reflects its policy orientation that has encouraged high-technology entrepreneurship. In the antecedent era, manpower programs sent students to study overseas, especially in the United States, and programs like the creation of Hsinchu Park worked to entice them back to join and lead high-growth firms. A thrust of employment policies has been around upskilling talent rather than encouraging entrepreneurship or midcareer movements. Over time, this ambition has only grown, targeting entrepreneurial capacity building in specific technologies (e.g., biotechnology, fintech, and green tech) and striving for an increasingly international pool of entrepreneurs. Thus, Taiwan's labor market is, so far, the most flexible, earning it a score of 3.5, as job movements, rather than lifetime employment, have only grown in its startup capitalism era.

Taiwan was an early mover, among the East Asian cases, in promoting early-stage equity markets for high-growth startups, with VC policies being implemented from the beginning of the 1980s. Given this orientation toward equity financing for innovation in the antecedent period, the starting point for financing is 3.5 on figure 4.1. That means it is relatively closer to a Mark I character than the Japanese and Korean cases, which both began much closer to Mark II (scores of 1). Over time, Taiwan's equity financing has only grown with the advance of VC markets and the expansion of startup-friendly stock markets. We illustrate this shift with a slight move outward, to a score of 4. This means that Taiwan began with, and still has, the financing for innovation scores closest to the Silicon Valley Mark I ideal type.

Continuing with this theme of having more of a Mark I character from the start, figure 4.1 depicts Taiwan's innovation in the antecedents period with a score of 2.5. This reflects our observation that, early on, Taiwanese policy focused on competing at the world's technological frontier, not on catch-up technologies. Taiwanese policy makers helped fledgling firms compete in cutting-edge industries by acquiring foreign technology and transferring it out of public institutes. Technological developments by ITRI were spun out to private companies, notably UMC and TSMC, so Taiwanese firms could compete in global value chains in the technology industry. The very success of Taiwan's semiconductor-centric miracle motivated policy makers to encourage startup-centric clusters around emerging technologies, such as biotechnology, LCDs, and green tech. The goal remains explicitly focused on the technological frontier, with startup capitalism aiming to bolster capabilities in new technologies. Owing to this approach, even incremental advances in the dominant semiconductor industry are not enabled by the state. Thus, the startup capitalism score for Taiwan's innovation is 4, placing it close to the radical innovation end of the continuum.

Also at an elevated level relative to Japan and Korea, which each scored 3, Taiwan's score for the mix of external and domestic social purpose is a 4 across the antecedent and startup capitalism eras. This is due to the more explicit national security link for Taiwan's startup-centric innovation efforts from the 1970s onward. In this sense, economic statecraft that links techno-competitiveness with national security is most striking in the Taiwanese case. Competing at the frontier of radical innovation was pursued in the context of semiconductors from the 1980s. As Taiwan established a foothold in semiconductor manufacturing, policies have focused on emerging technologies. The value of diversifying innovation capabilities in critical technologies has been central to policy making more so than job creation and social inclusion aims. Startup prowess does serve these domestic aims, especially at times when growth stalls and cost-of-living concerns are heightened. But techno-competitiveness retains primacy. For this reason, Taiwan's balance remains closer to the Mark I end of the spectrum, with a score of 4.

In sum, Taiwan remains closer to the Silicon Valley ideal than the Japanese and Korean cases. However, we note that creative destruction is not necessarily the aim of startup policy in Taiwan. Rather than disrupting large incumbents' positioning, the objective of startup policies is to foster new entrepreneurial pools in emerging technologies. The goal is to catapult capabilities in the next generation of critical technologies, not to disrupt the dominant position of oligopolies in established industries.

CHINA

Each employee needed to "return to the mindset of an entrepreneur," quipped Alibaba Chief Executive Daniel Zhang when the tech giant announced its plans to split into six different companies in March 2023 (Horwitz 2023).[1] The Alibaba split signaled, to many, the return of China Inc. and the end of the tech crackdown, as Jack Ma was able to again set foot in his home country and Chinese regulators offered big tech a way forward. Alibaba and the Jack Ma experience in some ways serve as a microcosm of China's dynamics, especially with respect to the state's engagement with companies in the consumer internet sector. After the Alibaba split was announced, the leadership detailed plans for the jewel in the crown—its cloud computing unit—to be spun out in an IPO. Just a few months later, headlines conveyed a retrenching of plans. Due to uncertainties, the Alibaba Group no longer planned to IPO the cloud computing unit (Zhou 2023). In the last weeks of 2023, Jack Ma announced that he was starting a new company (Hangzhou Ma's Kitchen Food, named after his hometown and focused on prepackaged food) (Wakasugi 2023). There is something to be said for the significance of such a storied founder (Jack Ma) creating a startup after stepping down from the market leader he built. This dynamism runs as a Mark I flavor across the Chinese case.

The China case stands in contrast to the enabling role of the state in boosting startups in open innovation ecosystems for the benefit of incumbents in the Japanese and Korean cases and is also different from the state's relative avoidance of oligopolies like TSMC in the Taiwanese context. This is because some large companies, like Alibaba in the platform economy, have faced existential threats from other competitors and from the regulatory reach of the state (McKnight et al. 2023). Companies operating in hard tech, strategic industries or critical technologies in China are flush with cash, while some firms in the consumer internet industry faced the brunt of the crackdown (*Economist* 2024a; Chen 2022a; Kroeber 2020).

In this sense, China offers the opportunity to study a unique hybrid of Mark I and II paradigms, depending on the industry, technology, and timing. For large state-backed firms, like SMIC, startup policy stands to complement or even benefit its capabilities, but in areas like the platform economy, sometimes oligopolistic positions face dismantling by the state and existential challenges by gladiatorial entrepreneurs (Chen 2015; Lee 2018). Even large firms hailed as essential competitors for China in its bid for self-sufficiency in various markets speak of fundamental threats posed by fellow Chinese competitors. For instance, the existential threat that ZTE Corporation posed to Huawei prompted Huawei to file an injunction against ZTE in the European Court of Justice in 2015 (Banasevic and Bobowiec 2023). This competition from fellow Chinese firms comes, of course, in addition to threats from Western firms and restrictions on market access (Fisher 2020a).

China's startup capitalism accelerated from the early 2000s but has experienced twists and turns vis-à-vis the treatment of big businesses since 2012. The eventual entry into the WTO and the EAFC—even if China was not directly affected by it—were critical junctures for policy makers, catapulting startup promotion. The government has implemented a wide range of policies to make startups a driver for innovation and, relatedly, industrial upgrading and job creation (Brandt and Thun 2016). For instance, the MIIT led a multi-agency plan around China's advance of its metaverse prowess in which five clusters of startup activity would be boosted (Deng 2023). In critical industries and technologies, such as semiconductors, however, the open innovation variety of startup capitalism is more evident, and large firms are championed (Pearson et al. 2023), aligning more closely with Mark II logics.

China is also a valuable case because it is often considered a late developer, a juggernaut that is understudied in comparative terms (Heberer 2016; Pempel 2021). Though not covered in the core developmental state scholarship, as China has developed, political economy scholars have revealed how the role of the state was crucial in the early stages as China sought to catch up with more advanced competitors (McNally 2012). From the outset, China adopted and adapted many of the policies used by the East Asian developmental states of Japan, Korea, and Taiwan. To start with, the central government strove to be in control of economic policy making, but considering its size compared to other East Asian countries, implementation was devolved to provincial and local governments. Thus, the

Chinese government's largesse for startups—across the 1978 to 2023 period—offers an opportunity to study a hybrid of Mark I and II logics operating differentially over time and across sectors.

Antecedents: China (1978–2000)

Scholarship on China's political economy emphasizes the role played by the state, often beginning with the foundations established by the Republican state (1927–1937) or the institutions created by the Maoist developmental state (Vu 2010; Bell and Feng 2013). The state not only managed economic activity, it owned the means of production and banned most, if not all, forms of private enterprise (Cai 2008). This changed in December 1978, when Chairman Deng Xiaoping announced domestic economic reforms and an open-door policy under the banner of *gaige kaifang* (reform and opening). In the ensuing years, China followed an economic growth model underpinned by gradual market-oriented reform premised on liberalization and greater privatization, export-orientation of domestic production, and ever-growing investment (Cao et al. 1999; Yao 2004). Over the years, therefore, China's politico-economic system has come to be known as "state capitalism" (Naughton and Tsai 2015).[2]

In terms of the size of the firm central to innovation, the Chinese context has been depicted for the centrality of its state-owned enterprise (SOE)s as well as the essential role played by its growing set of innovative entrepreneurs. From the 1980s, SMEs were expected to develop new "core" technologies (Segal 2003, 29), foster industrial upgrading, and create quality jobs. SOEs were not necessarily expected to drive innovation, instead mainly operating in utility types of sectors that would offer essential infrastructure for the rest of the economy—including small innovative firms (Song 2018). At the same time, the technology boom in Silicon Valley sparked interest in China, leading to questions about whether it could benefit from a similar brand of startup-centric innovation. The Torch Program and the Zhongguancun cluster were both established in 1988 (Ken 2022).[3] By the 1990s, with the rise of Electronics Avenue in Beijing and other technologically focused startups active across the country, small firms were acknowledged for their contribution to innovation activities (Ken 2022). Led by policy makers described as "red engineers" (Andreas 2009), both the Deng and Jiang governments passed regulations and established funding initiatives for new entrants and their technical upgrading abilities (Wan 2008; Child 2016).[4] Thus, in this antecedent period, startups were already construed as an engine of innovation. Indeed, some of China's best-known technology companies—and those competing with, or even outperforming in some metrics, American rivals like TikTok vis-à-vis Instagram (Campbell 2022)—were launched in this period, including Huawei (1987), Tencent (1998), Alibaba (1999), and Baidu (2000).

China's labor markets were more fluid in the antecedent period than those in Japan and Korea were. In line with thinking about new entrants as innovators and their ability to absorb surplus labor, employment in startups was promoted through initiatives such as the Torch Program's technology business incubator (Breznitz and Murphree 2011). In addition, the government set up different programs to attract both overseas Chinese students and international students interested in setting up a firm in China. For instance, in 1994, the Nanjing Municipal Government teamed up with the central government to launch the Nanjing Overseas Students Entrepreneurship Park, targeting overseas students. At the same time, the *hukou* social registration system began using the language of entrepreneurs to assign points for prospective residents in major cities. In 1998, the State Council approved the Notice of the Ministry of Public Security on Resolving Several Outstanding Issues in the Current Household Registration Management Work, which saw the first specific reference to entrepreneurial activities—"setting up" an enterprise. The entry of entrepreneurship on the *hukou* regulations signals efforts to encourage fluid labor markets by linking citizen rights to this form of (self-)employment. This all points to some degree of flexibility in the labor market, even in China's antecedent period.

In the antecedent period, China's financial system differed from those in the other cases in its greater openness to foreign sources of financing at an earlier stage and to a mix of credit and equity financing. On the one hand, the central government oversaw credit provision managed by state-owned banks, akin to those in other developmental states (Cheung 2018). At the same time, "back-alley banking" entrepreneurs proved resourceful in finding alternative, private sources of funding (Tsai 2002). While state banks provided preferential credit to SOEs, from the 1980s, there were efforts to avail equity-based financing for growing startups (Lewin et al. 2016). VC, for instance, was legally allowed in 1985,[5] and a year later, the government set up the China New Technology Venture Investment Corporation to provide VC funding (Kenney et al. 2002).[6] Managed by MoST and funded by MOF, Innofund was set up in conjunction with the Torch Program in 1999 to provide financial assistance to startups through a combination of interest-free loans, grants, and equity (Wang 2013, 133).

The state also expanded stock market access for startups. The Standing Committee passed the Revision of the Company Law in 1999, which allowed high-tech companies to be listed on the Chinese stock markets and set the groundwork for preparing to establish a separate high-tech stock exchange market. The existence of the Shanghai and Shenzhen stock markets and high-tech companies that could go public on those markets meant there were exit venues for high-growth startups. In this period, most tech firms listed in Hong Kong—with the city having rejoined China in 1997—and Shanghai or Shenzhen, plus, in some cases, New York. Thus, while large firms drew on debt financing, the state enabled financing through a mix of equity-based mechanisms (e.g., VC and stock exchanges) and debt (e.g., startup-focused loans).

The government put technological upgrading at the center of its development model. In 1980, the State Council established the Patent Office of the PRC. Set up only one year after the start of the reform and opening period, the office signaled that the Deng government wanted to make innovation part of the development and growth strategy (Simon and Goldman 1989). The Deng administration launched an innovation policy based on a dual strategy: to focus on catch-up development while planting the seeds for China to eventually compete at the frontier stage (Liu et al. 2011, 921). This period is depicted as evolving "from copying" to "fit for purpose" by George Yip and Bruce McKern (2016, 13), as entrepreneurs moved from imitation toward improving their products to address customer needs. The biggest institutional breakthrough came in 1985, when the Communist Party of China (CPC) Central Committee passed the Decision on the Reform of the Science and Technology System. This allowed for further decisions to expand the autonomy of R&D institutes, opening the gates to the establishment of high-tech industries development zones (HIDZ)—which paved the way for the Torch Program's business incubators—and for the institutes themselves to see members of their research teams spin-off into high-tech startups.

The ultimate motivation for the investment in upgrading technological capacity was clear; "indigenous technological capability would mean that" for the first time in centuries, "China would be actively involved in defining, not just accepting, international technological standards" (Segal 2003, 3). In 1986, the State Science and Technology Commission (SSTC) launched the State High-Tech R&D Program, also known as the 863 Program, to bolster indigenous innovation capacity (Zhi and Pearson 2016).[7] To be sure, China's antecedent period is characterized by the development of catch-up capabilities and incremental innovation prowess on a path toward indigenous innovation at the technological frontier.

The domestic aims of balanced regional development and job creation were central to China's social purposes in promoting small firms in the antecedent era. Domestic concerns in the form of equitable growth, particularly balanced regional growth across the country, have been central. This decentralization objective was an acknowledgment that the central government could not direct growth across such a geographically extensive and diverse country (Lin and Liu 2000; Cai and Treisman 2006). Local governments were motivated to develop economic activity, such as high-technology clusters of startups, as they could raise fiscal revenue through selling their land-use rights due to the 1988 constitutional amendment that allowed for the transfer of land use rights to private investors (Yip and McKern 2016). Launched in 1987, the Wuhan East Lake Hi-Tech Innovation Center therefore served this purpose, while the 1988 Beijing (Zhongguancun) New Technology Industry Experimental Zone helped bolster high-quality employment and production activities in Beijing (Zhou and Liu 2016). As in the other cases, there were some acknowledgments of external drivers in the form of techno-competitiveness contributing to national security. Technological development, fueled by a combination of SOEs and small firms, could help reduce China's dependence on foreign technologies and thus advance toward its aim of having a "rich country, strong army" (Segal 2003, 3).[8]

Thematic Analysis

Firm Size

State-backed firms, such as SMIC and ZTE, compete in critical technologies, semiconductors and telecommunications, respectively. The model for SOE technological prowess has included forming joint ventures with foreign manufacturers (Oh 2013). However, policy has also encouraged startups to develop technology and fight for market share, especially in the platform economy (Deng 2022). The elevation of startups came as SOEs were (relatively) sidelined by the Hu government—in power from 2002 to 2012—in its push to transform China into an innovation powerhouse. Startups were the focus of the Hu government's policies. This was visible in government procurement incentives, education, funding, and training to promote startups around universities and beyond (Lardy 2014).

The Xi government, since taking power in 2012, has been more mixed in its attention to both startups and large firms. Government policy from the Xi government has more to do with the technological application in which a company is operating and the degree of independence they assert. Certainly, under the Xi administration, the military and, to an extent, state-backed firms have been perceived as important components of the innovation ecosystem (Kania 2019). Startups access incentive packages, often once they have effectively navigated intensely competitive markets, if they were operating in the "right" technology sector (Lockett 2022). The competitive innovation context in China is such that technology firms regularly work "996"—9:00 a.m. to 9:00 p.m. six days a week (Dai and Tao 2019)—or even "007"—twenty-four hours a day, seven days a week.

State challenges to, rather than encouragement for, large incumbents reached a peak around 2020. Collective regulatory pressures constituted crackdown on Chinese tech firms in 2020 and 2021, as regulations served serious challenges to some technology sectors, such as online education, while taming others, such as video games. This crackdown was perhaps most publicly visible via the government's intervention to block the Ant Financial IPO in November 2020. Billed to be the world's largest-ever IPO, worth US$37 billion, Jack Ma's financial arm listing was halted by the Shanghai Stock Exchange just days ahead of when it was scheduled (Zhu et al. 2020). The widely reported reason for the regulatory crackdown was concern about Ant Financial operating as an independent technology firm rather than as a bank working in close collaboration with the Chinese state, as well as the off-the-cuff remarks Jack Ma made about the need for undertaking risk and innovation (Zhong 2020). The dramatic stop to the much-lauded IPO further instigated concerns about investing in the Chinese financial system. However, in June 2022, headlines abounded that approval for an Ant Financial IPO was likely (Chen 2022b), and in spring 2023, Alibaba announced plans to list its dismantled six entities on China's domestic exchanges—moving away from its US listing.

Didi also serves as a clear example of a big technology firm experiencing a crackdown and then a reprieve in the form of its listing on a foreign exchange. In July 2021, China's Cybersecurity Review Office announced a probe into data security practices and placed a ban on the ride-sharing app's ability to add new users (Yu et al. 2021). The crackdown on Didi occurred within days of its IPO on the New York Stock Exchange, with the stated reason being that paperwork filed for the IPO posed data security concerns. Didi, by listing on an American exchange, is said to have posed a national security risk—one that the Xi administration quickly acted on. Just under a year later, the Chinese regulator announced that they were concluding their probe and the Didi app would again be available to new users (Zhai and Lin 2022; Mitchell 2022). But in the intervening period, the message was clear: listing on a US exchange was increasingly discouraged, and instead, companies should should target mainland Chinese and Hong Kong exchanges for IPOs. In addition, there was speculation that Didi and other companies that had listed abroad were to offer the Chinese government a 1 percent equity stake and "a direct role in corporate decision" as compensation for their foreign listing (Zhai and Lin 2022).

The BATs (Baidu, Alibaba and Tencent) and also those that were subject to the crackdown, like Didi, publicly toe the party line. When Xi Jinping's thirty-one-point action plan was published in summer 2023, tycoons like Pony Ma, the Tencent founder, gushed, releasing a statement that he was "extremely excited and deeply inspired" by the plan (McMorrow and Leahy 2023).

The government's "techlash" and US-China trade war tensions have meant that contributing to national priorities is essential. Startups are welcome to partake in activities that align with national priorities (e.g., infrastructure-focused blockchain), while there are substantial blocks to activity in off-limits arenas, such as cryptocurrency (Hai and Klingler-Vidra 2022). Startups that were part of China's arms race in technological competitiveness, especially vis-à-vis the United States, have been awash with resources (Clover et al. 2017). Neil Shen, Sequoia China's storied manager, publicly advised Chinese entrepreneurs to align with the country's national priorities in 2021 (McMorrow et al. 2023). Entrepreneurs told journalists that they remain concerned about whether the changes "offer real protection of the entrepreneur class and private ownership" (Yuan 2023). Collectively, this augurs for a persistent need to fit with party plans, even if for publicity purposes, both for startups and incumbents.

Employment

Policies have advanced the fluidity of China's labor market in the twenty-first century in several ways. Status in the context of the party was boosted when entrepreneurship was elevated as a form of work in 2002 through Three Represents, in which the 2002 Sixteenth Party Congress "officially admitted entrepreneurs into the Party" (Roland 2023, 527). Thanks to a boom in foreign firm production facilities in China following WTO accession, worker mobility was growing, especially among university graduates. According to a survey conducted in 2010, 42 percent of university graduates from class year 2008 had already changed jobs at least once (Ibata-Arens 2019).

Before the GFC, explicit efforts were made to promote job creation by startups. This included the 2006 Tax Incentives for Technology Innovations by Enterprises, which allowed for staff training costs amounting to less than 2.5 percent of salary costs to be deducted before tax. This tax incentive could reduce costs that startups bear when hiring and expanding their workforce. Building on this, in early 2008, eleven government agencies collectively issued the "Guiding Opinions on Promoting Employment through Entrepreneurship" (State Council of the PRC 2008). Through this initiative, and as the GFC advanced, high-quality job creation became one of the key aims of startup promotion. In particular, the government was seeking to drive entrepreneurship among university graduates who hitherto would have preferred to join the best-known SOEs or any number of foreign firms operating in China.

In addition, the Hu government was widening the entrepreneurial pool by introducing policies designed to attract highly skilled overseas Chinese back to the mainland. Returnees could launch their own firms or join existing startups, reflecting a labor market embracing fluid job movement. As a notable example, the Ministry of Human Resources and Social Security launched the Chinese Overseas Students' Return and Entrepreneurship Support Program in 2009. The program offered returnees RMB200,000 (approximately US$30,000) if they had "outstanding" entrepreneurship projects and up to RMB500,000 (just more than

US$75,000) for "key" projects (Central People's Government of the PRC 2009). In short, policy increasingly aimed to widen the pool of would-be entrepreneurs who otherwise might have decided to try their luck in their country of study or with well-paid jobs with large firms.

The CPC Central Committee and the State Council teamed up to deliver a plan to attract highly skilled overseas Chinese into the country's entrepreneurial pool. This reinforced the point that this approach came from the top echelons of power. In 2010, the National Medium- to Long-Term Talent Development Plan Outline (2010–2020) was established to incentivize the return of overseas talent. These entrepreneurs would then receive incentive packages to launch their own startups or join existing ones (Central People's Government of the PRC 2010). Following this, the "Opinion on Supporting Overseas Students to Return to China and Start Businesses" was issued in 2011 (Central People's Government of the PRC 2011) to help returnees navigate funding, government programs, and other opportunities that overseas students might not necessarily be aware of when starting up in China.

Entrepreneurship—rather than lifetime employment—continued to be a priority when Xi came to power in 2012, with "mass entrepreneurship" coming to the fore. In 2015, the State Council issued its "Opinion on Furthering the Work on Employment and Entrepreneurship under New Conditions" (State Council of the PRC 2015b). The document specifies that entrepreneurship should help improve employment opportunities and talent development. The State Council also issued its "Opinion on Several Policies and Measures to Vigorously Advance the Mass Entrepreneurship and Innovation Initiative" (State Council of the PRC 2015a). This document sought to encourage mass entrepreneurship across the country, beyond the high-performing clusters in Shenzhen and Zhongguan. This aim for widespread entrepreneurship was amplified in 2018, as the State Council published the "Opinions on Promoting the High-Quality Development and the Establishment of an Upgraded Version of 'Mass Innovation and Entrepreneurship'" (State Council of the PRC 2018). While these efforts point to more fluid labor markets in the sense that entrepreneurship—not employment with established firms—was promoted, it was not necessarily focused on startup activity. In *The Labor of Reinvention*, Lin Zhang (2023) explains that as digital entrepreneurship has integrated with even low-tech rural entrepreneurs—through platforms such as Taobao—new firms encouraged by China's entrepreneurship policy are increasingly becoming part of the digital economy.

The "13th Five-Year Plan for the Development of National S&T Enterprise Incubators" did move explicitly in the direction of startup activity. Officially released by MoST in 2017, the plan set a target for startup incubators to create over three million jobs and employ at least half a million university graduates in the 2016–2020 period (MoST 2017). In 2018, Premier Li Keqiang stressed that mass entrepreneurship and innovation ought to help stabilize employment and drive economic growth (Xinhua 2018). Li reiterated this in 2018 (State Council of the PRC 2019). Earlier, in 2016, MIIT Minister Miao Wei had boasted that a national development fund set up one year before had already served 120,000 startups, leading to 4.2 million jobs being created (State Council Information Office of the PRC 2016a). In other words, the government was directly linking its startup policies to a quantifiable number of jobs more so than the creation of disruptive new entrants. The 2019 Mass Entrepreneurship and Innovation Week, where Premier Li gave his speech, was held to raise awareness of these policies across wider society (State Council of the PRC 2019).[9] Then, amid a slowdown in graduate job creation in 2021, the government introduced further preferential tax treatment and incentives for graduates launching their own startups (Huld 2023).

In addition to the significant scope and depth of its policies aimed at incentivizing fluidity through the promotion of entrepreneurship, the Chinese state has also enabled labor market flexibility by adapting its treatment of bankruptcy. Mark I contexts prize business dynamism, which means that firms need to be able to form and cease to exist. In this way, bankruptcy regulations shape the extent to which labor, and numerous other resources, can be reallocated. Enterprise bankruptcy was first enabled in China in 2007 for both private enterprises and SOEs (Falke 2007). This Hu government regulatory change encourages more flexibility, as firms have finally been able to wipe out debt and move on to new activities when they fail. However, in the Chinese context, personal bankruptcy has remained largely unavailable at the national level. In fact, Shenzhen was the only place in China "where local residents can file for personal bankruptcy, as a pilot scheme was launched there in March 2021" (Zuo and Huifeng 2023). Collectively, bankruptcy regulations have improved in China's startup capitalism era, which augurs for more fluid labor markets. However, there are still limitations that mean that China's employment context does not converge on the Mark I ideal type.

Finance

In its antecedent period, the Chinese government had launched a wide range of debt and equity funding initiatives to help fill the entrepreneurial funding gap. In the post-WTO accession period, the government significantly expanded entrepreneurial finance by following a dual strategy: direct (credit) funding by the state and development of a Silicon Valley–style (equity) financing system (Walter and Howie 2012; Pettis 2013). This included the Jiang government, at the end of its time in office, approving the "Provisions Concerning the Establishment of Foreign-Funded Venture Capital Enterprises" in 2001, which made foreign equity funding more available (State Council of the PRC 2016b).[10]

The government's direct startup funding, in both credit and equity forms, was substantially increased in the early twenty-first century.[11] For instance, in 2004, the government launched the Special Fund for SME Development. The fund would go on to provide RMB950 million by the end of 2007 to aid SMEs, especially innovative activities by micro and small firms (MoST 2004). In 2006, the commission issued the "Guidance Opinions Concerning Commercial Banks' Improving and Strengthening Financial Services for High-Tech Enterprises." As the name indicates, this initiative further targeted loans to high-tech firms specifically, so debt instruments remained part of the policy mix for financing startup-centric innovation.

Grants, subsidies, and incubator provision proliferated in the early 2000s. Innofund—China's version of the US SBIR program—continued to grow its subsidy disbursements throughout the early 2000s. In 2004, the Roadmap Scheme for the Growth of Tech-Based SMEs was launched. Its objective was to create a favorable environment for the development of tech-based startups at various stages, bringing together the efforts of different agencies such as the Shenzhen Stock Exchange (SZSE), the China Development Bank, the National Business Incubator Association, and the National VC Association. The number of firms that applied and received funding from Innofund roughly doubled between 2001 and 2008 (Li et al. 2020, 3).[12] In 2006, MoST launched an incubator capacity-building project as part of the "11th Five-Year Plan on Chinese Tech-Based Enterprise Incubators." The Silicon Valley–styled project included an annual budget of RMB20 million to create a national incubation information service platform, with local governments encouraged to contribute RMB100 million. Finally, the startup incubator system was to be boosted with a RMB200 million fund (MoST 2006a).

Access to equity funding was boosted via multiple channels throughout Hu's time in power. Government money was made available for equity VC investments, as the Government-Guided Investment Funds were established in 2008. The funds were a new form of a state-backed VC fund that had the objective of investing in startups alongside, and to contribute to, industrial upgrading and public infrastructure (Pan et al. 2021). Third, regulatory changes implemented from 1999 expanded the ability of domestic Chinese VCs to operate (Liu 2015).[13] Equity advances continued, as, in 2009, the NDRC and MOF established the Emerging Industries Venture Capital Program, which enabled the establishment of VCs for emerging high-tech industries. Funds had to manage at least RMB250 million, with the central government providing no more than 20 percent of total assets under management, local governments matching that share, and private funding exceeding 60 percent. As Vice Minister Zhu Zhixin stated, the Chinese government believed that the VC and private equity industry could contribute to economic development and industrial upgrading beyond what it had done in the past.[14] Collectively, regulatory changes and growing activity in the Chinese tech startup landscape meant that there was a significant increase in VC funds comprised of "ground beetles" and "sea turtles," foreign VCs, and government money (Mallaby 2022).

The balance further tipped in the direction of equity financing, as stock market access for high-growth startups was expanded. In 2004, the China Securities Regulatory Commission (CSRC) approved the SME Board (SMEB) plan to launch a stock market targeting high-tech startups. This would provide an essential exit venue for startups, especially those that had raised VC funding and needed to produce a sizable return for their investors. The SZSE also established a plan to launch ChiNext, a technology startup-friendly stock market. Plans for ChiNext had originally been mooted in 1999, and it eventually launched in October 2009 (SZSE 2020).[15] Together, these plans provided more robust exit options for entrepreneurs and, as a result, a more vibrant equity financing environment.

Incumbent firms—including the BATs, which had themselves been startups in the 1980s and 1990s—also began to make equity investments as they launched their own corporate VCs in the early 2000s (*Economist* 2018b). Tencent prioritized investments in seed-stage companies, whereas Alibaba and Baidu concentrated more on early-stage (e.g., A and B round) financing (Huang and Tian 2020). Investment from the corporate VC arms of the BATs provided a seal of approval to their portfolio companies, and they offered guidance and mentoring.

The Xi government continued the hybrid debt and equity financing strategy. On the state provision of debt front, the government overhauled the STI funding system in 2014 in a bid to provide structure to the hundred-plus preexisting and overlapping funding programs.[16] STI funding was reorganized into five pillars: three programs issuing tenders and two funds. The three programs were the National Natural Science Fund, focusing on basic and applied research; the Major S&T Projects (Megaprojects), focusing on major key products, technology, and engineering; and the National Key R&D Programs, focusing on social welfare and people's livelihood R&D. One of the two funds established—the Technology Innovation Guidance Fund(s)—focused on encouraging the growth and activities of innovative startups exclusively (State Council of the PRC 2014).[17] On the equity side, there have been marked increases in VC funding mechanisms. Starting from 2017, the RMB200 billion Venture Capital Guiding Fund for Emerging Industries operated through VC funds as well as fund-of-fund vehicles (China

Innovation Funding 2019). As for the National Fund for Technology Transfer and Commercialization, it facilitated the establishment of VC subfunds to enable the transfer and commercialization of new technologies (China Innovation Funding 2020a). Government guidance meant that VCs increasingly prioritized sectors in line with the national (security) interest, including software, IT services, and pharmaceuticals (Huang and Tian 2020).

Like its predecessor, the Xi government also saw *domestic* stock markets as a preferential exit strategy for startups. As the trade war with the United States intensified, the government eased the rules for startups to be listed in ChiNext by removing the requirement for CSRC preapproval, allowing loss-making companies to be listed and eliminating price limits during the first five days of listing (Liu and Galbraith 2020).[18] In June 2019, the Xi government also launched the Shanghai Stock Exchange Science and Technology Innovation Board (commonly referred to as the Shanghai Stock Exchange STAR market) (Cheng 2019). In a bid to be "China's NASDAQ," the STAR market adopted a registration-based IPO process consistent with the US process (Hawksford 2019). This new index was designed to focus on firms in the high-tech and strategic emerging sectors, such as IT, advanced equipment, new materials, new energy, energy-saving and environmental protection, and biomedicine (STAR 2020). To make listing easier, from the outset, startups listing on the STAR market did not need government preapproval, could be loss making, and could issue dual class shares so that entrepreneurs could retain control over operations (Lockett 2019). In a bid to further bolster domestic stock market access for startups, in December 2021, the Beijing Stock Exchange was launched as another venue for high-growth startups, complementing the growing set of options for domestic listings (Hsu 2021). This stock exchange specifically targeted innovation-driven startups, which could ultimately scale-up and then list on other domestic stock exchanges.

The Xi government has stepped up measures to keep capital flowing to Chinese startups, given a secular slowdown in global tech and rising US-China tensions around cross-border tech investments. China's VC market was jolted by news in summer 2023 that Sequoia China would be sawed off from its global operation, yielding to pressure that the US government had been applying to VCs investing in China (O'Keeffe et al. 2023). Sequoia China was a clear target, given the size of its fund; it had raised US$8.5 billion for its China fund, and its partner, Neil Shen, had led investments into some of the country's biggest success stories, such as ByteDance, since it was launched in 2005 (McMorrow et al. 2023). Then the Biden administration went further in August 2023, enacting an executive order explicitly banning US venture capital investments in Chinese startups in critical technology arenas, such as artificial intelligence, semiconductors, and quantum computing (Swanson 2023). While American VCs had been active investors in Chinese startups, given political tensions and explicit pressure on larger firms, reports show that Silicon Valley investments had already been declining since their 2018 peak (van Romburgh and Teare 2023). Given this context, the Xi administration has been mobilizing domestic capital for China's startups. In 2023, the government extended existing tax incentives for VCs and angel investors until 2027 (Xinhua 2023). However, as foreign and private sources of capital have decreased, Chinese state funding as a share of startup funding has grown.

In summary, since 2001, China's financial system has increasingly pursued the expansion of startup-friendly equity markets, ranging from VC funding to stock markets. While this bodes for an outward movement toward Mark I variety features, it is worth noting that the government has also continued its provision of credit to enable firms' innovation pursuits. As a result, the Chinese financing for innovation is closer to the Mark I end of the spectrum but remains a mix of equity and debt. While the government seems agnostic to the use of debt or equity, with time, there is an increasingly clear preference for the direction of financing: toward critical technologies.

Innovation

China has moved toward radical innovation and away from the catch-up capacity building that characterized its antecedent period. Even as the country was attracting a larger number of foreign firms, along with their technology transfers, the central government was focusing on creating the conditions for indigenous capacity to move from catch-up to frontier innovation. This was epitomized by the National Science and Technology Conference of 2006, where the Central Committee of the CPC and the State Council issued a Medium- and Long-Term Plan for the Development of Science and Technology. The plan indicated that the government wanted to turn China into an "innovation-oriented country" by 2020, with S&T contributing at least 60 percent of economic growth by that year (Liu et al. 2011, 920).

Part of the move toward radical innovation has involved attempts to simultaneously encourage both "go global" and indigenous innovation strategies. In 2006, the MoST and the Ministry of Commerce jointly issued "Several Opinions on Promoting Going Global of Technology Companies" (China Policy 2017). In this vein, Chinese accelerators in Silicon Valley, such as ZGC Innovation Center, which is backed by Zhongguancun, Beijing's answer to Silicon Valley, has been working to attract Chinese founders back (Qing and Rodriguez 2018). The idea is that Chinese founders working in Silicon Valley could bring their ideas and activities at the technological frontier to Beijing. The Thousand Talents Plan, launched in 2008, encouraged those who had been studying abroad for several years (the sea turtles, or *hǎiguī*) to return home. They received generous funding to set up their own research facilities, one-off payments, and other benefits (Jia 2018). Once based in a Chinese university or research center, these talents could also launch their own startup, or their research could be applied to others' innovative firms. On top of that, in 2001, the Ministry of Personnel issued the "Measures for Administrating Overseas Students Entrepreneurship Parks"—policy guidelines for local governments thinking about setting up facilities for overseas students to remain (Ministry of Human Resources and Social Security 2001). In 2009, the MoST released measures to guide technology companies in going global, encouraging them to carry out collaborative research and establish overseas R&D centers (Wang 2017).

The Chinese state has increasingly emphasized the protection of IP rights. China had been accused of disrespecting IP rights, with the country's firms moving the value-added chain by allegedly stealing IP from foreign firms (Fuller 2016, 102). Regardless of the merits of these accusations, Chinese bureaucrats determined that domestic firms would not be investing significantly in R&D-centric innovation if there was a chance of IP theft. Therefore, the government has developed more comprehensive IP protection frameworks. In 2001, an amendment to the Trademark Law of the People's Republic of China, a comprehensive review of all aspects related to trademark certification and protection, was introduced. At the same time, the central government also passed an amendment to the Copyright Law of the People's Republic of China. The amendment improved the level of copyright protection with reference to international treaties (Standing Committee of the National People's Congress 2001). Certainly, these amendments were linked to WTO membership, but the government also saw their benefit to stimulate indigenous innovation. It is worth noting that this advance in IP protection has not been foolproof; Kai-fu Lee (2018) notes that Chinese tech entrepreneurs engage in gladiatorial battles precisely because of the poor enforcement of IP protection.

A key reason for the government's drive to get returnees to launch technology startups is that they tend to have their headquarters and R&D facilities in China, unlike foreign firms or even the Chinese diaspora, whose firms tend to have their headquarters and innovation facilities overseas and assembly plants in China (Fuller 2016, 39–40). This explains why the Chinese government launched the Chinese Overseas Students' Return and Entrepreneurship Support Program in 2009 and issued the "Opinion on Supporting Overseas Students to Return to China and Start Businesses" in 2011 (Central People's Government of the PRC 2011). These policies were aimed at having young Chinese launch their startups at home rather than overseas, which would make it more likely that not only the headquarters but also R&D would remain there. In 2011, the Thousand Talents Plan was opened to foreigners working in S&T (China Innovation Funding 2020b). Going beyond what was on offer for Chinese talent, foreigners moving to China under the plan would receive additional benefits on top of a relocation bonus and research funding. The plan emphasized a preference for long-term relocation and set up a path for incentivizing R&D and innovation at the technological frontier in China.

For the Xi government, capabilities around critical technologies have been important, whether advanced by startups or large firms. As part of its emphasis on investing in capabilities in particular technologies, the Xi government has repeatedly identified "strategic emerging industries," including "electric vehicle manufacturers, biotechnology, renewable energy, artificial intelligence, semiconductors and other high-end equipment manufacturing" (Lockett 2022). The Little Giants program by MIIT, announced in 2018, was designed to foster innovation in high-tech sectors such as semiconductors, machinery, pharmaceuticals, or biotech—as identified in the Made in China (MIC) 2025 initiative. Little Giants program participants received preferential government investment, cheap loans, tax breaks, and help with recruiting talent to enable them to scale-up (McMorrow et al. 2023). Successful firms could then graduate to "Manufacturing Champions," receiving even stronger state backing as they achieve scale (MIIT 2022).

Chinese innovation policies have delivered on these aims of competing at the world's innovation frontier. The country has achieved world-class high-tech capabilities in sectors such as AI or 5G (see Allison and Schmidt 2022), but debate persists about the prowess of Chinese producers, especially SMIC, in the all-important semiconductor industry. The BATs had achieved remarkable positions in segments of the global technology sector, including Alibaba becoming "the world's largest business-to-business Internet portal" and Tencent achieving global success with the WeChat app (Yip and McKern 2016, 11). Taking the case of AI, many were startups launched from 2014 onward (Crunchbase 2020), and were already operating overseas only a few years after being set up (Ruehl 2020). In the semiconductor industry, repeatedly hailed as crucial to national security and specified as such in MIC 2025 as well as in the fourteenth five-year plan, which called for "technological independence" (Fuller 2019), assessments are more sanguine. HiSilicon, the semiconductor subsidiary of Huawei, and many of the other semiconductor firms are making marking advances in fabless chip design and foundry capacity (Klingler-Vidra and Hai 2024). However, China continues to have less than 1 percent of the global market in the end-product category, according to HIS iSuppli (Thomas 2021).

In contrast to the ongoing debate about whether Chinese capabilities are already *at* the technological frontier (especially in semiconductors), there can be no qualms about whether the ambition of China's startup capitalism is to deliver incremental or radical innovation. It has unabashedly moved outward, toward radical innovation, and thus closer to Mark I aims.

Social Purpose

China's post-WTO accession period coincided with a clearer strategy to develop Silicon Valley–style entrepreneurial ecosystems. Such startups were, by this period, increasingly featured in China's innovation policy (Fannin 2008). Startups and entrepreneurs received the greatest sociopolitical recognition possible when, in 2002, they were granted the right to join the CPC (Wilson 2007, 239). Membership in the CPC was implicit recognition that entrepreneurs were an essential component of the Chinese state. At a more material level, successive administrations increased financial assistance for startups.

China's startup policy continued to fulfill the two social purposes established at the outset of the reform and opening period: diversification away from SOEs and balanced regional growth. To begin with, private-sector-led technological catch-up supported the overarching goal of reducing dependency on SOEs in a gradualist way, accommodating differences among party leadership and across key institutions (Bell and Feng 2013).[19] The 2001 "Five-Year S&T and High-Tech Industries" plans made this clear and were followed by a set of programs and regulations to ensure that entrepreneurs had the best conditions to innovate (Standing Committee of the National People's Congress 2002b): the 2003 "Opinions on Further Improving the Operation of High-Tech Enterprise Incubators," issued to set up a special fund to launch and grow startup incubators (MoST 2003), and the 2005 "Measures for Accrediting and Administering Tech-Based Enterprise Incubators," issued to set up the guidelines for incubators (MoST 2006c). Through these policy initiatives, the Chinese government was diversifying the economy away from its SOE reliance (Wang et al. 2020).

The government's second domestic social purpose has been to decentralize the Chinese economy and achieve balanced regional development and economic growth. By the early 2000s, the government was making it clear that HIDZs were to be essential vehicles for creating clusters of innovation, jobs, and tax revenues at the local level (Huang 2008; Su et al. 2018). To promote decentralization, the Hu government released three key measures. First, the "Opinions on Further Improving the Operation of High-Tech Enterprise Incubators" established that local government should set up special funds to support incubators, on top of the funding to be provided by the central government (MoST 2003). Through this cluster-centric approach, the central government was indicating that local governments would prioritize largesse for startups. Second, the "Measures for Accrediting and Administering Tech-Based Enterprise Incubators" established certain quantifiable procedures for the accreditation of national HIDZ. To be accredited, a HIDZ needed to constitute over ten thousand square meters in size, over eighty incubated firms, over one thousand jobs, or ownership of over RMB3 million in seed or incubation funds (MoST 2006c). Through these metrics, the central government was laying out an objective benchmark for local governments to meet. Third, the "11th Five-Year Plan on University Technology Parks" set the goal of reaching eighty of these parks and incubating fifteen thousand high-tech firms as a way of better integrating entrepreneurial activity and university education and experience (MoST 2006b).

A third domestically oriented social purpose has advanced: startups as mechanisms for creating good-quality, well-paying jobs. Startups could attract younger workers, including those coming from other provinces or from overseas, thus expanding the tax base available to local governments.[20] Job opportunities for university graduates were becoming scarcer, since Chinese exports decreased in the aftermath of the GFC, and capital-starved foreign firms had to reassess their presence in China. As a result, the Hu government saw startups as a tool to promote high-quality employment. The government launched an unprecedented number of policies to link startups to high-quality jobs—especially for graduates and returnees. Prior to the GFC, the Hu government had already shown its concern with the number of dislocated workers that rapid reform was creating. The Hu government was also aware of rapidly growing inequality within and between the country's provinces—especially between the most prosperous cities and the still-backward (western) countryside (Cheung 2018). Startups, they contended, could help to address this issue.

Similar to how social inclusion became an aim in the Japanese, Korean, and Taiwanese cases, the Chinese government has increasingly sought to harness startups as a means of promoting inclusive economic growth. However, it has done so in a different tack; rather than focusing on diversifying the demographics included in the production of startups (e.g., increasing the share of female entrepreneurs), the Chinese approach has concentrated on inclusion in a regional, and rural, understanding. In particular, the Hu government targeted the geographic expansion of sellers engaging e-commerce platforms. Alibaba, in collaboration with various levels of the Chinese government, fueled the advance of Taobao Villages, which are rural hubs underpinned by Alibaba to sell food-stuff and handicrafts across the country (Peng et al. 2019). In partnership with Taobao, the government contributed to the development of logistics infrastructure, digital literacy, and, as a result, rural development (Li 2017). A village is a Taobao Village when it constitutes "a cluster of rural electronic retailers where at least 10 percent of village households engage in e-commerce and total annual e-commerce transaction volume in the village is at least 10 million Chinese yuan" (Tan et al. 2016, 2). The Taobao Villages served to foster a new set of rural "netrepreneurs" (Lowery et al. 1998). Even though Alibaba was a private company, the state was collaborating in a bid to fulfill the social purpose of regionally oriented social inclusion.

Finally, the external driver of techno-security has come to the fore, especially since Xi came to power in 2012. In 2015, the Xi government unveiled MIC 2025 as the national strategy to make China an innovation and high-tech powerhouse within a decade (Chen 2023). Analysts note that MIC 2025 is representative of a "more nationalistic" environment in which technological independence is a matter of national security (Yip and McKern 2016, 31). S&T and entrepreneurship were listed among the core areas for the government to support. As State Council of China President Lu Yongxiang had stressed shortly before MIC 2025 was announced, entrepreneurs and scientists were the two pivotal groups leading China's innovation drive (*China Daily* 2014). In this vein, national and provincial governments continue to provide assistance to startups to pursue innovation at the world frontier, especially technologies considered central to national security, such as blockchain, robotics, and semiconductors (Fuller 2019).

Though the state allowed an open environment for platform economy firms like Alibaba and Tencent to grow, as they matured and came to serve as an essential infrastructure (Plantin and de Seta 2019), they began holding significant stores of data on Chinese citizens and enabling massive volumes of transactions. With the expanse of the digital platforms, the provision of the service and the holding of this granular data on the numerous activities and whereabouts of citizens came to inform national security and, as such, part of the state's social purpose (see Zheng and Huang 2018; van Dijck 2021).

As part of its efforts to compete in emerging and critical technologies, the Xi government implements policies to encourage innovative startups. The urgency of self-sufficiency in 5G and semiconductors spiked following US bans (Fisher 2020b), with Huawei's ability to compete dependent on China's domestic production capabilities. When Huawei launched its Mate 60 Pro with 5G capabilities in late summer 2023, headlines abounded hailing it a victory for China's self-sufficiency in chip production (Pan et al. 2023). Yet, it is unclear whether the phone's semiconductor was made by Huawei or SMIC. What seems sure is that it is likely to instigate even tighter US restrictions on Huawei in a bid to slow down China's advance toward the technological frontier in this critical technology.

Continuity and Change in China

China's startup capitalism comprises continuity and change in how it combines aspects of both Mark I and II modes. Figure 5.1 summarizes the evolution of firm size, finance, employment, innovation, and social purpose in China, which shows change in the direction of—though far from full alignment with—Mark I in each domain. Similar to that of Taiwan but different from those of Japan and Korea, the Chinese case is depicted as the relative balance of social purposes moving increasingly toward the external priority of national security.

Figure 5.1 reveals that, relative to the other country cases, China has experienced the most significant change. It has seen a remarkable move toward the technological frontier, to one of the world's largest VC markets and a labor market that celebrates entrepreneurship.

In terms of the size of firm central to innovation, China's antecedent position on figure 5.1 is designated with a score of 2, reflecting this balance of SOE primacy coupled with some startup involvement. SOEs were essential producers, though already by the 1980s, they served as a platform for the growth of Silicon Valley–style startups. This score places China's antecedent position further away from the oligopolistic ideal that Japan and Korea were closest to, though it is not as startup-centric as Taiwan's antecedent era. There has been an overall rise in the focus on startups as engines of innovation in China.

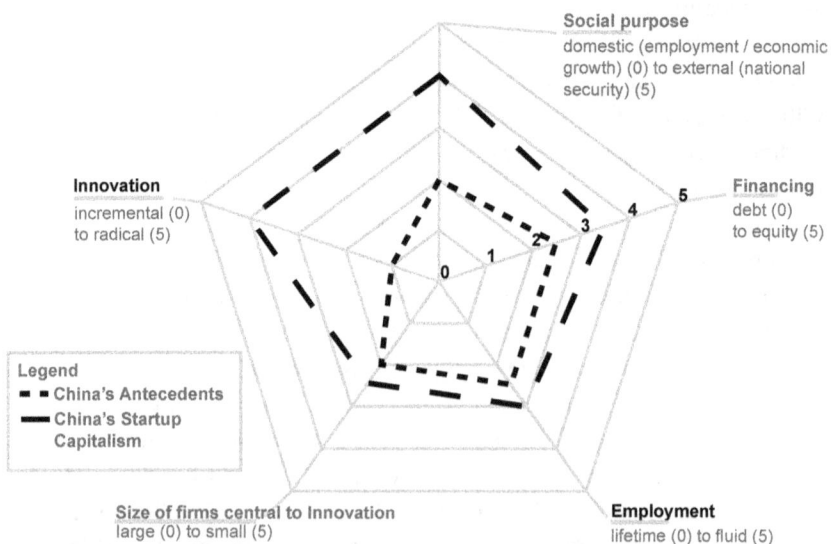

FIGURE 5.1. Analyzing China's institutional evolution: antecedents to startup capitalism

However, there is marked variation across industries, which is why the score only increases to 2.5—smack in the middle of the oligopolistic and startup-led modes. State support for critical technologies, such as semiconductors, has maintained a focus on large firms. For instance, the state has invested significantly in SMIC, its state-backed semiconductor champion, and provides financial assistance to numerous startups operating in related, but not competing, areas within the semiconductor industry. At the same time, the tech crackdown speaks to the state's propensity to engage antagonistically with large firms. Platform giants like Alibaba have seen the Chinese state block the IPO of Ant Financial as well as an order to repatriate the stock listing to Chinese equities markets, splitting it into six distinct entities. These Xi-era moves to break up large firms epitomize, in some ways, the state's orientation toward challenging, rather than reifying, oligopolistic market power. Collectively, we depict China's path as one in which large firms were—just slightly—more central in the antecedent period. Interestingly, even large firms that may otherwise be considered national champions in their respective technology sectors (e.g., Huawei in telecoms infrastructure) have been described as continuing to face existential threats in the form of other large Chinese firms (e.g., ZTE). This speaks to the aura in which Chinese companies operate—one in which oligopolistic competition and existential threats are both possible.

China's labor market was—relative to the other cases—fluid in the antecedents period, in the sense that startup employment has long been encouraged. This has only grown. Notably, startups as creators of high-quality jobs became an explicit goal for the government following the 2008 GFC. The importance of startups as employer, innovators, and agents of regional economic growth was underscored by the Hu government issuing the "Guiding Opinions on Promoting Employment through Entrepreneurship" in 2008. Startups continue to be a source of job creation, with the mass entrepreneurship scheme, among others, aimed at boosting the regional distribution of activities. There are still restrictions related to closing a business, though, which dampens the fluidity of the labor market. Thus, while China's labor market is characterized as being in the middle of fluid and lifetime employment (at a score of 2.5) in the antecedent period, the significant efforts to encourage entrepreneurship across society and to improve regulations around starting and closing businesses underpin the modest shift outward to a score of 3 for the startup capitalism era.

China's provision of financing for entrepreneurs and startups began with a mixed debt/equity starting point. Again in the middle at 2.5, China's antecedent period purposefully availed both credit and equity financing for innovation, especially for entrepreneurs. For instance, in 1985, the CPC Central Committee Decision on the Reform of the Science and Technology System created the legal framework for VCs to be launched. In 1986, the China Venturetech Investment Corporation became the first VC firm in China. From the onset of the startup capitalism era in 2001, several government mechanisms for equity financing, specifically VC funding and startups' access to public equity markets, ensued. This includes the "Provisions Concerning the Establishment of Foreign-Funded Venture Capital Enterprises" of 2001, which led to a sharp growth in the number of VCs backed by foreign investors. Stock market access was boosted; in 2009, Shenzhen's ChiNext became China's first answer to Nasdaq, and in 2019, Shanghai's STAR market joined it. Over the course of the Xi administration, access to foreign capital, including stock markets and VCs, has retrenched, and in its place, there is an emphasis on listing on these domestic exchanges and relying on public coffers to finance growth.

China's innovation trajectory is characterized by its move toward the technological frontier. China's antecedent period focused on catch-up capabilities, and thus the score on figure 5.1 for that era is 1, placing it closest to the Mark II end. Throughout the 1980s and 1990s, China was pursuing high growth and did so by entering, and then upgrading, within global value chains. This model continued in the years following WTO accession. There was a fear that Chinese technological innovation would become a paper tiger, with innovation being driven by foreign firms and their Chinese counterparts acting as mere suppliers or bystanders. Thus, the Hu and Xi governments doubled down on putting Chinese firms at the world's technological frontier. To achieve this goal, HIDZs, universities, and research institutes received extra financial and other support from the government *if* they were operating in line with national aims, particularly in AI, blockchain, robotics, and semiconductors. Given the remarkable jump toward the world's technological frontier, perhaps best epitomized by the MIC 2025 initiative, China's startup capitalism score for innovation is an impressive 4, placing it closest to the Mark I ideal type.

The arena to see the second largest jump between the antecedent and startup capitalism scores on figure 5.1 is social purpose. It began with a score of 2, reflecting the primacy of domestic aims of decentralization and regional growth, and shifted out to a score of 4, owing to the significant rise in the link between startup-led innovation and national security. During the reform and opening period that preceded WTO accession, economic growth drove the Chinese developmental state. When this period started, China was a poor, underdeveloped country, so policy motivations were around inclusive growth. Following WTO accession, the social purpose shifted to job creation as well. Partly, this reflected China's changing employment structure. SOEs were shedding jobs as they automated processes to become more competitive. Private-sector jobs had to absorb a growing share of total employment. Innovative startups were seen as an important part of the overall jobs mix. Post-GFC, startups became even more integral to job creation, as mass entrepreneurship would see the encouragement of founders creating their own jobs and growing their startups, thus employing others. Yet, the social purpose of startup promotion in China has experienced a move toward more external motivations, with national security at the fore. External motivations, particularly what Tai Ming Cheung (2022) calls techno-security, have ascended considerably since Xi came to power in 2012.

In summary, starting from the reform and opening period, small firms received support from the government as agents of innovation, in some ways more like the approach taken by Taiwan. But this encouragement for widening entrepreneurial pools became more systematic and better defined following China's WTO accession, when its startup capitalism came to fruition. In the first decade of the twenty-first century, startups received targeted economic largesse as well as social recognition, with equity funding growing, a shift toward radical innovation, and the promotion of entrepreneurship toward more fluid labor markets. This all points to a move toward Mark I. Yet, in China more than the other cases, there is significant variation across industries. There has also been an increasingly difficult regulatory environment to navigate, with startups finding that some markets become off-limits overnight (e.g., cryptocurrency) and that (foreign) capital markets are more difficult to access. In critical technology arenas, government tactics entail startups being regarded as external resources for national champions, like SMIC, to benefit from. For this reason, the China trajectory also retains elements closer to the oligopolistic competition mode.

Conclusion

East Asian states have been widely studied for their developmental trajectories and their different state-led strategies as well as to determine whether innovation was led by startups or big business. The region of developmental states offers two archetypal examples of large firm–led systems (Japan and Korea), a small firm–centric approach (Taiwan), and a mix of state-owned enterprises and private entrepreneurs (China). In their antecedent periods, which largely correspond to their classic developmental state eras, this large- or small-firm focus was reinforced with complementary institutional dynamics across employment, finance, innovation, and social purpose.

Looking at the four cases in comparative terms, how can we understand the continuity and change experienced from the antecedent era to their pursuits of startup capitalism? To inform the analysis, figure 6.1 illustrates all four cases' antecedent conditions in terms of the radar chart used in the case chapters. The Mark II type constitutes the starting point (0) for the quintessential developmental state, which Japan and Korea approximate most closely in terms of firm size central to innovation (large), the financing of innovation (debt), the employment (lifetime), and the nature of innovation (incremental). In contrast, the Mark I setting is depicted as constituting the opposite ends of the spectrum in terms of the firm size central to innovation (small), the financing of innovation (equity), employment markets (fluid), and the nature of innovation (radical).

In figure 6.1, Japan and Korea have the same starting scores, indicated by their full black lines touching on 1s for each arena other than social purpose. The antecedent period in Taiwan was closest to the Mark I variety and thus is the most

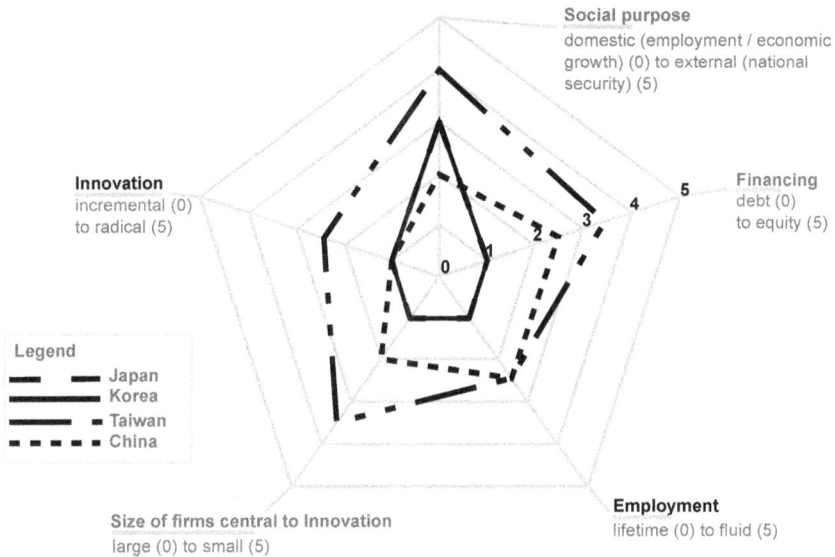

FIGURE 6.1. Antecedents in Japan, Korea, Taiwan, and China

distant from the Japanese and Korean depiction in figure 6.1. Taiwan's antecedent score reflects the fact that financing (equity), employment (fluid), and efforts
to compete in the technological frontier while advancing process-based innovations (mix of incremental and radical innovation) combined with an emphasis on
small firms as essential engines. In between these two shapes are China's antecedent characteristics. China is in the middle because of its mix of large state-owned
firms and small-scale entrepreneurs, the availability of a combination of debt and
equity financing, the relatively fluid labor (given early promotion of entrepreneurial careers), and its pursuance of "catch-up" innovation (incremental). This
gave it a mix of Mark I and II attributes and thus scores ranging between 1 (for its
catch-up innovation), 2 (for firm size and social purpose), and 2.5 (for financing
and employment).

From these distinct starting points, did East Asian states converge on an ide-
alized version of Mark I? Does this examination of startup capitalism serve as
further evidence of a convergence on the LME variety of capitalism? Or do East
Asia's approaches to startup capitalism align better with the *reality* of Silicon Valley? By this, we mean that startups are largely perceived as resources for big businesses that have only expanded their competitive positions. Do the trajectories
mostly suggest continuity in each state's own approach?

Let us start with Japan. Since the Heisei recession in 1990, the Japanese developmental state has increasingly promulgated startup largesse. But rather than a

rejection of its large firm–led developmental state apparatus in which pension savings and main banks reinforced lifetime employment and incremental innovation prowess, there has been continuity. Japan's startup capitalism is one of fostering open innovation systems in which the keiretsu and main banks have emerged as crucial partners, investors, and beneficiaries. Prominent programs like the 2018 J-Startup Initiative and the 2020 Startup Ecosystem Consortium center on the participation of keiretsu and main banks, which play vital roles in selecting startups and are recognized as essential investors and potential acquirers. Prime Minister Kishida's 2022 "Startup Development Five-Year Plan" even emphasized that large, existing companies engage with startups in open innovation as a means of sustaining their business operations.

Thus, Japan's startup capitalism constitutes some change but not a radical departure from its developmental state starting point, as illustrated with a modest shift outward in figure 6.2. More equity-based investment vehicles have been promoted, lifetime employment has been modestly eroded, and the nature of innovation has, for many years, been at the world's technological frontier. However, the size of firms still regarded as essential to national innovation capacity remains large. The keiretsu are beneficiaries of startup activities, including talent. The financiers of the previous epoch are involved in startup capitalism as active investors, judges, and ecosystem actors. It cannot be said that the keiretsu fear competition from startups nor that the Japanese government has discontinued its backing of big business.

Korea was the second country examined, given that it is also often characterized as an archetypical developmental state. In the chaebol-dominated era, the state acted to encourage the upgrading of the technological capacity of SMEs that could provide high value-added employment in addition to being suppliers to the internationally competitive chaebol. The Korean context closely aligned with an open innovation variety of the Mark II mode. Since the EAFC in the late 1990s, policies have publicly attested to a rising dedication to startups as employers and innovators. Every government since the crisis, whether liberal or conservative, has stated its championing of startups. High-profile initiatives, such as President Park Geun-hye's implementation of the Creative Economy Action Plan and President Moon Jae-in's establishment of the MSS in July 2017, have amplified those messages in a very public way.

While institutional change has occurred, particularly in the extent to which innovation is now radical, equity is more prevalent, and the employment market is more fluid, the Korean startup capitalism mode remains best depicted as fitting the open innovation variant of the Mark II type. Startup initiatives often foster partnerships between startups and chaebol, with the aim of injecting innovative DNA into the country's leading firms. Startup capitalism offers a different, and less publicly visible, way of backing large firms than the credit-centric tools linked to exports in the classic developmental period. Sentiment expressed across the media suggests that the chaebol are aware that the promotion of startups by successive governments aims to reinforce them and expand their offerings through the integration of new technologies rather than foster their replacement by new firms. While startups are presented as key beneficiaries of innovation policies, we observe that the chaebol often act as vital partners and ultimate recipients of this help. The K-Startup Grand Challenge, for instance, sees a licensing agreement with a chaebol as a KPI. The Korean startup capitalism mode, then, has seen movement outward in several institutional arena, as illustrated in figure 6.2, but remains most closely aligned with the Mark II variety (one fueled by open innovation logics).

In the antecedent period in Taiwan, the state stands out relative to the others in East Asia in its early orientation toward small technology-centric firms as central to technological upgrading capacity. The government's policies focused on enhancing the capabilities of small firms by incentivizing R&D and export activities. Entrepreneurship was encouraged as it provided a form of employment; early-stage equity markets for high-growth startups were developed already in the 1980s, and government entities facilitated the competitiveness of nascent firms by acquiring foreign technology and transferring it from public institutes like ITRI. However, by the turn of the twenty-first century, the government publicly advocated for startups in emerging sectors and technologies, and not in collaboration with, or necessarily for the benefit of, large firms (like TSMC) or their technologies. The primary focus has been on widening the entrepreneurial pool by attracting foreign talent and directing attention to emerging technologies. The government routinely asserts that the success of Taiwan's personal computer and semiconductor-focused miracle has prompted them to encourage startup activity in emerging technology sectors such as biotechnology, LCDs, and green tech.

Thus, Taiwan's startup capitalism began as the closest to the Mark I ideal type and remains the most oriented toward startups as innovators in their own right. Taiwan's social purpose in helping startups remains to encourage more new entrants who can disrupt firms in world markets—but not domestic firms.[1] The aim of backing startups is not to prop up domestic industries or firms, nor is it to challenge them. The aspiration to achieve more radical innovation has grown, shifting from acquiring foreign technology and catching up in manufacturing to competing as front-runners in design capabilities in the semiconductor industry. However, large firms like TSMC, despite its essential position in the world's critical technology, are not considered the ultimate beneficiaries, unlike such an orientation in the two East Asian developed counterparts. Collectively, Taiwan's movement from antecedents to startup capitalism reflects the outward shift toward (more) radical innovation and the persistence of its focus on small firms, equity financing, fluid employment, and external security threats as its great motivator.

China's political economy is often depicted as opposing the neoliberal approach of the United States, with the state actively shaping firm-specific capabilities and allocating resources toward critical technologies. Its antecedent period is characterized by its mobilizing of resources to bolster catchup technological capabilities across a combination of firms, including state-owned enterprises and large private firms. This gave the Chinese antecedent more of a Mark II character. Even in the antecedent period, however, startups were already conceptualized in playing a role, and clusters of innovative startups were developed across major cosmopolitan areas. So while the antecedent period was *closer* to the Mark II ideal, it did not fully align with that ideal type.

The striking finding in the Chinese context is the magnitude of the change. While all cases experienced movement in the direction of Mark I, the size of the evolution in the Chinese case is the greatest. Yet, like the other cases, it comprises a mix of Mark I and II elements. This is seen as policy makers not only encourage new entrants to foster capabilities in emerging technologies but also strive to dismantle the dominant positions held by giant corporations like Alibaba. In the consumer internet or platform economy, efforts encourage China's entrepreneurs to fight against each other as well as against industry leaders for their place. This consternation has been mirrored in market dynamics. The *Economist* (2024a) notes that "capital for the consumer internet has all but dried up," while, in the same period, "hard-tech developers have collectively raised about 550bn yuan through initial public offerings."

In technologies like semiconductors, renewable energies, or 6G, the state finances its large would-be national champion firms, such as SMIC, which was given a US$282.1 million subsidy in 2022 (Cao 2023). This is a telling example, as it reveals that SMIC was far from being the sole recipient; more than 190 Chinese companies operating in the semiconductor industry received funding as part of a US$1.75 billion package. This semiconductor package is in some ways emblematic of China's startup capitalism; large companies receive financing, but so do would-be startups operating in the space. What is more, China's crackdown on the oligopolies of large private firms is consistent with China as a Mark I variety only in the sense that the destruction of dominant positions occurs. However, this is not fueled by startups as engines of this existential threat. At the same time, the Chinese approach includes the marshaling of state resources in key technologies, which represents a continuation of some of its Mark II attributes from the antecedent period. As a result, the Chinese evolution toward startup capitalism contains a mix of contradictory elements from both the Mark I and II varieties.

Collectively, the continuity and change trajectories reveal movements of inter-locking institutions underpinning East Asia's antecedents through to the startup capitalism modes in each country. Overall, relative to figure 6.1's concentration by Japan, Korea, and China in the center of the radar chart, figure 6.2 shows that each country has adapted such that employment markets are now more fluid, innovation aims are more radical, and financial systems are more comprehen-sive, with equity offerings alongside the provision of credit. There are varying degrees of outward movements toward small firms as the locus for innovation activities, with Taiwan remaining so and China moving more in that direction. For most countries, the motivating social purpose has remained a mix of exter-nal and domestic elements, but the national security imperative has grown more noticeably for both China and Taiwan compared to Japan and Korea. In this sense, there has been a convergent trend across the countries, with hybridity moving in the direction of, but not coming close to reaching, Mark I paradigms.

What should we make of this continuity and change? One read is that there is an overall convergence toward a Mark I mode across the cases. None of the cases have seen their trajectories shift inward, toward the Mark II ideal type (e.g., no scores have gotten closer to zero). What is more, we do not observe a mere con-tinuation of previous approaches. No country's scores remain at the same posi-tion across their antecedent and startup capitalism eras, as illustrated in figures 6.1 and 6.2. There have been shifts *away from* Mark II logics in all four countries. Each case has seen movement in the direction of Mark I in terms of radical inno-

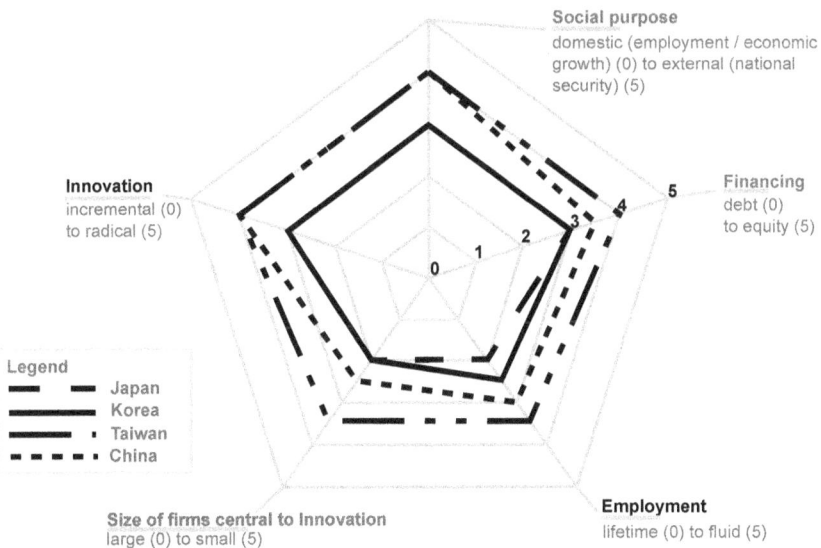

FIGURE 6.2. Startup capitalism in Japan, Korea, Taiwan, and China

vation and the inclusion of equity financing and startups as innovation engines. In Taiwan, there has not been a retreat of its small firm antecedents, even though the economy is dominated by just a handful of firms that operate in a small set of industries, with TSMC's position in the fabless manufacturing of semiconductors being the most prominent and well-known. Startup initiatives strive to bolster the widening of entrepreneurial pools in emerging industries, like biotech and green energy, not as innovative DNA to inject into the semiconductor giants.

However, it would be wrong to conclude that there is a broad convergence on the Silicon Valley–styled mode (Mark I). As we showed in the Japan and Korea cases, startups fuel the pursuit of large firms' capacity to compete at the world frontier in a more complex and competitive international environment. Incumbents themselves provide equity financing for the startups that benefit them and serve as the beneficiaries of more fluid labor markets, where startups help them develop their long-term access to talent. In at least these two countries, the expanse away from 0 and toward 5 on the radar chart is in collaboration with, and primarily for the benefit of, large firms, not instead of them. Startups are construed as engines of innovation and talent creation in incumbent-led open innovation systems, where it is big businesses that are key investors and acquirers. Thus, the size of the shift in Japan and Korea is from 1s to 3s, rather than 1s to 5s. This augurs for the pursuit of an open innovation variety of startup capitalism rather than convergence on creative destruction logic.

In fact, even in cases where startups are scored as essential agents for innovating in new technologies (e.g., Taiwan's score of 3.5 for startup centrality), none of the cases strongly position startups as engines of creative destruction. Startups are portrayed as agents capable of spurring economic growth through the enhancing of capabilities for incumbents or as essential stewards of emerging technologies. Initiatives incentivize the widening of entrepreneurial pools who are pursuing emerging technologies. These startups complement, rather than challenge, big businesses. They are not creative destruction agents in any case.

Given that startup promotion is not necessarily striving to transform the system, we conclude that startup capitalism can be best understood as a form of institutional coevolution (Breznitz 2007; Edmondson et al. 2019). One reason for coevolution is that the organizations that were once responsible for developmental state policies are often the same organizations leading startup initiatives. In Japan, METI plays a central role. In China, the State Council, the NDRC, and MoST lead entrepreneurship and startup promotion initiatives. In Taiwan, what was the CEPD—then the MoST, and then, since summer 2022, the National Science and Technology Council—is a leader in orchestrating startup advancements in emerging industries. Pauline Debanes (2017) calls this "institutional layering" in Korea, as organizations such as the MSS have been merely changed in name, toward startups and the technological frontier rather than shepherding the country's less-productive small firms. The ministry became the MSS in 2017, which served as an explicit indicator that the movement toward viewing small firms as innovators that had been underway since the EAFC was officially enshrined in the governance structure (Klingler-Vidra and Pacheco Pardo 2019). But these organizations are not new; they are new iterations of those that helped propel growth in the past and from which they evolved.

Across the four countries, there has been a shift outward in the context of the nature of innovation, when comparing figures 6.1 and 6.2, from incremental (score of 0) to radical (score of 5) innovation. Startups are increasingly envisaged as driving radical innovation rather than participating in the catch-up, incremental manufacturing that was the focus in the antecedent period. In Japan, Korea, and Taiwan, shifts were already well underway by the 1990s; the first developer in this context, Japan, was pushing (though not always successful in reaching) for the technological frontier by at least the 1980s, with personal computing software, semiconductors, and even AI and machine learning (Callon 1995). In the case of Korea, this move toward the technological frontier was clearly underway by the 1990s, when both the government and the chaebol became aware that the phase of catch-up development was over. In the aftermath of the EAFC, the ambition of producing radical (open) innovation with startups as a crucial component became more open and obvious. Taiwan's Hsinchu Park, for its part, was already on the world map of semiconductor foundries in the same decade, with TSMC being catapulted to international innovation importance shortly after its establishment in the 1980s. Startup policies' aims in Taiwan have clearly been, since the dawn of the twenty-first century, to cultivate entrepreneurship in emerging technologies rather than to achieve incremental innovation capacity for giants in established industries. In China, the thrust of efforts shifted toward indigenous innovation capabilities at the technological frontier later, especially in the early 2000s and then even more so since Xi took office in 2012, enabling it to compete in specific world-leading technologies, again bringing it toward Mark I in this respect.

As each country moved to incorporate the promotion of startup-centric innovation at the technological frontier into its suite of industrial policies, the institutional foundations have adapted in step with one another, having an interlocking effect. The institutional complementarities of finance and labor have moved, in varying degrees, toward equity funding (VC and stock markets) and more fluidity (less lifelong employment).

To different extents, the financing of innovation had already expanded to include equity funding means, especially VC and stock market access for high-growth firms, in the antecedent period. Beginning in Taiwan in the early 1980s, governments have themselves acted as VC investors by running VC funds that invest in startups. They have also increasingly improved the regulatory environment for VC by ensuring that legal structures such as the LP are available and offering tax incentives. In this way, each country has acted as a "venture capital state" (Klingler-Vidra 2018), seeing early-stage equity financing as essential to startups' ability to innovate. Stock markets have been launched in each country that cater to high-tech startups that do not have many years of profitability under their belt, which is typically required to list on a stock exchange. In Japan, JAS-DAQ was launched (with the backing of SoftBank); the Emerging Stock Board was created within the Taipei Exchange in 2002; KOSDAQ was established in 1996 and KONEX in 2013 in Korea; and ChiNext, the Shanghai Stock Exchange's Sci-tech Innovation Board, or STAR market, and the Beijing Stock Exchange were launched in China.

The varying moves toward a greater use of equity-based financing has not necessarily come as separate from large firms, banks, or national pension funds. The rise of startup-focused equity investment activity has reflected an evolution in the comprehensiveness of the country's financial systems, not in opposition to debt financing. In Japan and Korea, the keiretsu and chaebol, respectively, are active VC investors openly courted by the government, investing along with, and in addition to, government programs and national pension funds. In Taiwan, the government leveraged financing from big businesses, like Acer and Formosa Plastics, to initially seed its VC industry in the 1980s. In China, the remarkable rise of equity financing—by some measures, China is the world's largest VC market—reflects an increasingly enabling regulatory environment and mobilization of state investment for early-stage equity investment. Rather than a rejection of debt financing, then, the embrace of equity investing has been ushered in by stalwarts of the antecedent era, including large firms, main banks, and state funds. In this sense, financing models have not seen a break with the past but instead added new tools to preexisting ones.

Employment has also, broadly speaking, become more fluid. Lifetime employment has been eroded in each case. In Taiwan, policies have long aimed to widen entrepreneurial pools. From the antecedent period, the thrust of employment-related startup policies in Taiwan has been on ensuring skills for what has been deemed the technological frontier or an emerging industry. With the onset of crises and recessions in Japan and Korea in the 1990s came a challenge to the ubiquity of the permanent employment system; companies faced such dire situations that they were forced to conduct layoffs (Pempel 1998; Vogel 2006, 2018) and reduce numbers through natural attrition. Crucially for labor market fluidity, pension fund regulations were relaxed, so employees did not have to stay with their company for the duration of their career. Over time, secondment programs and the normalization of midcareer moves contributed to a modest increase in the fluidity of the Japanese and Korean labor markets. In China, the most notable change in the employment arena toward fluidity is the way in which government efforts, particularly the *hukuo* system and talent incentives, began to target entrepreneurs. Entrepreneurship has—from 1998—counted as a form of employment that could help secure access to social services. It has been accepted in party circles, and high-tech startup activity has been promoted among graduates and returnees.

Yet, labor market fluidity, in practice, continues to fall short of the Mark I ideal. There are numerous drivers of this. For one, practices have helped enable flexibility *within* the existing system. For instance, in Japan, secondments have enabled permanent employees to gain startup experience without leaving their job for life. In Korea, while startup experience is more socially acceptable, the path of attending a SKY university and then working for a chaebol remains the most sought after. In Taiwan, startup policies encourage widening pools of entrepreneurial activity in emerging technologies. China's intense "007" technology work culture, which refers to working midnight to midnight seven days a week and is the newer and even more intense version of the "996" pattern (working 9:00 a.m. to 9 p.m. six days a week), does see movement across firms as well as mavericks who leave to set up their own startups.

Social purpose does not necessarily align with external or domestic drivers, according to our articulation of the Mark I and II types. Some scholars do expect that "creative insecurity" (Taylor 2016) instigates innovation prowess, so a relative focus on external concerns could motivate more investment in radical innovation. As we saw with the four cases, the need for innovation—even radical innovation—does not necessarily align with a focus on either startups or large firms. As a case in point, external determinants have been essential to Taiwan's pursuit of its Mark I version of startup capitalism for decades, while China's investment in critical technologies has centered in some ways on startups as resources for large firms. However, innovation in critical technologies has become a more explicit social purpose underpinning government efforts. In this sense, startups and economic statecraft have converged. Economic statecraft is not only the domain of large military contractors. Interestingly, given the region's geopolitical context, China and Taiwan are similar in the emphasis on techno-national security, whereas Japan and Korea show more of a hybrid aim of delivering on domestic and external arenas.

More often, there has been a mix of external and domestic social purpose motivating efforts that have varied over time. Here Japan offers a clear example. The Japanese government has aimed, through startup promotion, to generate high-quality employment opportunities, first motivated by job losses suffered in the 1990s. Entrepreneurial experience has also been regarded as a means of training talent for the keiretsu. Secondly, Japanese startup assistance seeks to enhance the technological capabilities of large firms as a means of propelling economic growth and competing in key world technology niches. Collectively, these efforts are aimed at advancing Japan's relative technological security (external) and fostering job creation and economic growth (domestic). Another domestic motivation has come to motivate startup promotion across the cases. Startup initiatives have increasingly been positioned as means of improving social inclusion, especially in terms of gender participation rates in Japan, Korea, and Taiwan and in the context of regional inclusion in the Chinese case.

Thus, across all four cases, a domestic source of social purpose has emerged: a means of fostering social inclusion. In China, there has been a strong thrust for decentralization, with the promotion of mass innovation and entrepreneurship aiming to better distribute high value–added activity across China, especially to small towns and villages away from the glittering lights of Beijing, Shanghai, or Shenzhen. Through the government's bankrolling of infrastructure alongside the e-commerce platforms of Taobao and Pinduoduo, local "makers" are encouraged to become digital entrepreneurs (Li 2017). However, there remain debates about the extent to which such efforts have reduced inequality, as China's coastal, urban hubs continue to dominate (see Klingler-Vidra et al. 2022). In the other cases, especially Japan, employment in technological startups is a solution to demographic challenges (aging population, gender-based exclusion, and regional inequalities) as well as social exclusion concerns. Korea's startup policies speak of addressing gender inequalities, with the aim of increasing the participation of female entrepreneurs. In the Taiwanese context, dynamic startups have long been construed as important employers; this has continued to be the case, with greater efforts to drive social inclusion in terms of who is employed by, or able to establish, these firms, especially in gender terms.

The Emperor's New (Startup) Clothes

In this book, we contribute to the "developmental state: dead or alive" debate. We do so by showing that even in empirical arenas that suggest a decline in state direction, the state (the emperor) has not retired but instead has adapted the means of intervening (the new clothes in the form of startup capitalism). The fact that there are outward movements toward Schumpeter's Mark I type, which aligns in many ways with a stylized version of Silicon Valley, does not signify a death of the developmental state. Instead, we argue that the developmental state is very much alive. It has adopted equity financing tools, enabled more fluid labor markets, and worked to compete at the world's technological frontier by embracing startups as engines of innovation capabilities. In other words, the developmental state has adapted to the realities of today's innovation paradigm.

As a result, we argue that an assessment of the persistence (or not) of the developmental state's focus on large firm is too narrow of an analytical lens. In a similar way, studies of the entrepreneurial state are too narrow, as they miss the role of large firms, and see startup help as something distinct or even at odds with long-standing industrial policy. As evidenced here, these two modes of analysis—one focused on state–large firm relations and the other on state–entrepreneur interactions—are both incomplete. Thus, we contend that political economy scholars need to assess interactions between the state and the wider innovation system, one that is more of an open innovation system composed of startups as well as national champions, universities, research institutes, and multinationals, to understand the contemporary innovation mode.

We contend that East Asia's startup capitalism constitutes modern forms of their respective developmental state orientations rather than a decline or death. For some, they have continued along a variety of Mark I logic in which startup capitalism boosts high-growth entrepreneurs in emerging industries (Taiwan); for others, oligopolistic competition remains the organizing logic (Japan and Korea), bringing them closer to a Mark II type. We are not alone in our finding that startup capitalism constitutes continuity *and* change. Debanes (2017) refers to this as institutional layering in Korea, and Ulrike Schaede (2020, ix) depicts this as Japan's "new corporate culture that foster[s] coexistence of mature and new businesses." China's developmental state operates according to some Mark I logics, as it actively encourages startups and breaks the centrality of some large firms (most famously, Alibaba) while also funding startups alongside large firms competing in even critical technology markets, which aligns more with a Mark II approach.

We reveal that through startup capitalism, developmental states pursuing an open innovation variety of a Mark II approach have found a way to continue backing national champions. The nature of the assistance is less direct and more nuanced than in the classic developmental state era. Rather than organizing consortia and endowing preferential credit access, which is direct and highly visible, governments can invest in and give tax breaks to startups that then partner with, or are acquired by, large firms. This tack helps limit political contestation over state–large firm relations by framing startup efforts as open innovation initiatives (Hsieh 2018; Klingler-Vidra and Pacheco Pardo 2022). Korea's CCEIs make for one clear example. Each of the country's nineteen centers have a chaebol partner that helps finance the center, which appears like the large firm's contribution to society. In reality, the CCEIs are aligned with the strategic direction of the chaebol; they fit with its business lines and help it to source solutions to "what keeps it up late at night."

The CCEIs embed the chaebol at the heart of the entrepreneurial ecosystem, which endows the large firms with access to entrepreneurial talent and ideas. By the chaebol advancing their sector-specific positions in Korea's open innovation system, they can showcase their innovativeness to their workforce and also to their customers and suppliers (Pacheco Pardo and Klingler-Vidra 2019). Similarly, in Japan's J-Startup Initiative, select main banks and keiretsu work with METI bureaucrats to choose the startups that can participate in the program. In the process of judging and then collaborating with METI in the running of the program, the large firms have insight into new ideas, talent, and prospective customers. The keiretsu, as a result, align their brand with startup-fueled innovation. Startup policy, in both cases, is designed in collaboration with—and for the benefit of—large firms.

Startup Capitalism's Global Implications

The story goes that the phrase "what's good for GM is good for America" was uttered by the president of General Motors, Charles Wilson, when he was answering questions about his ability to hold company stock while serving as the US secretary of defense in 1953.[2] What Wilson meant was that big businesses like GM were essential employers, taxpayers, and contractors for national security aims. For Wilson, there was a mutually beneficial relationship between big business, the US government, and society that propelled his company's alignment with the American people. This story speaks to long-standing relations between big business and the state in even the quintessential LME and the home to Silicon Valley.

This raises questions: Is our observation that startups can be construed as resources for large firms in East Asia specific to the region? Why could the interests of large firms not feature in startup capitalism in other countries, even in the United States? We return to that crystalizing moment for us in the early days of writing this book, when the manager of the CCEI in Seoul explained that a key aim was to inject innovative DNA into the country's largest employers, producers, and taxpayers. It makes sense, from that lens, that startup capitalism does not necessarily manifest as separate from big businesses, let alone have the aim of disrupting them.

At the same time, the societal position of big business is now more contentious. Unlike the description of the alignment of GM and American interests, big businesses are criticized for their dominance of markets and exploitation of consumers. They are more likely to be described as strictly operating according to self-interest than as being motivated by what is good for America. Congressional hearings comprise business leaders like Mark Zuckerberg testifying to their good intentions in the face of antitrust cases and scandals. Playing on this sentiment, Jonathan Tepper (2023, 15) asserts in *The Myth of Capitalism* that "what is good, right, and logical for the corporation is not good, right, or logical for the economy as a whole." The critique being that the US economy is increasingly concentrated in the hands of oligopolies that build "moats" that protect their competitive advantage.

Thus, in contrast to popular depictions of the United States as a—*the*—neoliberal, free-for-all market economy and the home to the world's leading startup cluster, Silicon Valley, which policy makers across the world seek to replicate in their own home countries, there is a growing chorus of critiques. US markets, some critics posit, are less competitive, with sector after sector being dominated by a handful of companies protecting their oligopolistic, and even monopolistic, practices. "Not only are the big companies gobbling up the small," according to Tepper, the United States has "not seen a new wave of startups coming in to compete with the Goliaths" (Tepper 2023, 11). This sentiment about worrying levels of industrial concentration has been echoed in popular media, too. For instance, the *Economist* found that in the 900 sectors it tracks, "the number where the four biggest firms have a market share above two-thirds grew from 65 in 1997 to 97 by 2017" (*Economist* 2023d).

Why is this happening? One explanation is that large firms are simply acting in line with prevailing business strategy logic, such as Michael Porter's "five forces" and Warren Buffet's sage investment advice. The economics discipline has linked this to a decline in economic productivity, even in the face of the supposed rise of Silicon Valley and its brand of startup-centric innovation (e.g., see Decker et al. 2016a).

A second reason is that the nature of technology today may lend itself more to monopolistic positions. Silicon Valley platform economy firms like Amazon and eBay achieve dominance over markets, and there are little means for the public—and even the state—to hold them accountable (Culpepper and Thelen 2020; Moore and Tambini 2021). Antitrust laws and calls for decentralizing the internet giants have proven difficult to action, as these companies continue to accumulate massive amounts of data, expand their physical infrastructure, and enter new market domains (Lehdonvirta 2022). The US government has, however, made some initial advances. Notably, the Federal Trade Commission is suing—along with seventeen state governments—Amazon for an illegal protection of its monopoly in online retail (McCabe 2023).

A third driver of the increased market concentration and declining business dynamism may be the widespread embrace of open innovation. As evidenced in our examination, even public policy makers tasked with promoting startups are often working to connect startups as customers of, and resources for, large firms. Startups are linked with large companies and, as such, do not instigate creative destruction's productive forces. Rather than viewing them as competitors to be feared, big businesses see startups as customers, as outsourced R&D, and as marketing partners.

The aim of integrating startups as customers is neatly exemplified by the case of the Amazon Web Services accelerator. Early cohorts of their accelerator received coaching, mentorship, and a monetary investment. By the early 2020s, startups selected for the AWS Startup Loft Accelerator received AWS credits rather than money. The accelerator program, in this way, helped establish AWS as core to startups' tech stack. The head of Microsoft's corporate VC unit spoke of a similar shift toward a more strategic, rather than financial, orientation, as she "transformed the CVC's startup investments so that they more closely align with the parent company's business" (Rivera 2023). These approaches fit Linus Dahlander and David M. Gann's (2010) depiction of open innovation as potentially taking inbound and outbound orientations, with startups being capable of constituting sales channels and R&D inputs. This reality—that startup-incumbent engagement in the form of accelerators is a potential sales boost for big businesses—raises important questions about whether this form of open innovation is subduing, rather than fueling, business dynamism.

Simultaneous to the growing dominance of oligopolist firms in open innovation systems, a culture of celebrating disruptive entrepreneurs has become ubiquitous. Successful startup founders, like Jack Ma or Steve Jobs, are idolized. University graduates aim to start their own world-changing business rather than work for a large company. The connotation of startups is that of exciting, nimble innovators intent on displacing the unloved, pedestrian, and sometimes even mocked big businesses. The cultural salience of startups is enshrined in hit shows like *Silicon Valley*, the proliferation of documentaries, and, in some prominent cases, Hollywood movies on the lives of tech founders.

Researchers have begun to lament the entrepreneurial obsession. Some have noted the problem of conflating gazelles and unicorns with the wider population of entrepreneurs (Aldrich and Ruef 2018). Books like *Big Is Beautiful* (Atkinson and Lind 2019) contend that large firms do bring societal value as employers and innovators, and as a result, government efforts should adopt innovation-centric and size-neutral policies rather than favoring firms based on their small size. Perhaps unsurprisingly, technology industry leaders have bemoaned the hollowing out of large-scale, cutting-edge manufacturing in the US. Already in 2010, Andy Grove, the former head of Intel, made the case for American policy that would incentivize high-end manufacturing in the semiconductor industry, and in so doing, create quality jobs and bolster US prowess in end-to-end chip capabilities (Grove 2010).

The critique of prioritizing entrepreneurship has been boosted by studies that question the relationship between startups and economic performance indicators. For instance, one analysis (Fairlie et al. 2023) of US Census Bureau data revealed that job creation and survival rates of startups are much lower than otherwise reported by the government. This adds to the call to arms around policy makers' need to clearly define and distinguish different types of entrepreneurship and the policies required to aid their growth (Acs et al. 2016). The implication here is that there is a growing need for public policy makers to reconsider how to best encourage innovation.

Bringing these different strands together, we distill two simultaneous but paradoxical observations. The first is the reality of large firms dominating the economy. Incumbents have a greater share of markets and the ability to shape the information and products available to society, now more than ever. Business dynamism is down, in part because of the inability of high-growth firms to realize their potential due to the entrenched position of large firms serving as barriers to scale in numerous markets (Decker et al. 2016b). The second observation is that the myth of this being the era of the audacious entrepreneur persists. Within this guise, governments publicize their startup promotion efforts, like Start-Up Chile and Japan's J-Startup Initiative, showcasing their intentions of building Silicon Valley–style clusters. Now more than ever, governments around the world communicate their desire to bolster aspiring entrepreneurs and their startups. Large companies often do the same by organizing a range of corporate venture programs that excite their employees and show external stakeholders that they are innovative.

What, then, can be said about the aims of the ubiquitous international efforts to foster local Silicon Valleys? On the surface, the ambition of startup capitalism is to build cohorts of high-growth startups that will create high-quality employment, launch innovative products, and help drive economic performance and national security. But is the goal to encourage disruptive startups that challenge large companies or instead to service the competitive positioning of the domestic economy's Goliaths? We show that startup capitalism should not be viewed as separate from the treatment of large firms, from San Jose, to Seoul, to Tokyo. We call for a critical discussion around what really is the aim of public policies with Silicon monikers around the world. The point of governments fostering local Silicon Valleys is especially poignant, as Silicon Valley itself is under attack for being incumbent dominated.

We reveal that startup capitalism is not necessarily about creative destruction. Schumpeter's (1934) Mark I understanding of the industrial dynamics that best foster innovation and economic growth emphasizes the value of the existential threat that new entrants bring. The conventional understanding of the Mark I pattern of innovation hinges on the notion of creative destruction in which new entrants displace the position of large firms and their technologies. Even the competitive threat of new entrants is enough to spur innovation from existing firms, for fear of being replaced by more nimble and hungrier startups.

However, we find that in startup capitalism, this rationale does not necessarily underpin startup policies, which instead strive to widen entrepreneurial pools in emerging technologies. What is more, we find that policies often take a Mark II tack, as they—sometimes explicitly but more often implicitly—aim to benefit big businesses rather than challenge them. The underlying logic is that large firms, especially those that are important to society's job creation, economic output, and national security, such as Japan's keiretsu and Korea's chaebol, but also many large American firms that are too big to fail, should benefit from startups. Rather than fear startups that could displace them, leaders of large firms, such as those represented by Japan's powerful and decades-old business group, the Nippon Keidanren, lobby the government for more investment in startups. As an example, in July 2023, Tomoko Namba, the vice chairperson of the Keidanren, told the *Japan Times* that "it is crucial to produce more globally successful startups" (Nagata 2023). Startups, the Keidanren chair contends, will not compete with them directly, as they will instead offer them new technologies to integrate into their business operations, products, and services. As such, even the Keidanren were "urging the government to boost support" to startups, stressing "the importance of Japan attracting foreign talent and major overseas venture capital to reinforce global networks" (Nagata 2023).

In Schumpeter's work, incumbents aim to preclude new entrants, seeking to instead deepen their position. This can be understood as the human self-preservation instinct applied to the firm level, with large firms seeking their own continuation in business. We find that industry giants—and policy makers—today engage startups as external (technology-centric) resources or customers that benefit large firms. Thus, rather than preventing startups from coming into existence or scaling up in the name of open innovation policies, big businesses collaborate with their local governments to help them access new ideas and talent from startups. Policy makers often pursue startup capitalism as a hybrid of Schumpeterian thinking, as they strive to create new cohorts of unicorns while also ensuring the competitive positioning of large firms.

Creative Destruction or Oligopolistic Competition?

Schumpeter was ultimately interested in understanding which industrial dynamic was optimal, given the attributes of the historical setting, such as the maturity of the industry and technology. At the dawn of the twentieth century, he contended that it had been dynamic new entrants that incentivized or directly caused innovation advances. But a few decades later, he opined that large, well-capitalized companies like US Steel were able to take big bets that their smaller competitors could not consider. The human resources and deep pockets of oligopolies meant that they were capable of driving society's transformative innovation. The two modes of innovation operated at different historic moments, according to distinct logics.

In this book, we contend that startup capitalism is underpinned by the widespread acceptance of the following three presumptions: (1) startups are essential motors of economic growth and innovation; (2) large firms, which are important actors in open innovation systems, bring value to fledgling startups, and incumbents likewise benefit from startups' ideas and talent; (3) markets are competitive, with high-growth startups capable of disrupting the position of big businesses.

In open innovation systems in which large firms deepen their position by leveraging external resources, incumbents do not fear startups; rather, they seek out collaboration with startups to help boost their competitive position. As Baslandze (2023) argues, this orientation toward seeking out collaborations with new entrants makes sense at the level of the individual big firm. Large companies want to work with startups for inbound and outbound activities (Dahlander and Gann 2010), to know what challenges may loom, to access new product ideas that may escape them, to sell to new markets, and to find new talent. The complementarity, rather than contention, of startups from the eyes of incumbent firms aligns with Henry Chesbrough's expectation that the proliferation of the knowledge economy and ICT fundamentally changed the nature of innovation; digital prowess can be perceived as an exogenous resource to be layered in rather than an existential threat to an established firm (see Chesbrough and Bogers 2014, 16). However, more cynically, it could be that large firms pursue open innovation strategies in a cloaked attempt to suppress threats to their business by acquiring teams and developing startup ideas as their own. Regardless of the motivation, we note that it is rational for the individual incumbent firm to lobby the government to facilitate their engagement of startups (Bombardini et al. 2023), repurposing startup assistance in a way that benefits, rather than threatens, their business. For big companies, open innovation offers multidimensional access to startups in ways that can engender innovation and simultaneously undermine their direct competition. Their motivation to shape startup help is clear.

It remains to be seen whether startup capitalism is optimal for innovation in the twenty-first century. There are various approaches taken, depending on the novelty of the technology and its accompanying industry. Policy makers strive to widen the entrepreneurial pool (closer to Mark I), and some aim to deepen the innovative capabilities of the large firms (closer to Mark II). Startups may be invoked as essential engines in areas of high uncertainty, when radical innovation is likely; oligopolies take the fore in more mature settings, and thus innovation advances are more incremental. Kai-fu Lee's (2018) assessment of who will win the AI competition—the United States or China—invokes this logic, as he contends that AI is a mature technology, given that its major breakthroughs occurred in the mid-twentieth century. He asserts that large datasets will now dominate, not nimble entrepreneurs writing genius code. The implication is that the government should encourage scale and therefore an innovation pattern more aligned with an open innovation orientation.

Pure Mark I approaches that strive for creative destruction could challenge or alienate some companies, which would be met with pushback from business leaders—potentially the same leaders who offer crucial support for politicians and political parties. Japan's powerful business group now lobbies for more state bankrolling for startups under the veil of open innovation aims in which startups are not threatening, but it would campaign strongly against startup policies that sought to challenge its position. This does not mean that it is politically impossible.

The Taiwan chapter opened with a public debate that unfolded for years between the TSMC founder Morris Chang and Taiwanese President Tsai Ing-wen. TSMC is central to the Taiwanese economy, but the state's startup help is dedicated to a hybrid version centered on widening entrepreneurial pools in emerging technologies, not on fostering open innovation to benefit TSMC and its semiconductor dominance. High-profile initiatives, such as the 5+2 innovative industries strategy or Asia's Silicon Valley Plan, continue to focus on widening entrepreneurial pools around emerging technologies. Morris Chang (2017) has been outspoken about his frustration about the lack of aid. The Tsai administration did not retract its position, but future governments may. This means there is precedent for policy makers pursuing efforts that is primarily in service of startups. However, this is not creative destruction per se.

Our analysis revealed that one of the motivations is that startup support is politically cleaner than directly underwriting long-established firms that may be perceived as cronies. This is clear in the Korean case, as successive governments work to distance themselves from headlines about their cozy relations with big business. More broadly, assistance for entrepreneurs is more acceptable to the public, as big business has come to have negative connotations, whereas the public roots for individual entrepreneurs and their growing firms. The techlash—US society's strong negative reaction to the growing power of Silicon Valley's large tech firms (Wladawsky-Berger 2020) and now the Amazon antitrust case—serves as evidence of this sentiment opposing more help for large firms. Unlike the GM refrain, what is good for Amazon is not widely thought to be good for America.

The Social Purpose of Startup Capitalism

We conclude by returning to the big *so what?* Schumpeter was interested in. He asked: What is the pattern of innovation that is best for society? He posited that either oligopolies or new entrants could best propel economic growth and innovation outcomes. But what if we cast a wider understanding of the aim—or what we have called here *social purpose*—of public largesse to encourage startups? What if the social purpose of startup capitalism had to do with the (re)distribution of benefits, decreasing inequality, and incentivizing technological innovations that benefit the environment and underrepresented members of society? To what extent does the pursuit of startup-led innovation to compete at the world's technological frontier align with, or contrast with, stakeholder capitalism, which emphasizes a distribution of gains across people and planet (Schwab 2021)?

E. F. Schumacher (1973), a leader of the Appropriate Technologies movement in the 1970s, argued that *Small Is Beautiful*. This in some ways counters the emphasis on innovation at the technological frontier and in pursuit of economic growth. Schumacher argued that we should organize innovation capabilities in a way that prioritizes our communities and technologies to solve local challenges rather than to compete at the world's technological frontier. The contemporary lexicon for this idea is *inclusive innovation*, which acknowledges that innovation has a direction and that efforts should consider the environmental and societal aims as well as who participates in and benefits from innovation (Klingler-Vidra et al. 2022).

In the social purposes analyzed across the cases, we saw job creation as central in the antecedent period and even more strongly invoked in startup capitalism. Employment opportunities, rather than competing at the technological frontier, are often named in public communications of startup policies. Our analysis of social purpose also reveals the rise of inclusion and redistribution aims especially focused on women and rural populations. Distribution considerations, in spatial terms, were most prominent in the Chinese context, acknowledging that the participants—and beneficiaries—of startup-fueled innovation are often urban populations. So, efforts strive to encourage greater regional distribution of opportunities. Women's participation in startup clusters has adorned initiatives in Japan, Korea, and Taiwan, with the aim being to increase the number of female founders as well as the level of equity financing available for their startups.

There has, however, been less evidence of explicit links to startups as a mechanism for addressing environmental degradation. This is interesting, as elsewhere, evidence suggests the state—including in East Asia—has taken a central role in environmental action. Elizabeth Thurbon and colleagues (2023) call this "developmental environmentalism," based on their study of China and Korea. While the state takes a strategic role in the green energy shift, our examination suggests that large firms are likely at the center of its open innovation efforts. Startups as a means of instigating environmental innovation did not feature prominently in our analysis. Perhaps policy makers instinctively see large firms are better resourced and capable of leveraging their scale to drive widespread impact. If this is the case, it explains why environmental degradation and protection efforts focus on the activities of large firms rather than incentivize startups to develop solutions.

The challenge for wider society and especially for bureaucrats is to determine the relative priority of the different social purposes underpinning startup capitalism. Which domestic priorities should motivate efforts? Are economic growth, stability, and job creation the priority? Should redistribution and environmental stewardship be the focus? Or should it be supremacy at the world's frontier in critical technologies to advance national security that is primary? Should startups be bankrolled as a purposeful constraint on the growing dominance of platform businesses (Srnicek 2016; Thelen 2018; Kenney et al. 2020; Boyer 2022), like Amazon and Alibaba, which otherwise stand to hold massive amounts of data and control over market activities and society (see Cioffi et al. 2022)?

No single startup initiative can deliver cutting-edge innovation, national security, equitable growth, job security, and environmental benefit. Depending on the motivating social purpose, startup capitalism will take different forms. We argue that startup capitalism should be viewed as a contemporary mode of socioeconomic management well beyond the confines of high-tech startups. Startup capitalism—in its different forms, which involve large firms as well as a myriad of government bodies—is how governments are delivering economic statecraft in the twenty-first century.

Appendix

EAST ASIAN STARTUP POLICIES

TABLE A1. Japan's startup-centric innovation policies (1948–2023)

YEAR	INITIATIVE	INNOVATION POLICY TYPE	IMPLEMENTING ORGANIZATION
1951	Guarantees loans of up to twenty-five million yen for companies within five years old	Funding	JFC
1953	JFC for SMEs established with thirteen billion yen	Funding	Central government
1959	Patent Act, Design Act, and Trademark Act all passed into law	Regulation	Central government
1963	Establishment of the Small and Medium Enterprise Basic Law	Regulation	Central government
	Three Small Business Investment Companies (SBIC) were formed, in Tokyo, Osaka, and Nagoya, fashioned after the US SBIC program	Funding	MITI
	Tsukuba Science City established	Clusters, networks, institutes	National government and Ministry of Education
1967	Tax deduction (20%) on experimental and research expense increments	Taxation	National Tax Agency
1971	Kyoto Enterprise Development, first VC firm, launched	Funding	Local government and private partners
1972	Small and Medium Enterprise Vision	Regulation	MITI

(continued)

TABLE A1. *(continued)*

YEAR	INITIATIVE	INNOVATION POLICY TYPE	IMPLEMENTING ORGANIZATION
1975	New Business Support Fund: loans to new businesses (within five years of founding)	Funding	National Finance Corporation
	Venture Enterprise Center established	Funding	MITI
1982	Japan Associated Finance Co. Ltd. (JAFCO) launched the first limited liability company VC fund in Japan	Funding	Consortium of financial institutions
1983	Deregulation of initial listing requirements for over-the-counter market	Stock market	MOF
1985	Tax deduction (6%) to strengthen SMEs' Technology Foundation	Taxation	National Tax Agency
1993	Tax deduction on Special Experimental and Research Expense increased to 12%	Taxation	National Tax Agency
1995	New business development program	Funding	Development Bank of Japan
	Venture Plaza	Clusters, Networks, Institutes	SMRJ
	SME Creative Business Promotion Law	Regulation	Diet
1997	Angel tax incentives launched	Taxation	National Tax Agency
	Stock options issuance law passed	Regulation	Central government
1998	Limited Partnership Act for Investment passed	Regulation	Diet
	Venture Fair: matching event to introduce products and services of select startups and help them to expand their marketing channels	Clusters, networks, institutes	SMRJ
	Government-backed loans (forty trillion yen) for SMEs	Funding	MOF and MITI
1999	Small Business Innovation Research (SBIR)	Funding	SMRJ
	Venture Fund: investing in startups at the early stage, less than seven years after foundation	Funding	SMRJ
	Industrial Revitalization Law	Regulation	Central government
	Mothers (Market for High-Growth and Emerging Stocks, on the Tokyo Stock Exchange) and Centrex (Nagoya Stock Exchange) are launched to encourage growing high-tech company listings	Stock market	Central government
	Temporary Work Agency Law and Employment Security Law revised to expand employment placement and job-seeker support	Regulation	Diet

TABLE A1.

YEAR	INITIATIVE	INNOVATION POLICY TYPE	IMPLEMENTING ORGANIZATION
	Improvement of entrepreneurship education: for elementary and secondary school students to develop their "entrepreneurship"	Education	MITI
	Venture School: short-term intensive training	Education	Local governments
	Small and Medium-Sized Enterprise Basic Act amendment: Promotion of Startups	Regulation	Diet
2000	Nasdaq Japan (JASDAQ) launches	Stock market	Central government
	New Business Development Fund	Funding	Japan Finance Corporation for Small and Medium Enterprise
	Launch of incubation facilities	Clusters, networks, institutes	SMRJ, local governments
	Japan Venture Awards	Clusters, networks, institutes	SMRJ
2001	New Business Financing Program: providing loans without security/surety	Funding	JFC
	Industrial Cluster Policy	Clusters, networks, institutes	METI
	e-Japan strategy launched to boost IT sector competitiveness	Regulation	Cabinet
	Pension fund portability	Regulation	MOF
	Commercial Law amended to make the system of classified stocks more flexible	Stock market	Diet
	J-Net 21: portal site for SMEs	Infrastructure	SMRJ
2002	Cluster Plan	Clusters, networks, institutes	METI
	Deregulation of Share Issues and Stock Options	Regulation	MOF
	Basic Law on Intellectual Property reformed	Regulation	Diet
2003	IT Startups Support Program	Funding	METI
	Tax deduction on the Total Experimental and Research Expense (increased to 10%)	Taxation	National Tax Agency
	Dream Gate, startup support platform	Clusters, networks, institutes	VEC
	Plan to Promote IT among SMEs	Infrastructure	METI
	Program for Training of Venture Capitalists	Education	METI

(continued)

TABLE A1. *(continued)*

YEAR	INITIATIVE	INNOVATION POLICY TYPE	IMPLEMENTING ORGANIZATION
	Challenge Community Creation Program	Education	METI
	Business Startup Support Fund	Funding	SMRJ
	SME Growth Support Fund and SME Revitalization Fund	Funding	SMRJ
2005	New limited liability corporate and limited liability partnership structures for VC funds	Regulation	Central government
2006	Comprehensive Support Program for Creation of Regional Innovation	Clusters, networks, institutes	JST
	Companies Act Amendment	Regulation	Central government
2008	New Startup Fund, the New Business Startup Loan Program, Provision Scheme for Challenge Support and Capital Enhancement, and Loan with Stock Acquisition Rights	Funding	JFC
	Re-challenge Support Loans	Funding	JFC
2009	Innovation Network Corporation of Japan Investment program	Funding	METI and 19 corporations
	University & Graduate Schools Entrepreneur Education Promotion Network (Japanese)	Education and training	METI
2010	New JASDAQ	Stock market access	MOF
2011	Act to Facilitate Technology Transfer from Universities to the Private Sector Law)	Regulation	Diet
2012	Program for Creating Startups from Advanced Research and Technology	Funding	JST
	The SME Business Capabilities Enhancement Support Act	Regulation	METI
	Entrepreneurs' Challenge	Education and training	MIC, NICT
	Startup Subsidy	Funding	SMRJ
2013	Center of Innovation Program	Funding	Ministry of Education, Culture, Sports, Science, and Technology (MEXT), JST
	Next Generation Technology Transfer Program (NexTEP)	Funding	JST
	Micro Enterprise Revitalization Project	Funding	METI
	Super Cluster Program	Clusters, networks, institutes	JST
	Mirasapo (SME portal)	Infrastructure and government procurement	METI

TABLE A1.

YEAR	INITIATIVE	INNOVATION POLICY TYPE	IMPLEMENTING ORGANIZATION
	Article 18 of the Labor Contracts Act	Regulation	Diet
	National Strategic Special Zones	Attracting talent and investment	Cabinet Office
	High School Student Business Plan Grand Prix	Education and training	JFC
2014	ICT Innovation Creation Challenge Program (I-Challenge!)	Funding	MIC
	Government-Public Innovation Program	Funding	MEXT
	Support Program of Capital Contribution to Early-Stage Companies	Funding	JST
	Taxation to promote companies' venture investment	Taxation	National Tax Agency
	Enhancing Development of Global Entrepreneur Program	Education and training	MEXT
2015	Seed-Stage Technology-Based Startup Support Program and Startup-Up Innovation	Funding	New Energy and Industrial Technology Development Organization
	Strengthening the global venture ecosystem	Clusters, networks, institutes	METI
	Act for Demand Creation for SMEs amendment	Infrastructure and government procurement	Diet
	Startup Visa in National Strategic Special Zones	Attracting talent and investment	Immigration Bureau of Japan
	Jump Start NIPPON	Education and training	METI
	Promote the global alliance of Japan's core companies and SMEs	Attracting talent and investment	METI
	Project Creating a Bridge of Innovation between Silicon Valley and Japan	Attracting talent and investment	METI
2016	Open Innovation Platform with Enterprises, Research Institute and Academia	Clusters, networks, institutes	JST
	Entrepreneurial Experience Promotion Project for Elementary and Junior Schools	Education and training	MEXT
	Female entrepreneurs support network (ten hubs)	Clusters, networks, institutes	METI
	Startups in Corporate Alliance Subsidies of up to seventy million yen for R&D in startups in the program	Funding	NEDO
	Formation of Regional Innovation Ecosystem	Funding	MEXT

(continued)

TABLE A1. (*continued*)

YEAR	INITIATIVE	INNOVATION POLICY TYPE	IMPLEMENTING ORGANIZATION
2018	J-Startup Initiative	Clusters, networks, institutes	METI, New Energy and Industrial Technology Development, JETRO
	12-Month Startup Visa Program	Attracting talent and investment	METI and Ministry of Justice
2019	Start Next Innovator 2019	Attracting talent and investment	METI
	25% tax incentive on startup investments	Taxation	National Tax Agency
2020	Startup Visa scheme requirements relaxed	Attracting talent and investment	METI and regional governments
2021	Startup Visa eligibility extended to students already residing in Japan	Attracting talent and investment	METI and regional governments
	Guidelines for Business Collaboration with Startups	Clusters, networks, institutes	Japan Fair Trade Commission and METI
	Startup City Acceleration Project	Clusters, networks, institutes	JETRO
	Open innovation tax relief program allows existing companies to deduct from their taxable income 25% of the value of their investments in startups	Taxation	National Tax Agency
2022	Government Pension Investment Fund to increase investment in startups	Funding	Cabinet
	Startup Collaboration Strategy	Clusters, networks, institutes	Tokyo Metropolitan Government
	Startup Development Five-Year Plan	Clusters, networks, institutes	Cabinet
	Tax reforms recommended to enable stock option issuance to nonpermanent employees	Taxation	National Tax Agency
2023	Open innovation tax incentive extended to allow a domestic business corporation or its domestic corporate VC arm to deduct 25% of the cost of a startup acquisition from the income	Taxation	Industry Creation Policy Division, Economic and Industrial Policy Bureau, METI Small and Medium Enterprise Agency

TABLE A2.   Korea's startup-centric innovation policies (1961–2023)

YEAR	INITIATIVE	INNOVATION POLICY TYPE	IMPLEMENTING ORGANIZATION
1961	Small and Medium Enterprises Cooperatives Act	Regulation	Central government
	Industrial Bank of Korea Act	Regulation	Central government
	Small and Medium Industry Bank established	Funding	Small and Medium Industry Bank
	Comprehensive Plan on the Promotion of Small and Medium Business	Regulation	Central government
1977	Loan program for SMEs technology development	Funding	Small and Medium Business Administration (SMBA)
1978	Small and Medium Enterprises Promotion Act	Regulation	Central government
1979	Small and Medium Business Promotion Fund	Funding	Small Business Corporation
1982	Ten-Year Long-Term Development Plan for SMEs	Regulation	Central government
1986	Support for Small and Medium Enterprises Establishment Act	Regulation	Central government
1989	Korea Technology Credit Guarantee Fund	Funding	Korea Technology Finance Corporation
1996	Small and Medium Enterprises Promotion Act	Regulation	Central government
	Establishment of KOSDAQ	Stock market	KOSDAQ, MOF
1997	Act on Special Measures for the Promotion of Venture Businesses	Regulation	SMBA
1998	Fostering Venture Businesses	Clusters, networks, institutes	Central government
	Special Law to Promote Venture Firms	Regulation	Central government
	Act on the Special Cases Concerning Support for Technoparks	Regulation	Regional governments
	Venture Business Startup Program "Restart Fund"	Funding	Small and Medium Business Corporation
1999	Science and Technology Vision 2025	Clusters, networks, institutes	Central government
	National Science and Technology Council (NSTC)	Clusters, networks, institutes	Central government
2001	Act on the Promotion of Technology Innovation of Small and Medium Enterprises	Regulation	SMBA
2002	Korea BioValley (San Diego)	Funding	Federation of Korean Industries
2003	Innovate Korea	Clusters, networks, institutes	Central government

(continued)

TABLE A2. (continued)

YEAR	INITIATIVE	INNOVATION POLICY TYPE	IMPLEMENTING ORGANIZATION
2004	Office of Science, Technology, and Innovation	Clusters, networks, institutes	MoST
2005	Act on the Promotion of Collaborative Cooperation between Large Enterprises and Small-Medium Enterprises	Regulation	SMBA
	Korea Venture Investment Corporation (KVIC)	Funding	KVIC
2008	577 Initiative	Clusters, networks, institutes	Central government
	Ministry of Education, Science, and Technology (MEST)	Education and training	Central government
	Institute for Korea Entrepreneurship Development, Korea Institute of Startup and Entrepreneurship Development (KISED) from 2011	Clusters, networks, institutes	IKED/KISED
2009	Act on the Facilitation of Purchase of Small and Medium Enterprise-Manufactured Products and Support for Development of Their Markets	Infrastructure and government procurement	Central, regional, and local governments
2011	Act on the Fostering of Self-Employed Creative Enterprises	Regulation	SMBA
	Angel Investment Matching Fund	Funding	KVIC
2012	Korea Technology Finance Corporation Act amendment	Funding	Korea Technology Finance Corporation
2013	Creative Economy Action Plan	Clusters, networks, institutes	Central government
	Ministry of Science, ICT, and Future Planning	Regulation	Ministry of Science, ICT, and Future Planning
	Fund of Funds for Industrial Technology Commercialization	Funding	KVIC
	Foreign VC Investment Fund	Funding	KVIC
	Korea New Exchange (KONEX)	Stock market access	KONEX
2014	Creative Economy Innovation Centers (CCEIs)	Clusters, networks, institutes	Regional and local governments
	Act on Support for the Protection of Technologies of Small and Medium Enterprises	Regulation	Central government
2015	Special Act on Support for Small Urban Manufacturers	Regulation	Central government
	Angel Fund of Funds	Funding	KVIC
	Youth Development Fund	Funding	MOSF
	Korea Electric Power Corporation Fund of Funds	Funding	KVIC and Korea Electric Power Corporation
2016	K-Startup Grand Challenge	Attracting talent and investment	National IT Industry Promotion Agency and MSS from 2017

TABLE A2.

YEAR	INITIATIVE	INNOVATION POLICY TYPE	IMPLEMENTING ORGANIZATION
2017	Ministry of SMEs and Startups (MSS)	Regulation	Central government
2018	Scale-Up Co-Investment Fund	Funding	KVIC
	KEBHana-KVIC Unicorns Fund of Funds	Funding	KVIC and KEBHana
2019	Strategy to Promote Second Venture Boom	Funding	Central government
	SME Policy Deliberation Committee	Regulation	MSS
	Global TOP 5 Start-Up City Seoul	Clusters, networks, institutes	Seoul Metropolitan Government
	Masterplan for Promoting Women's Entrepreneurship Activities	Funding	MSS
2020	K-Unicorn project launched	Clusters, networks, institutes	MSS
	Pledge to increase the number of energy-related startups to four thousand by 2025	Clusters, networks, institutes	Ministry of Trade, Industry, and Energy
	Commitment to invest US$2.2 billion in two thousand green startups over the next five years	Funding	Ministry of Environment
	Digital startup investment fund launched with US$339.6 million	Funding	Ministry of Finance
	Regulatory change to the Fair Trade Commission Law to allow nonfinancial holding companies to run corporate VC funds	Regulation	Ministry of Economy and Finance
2021	National Pension Service committed US$127.2 million to four Korea VC funds	Funding	National Pension Service
2022	New Entrepreneurship initiative for chaebol, tech giants, and startups to create jobs and tackle social issues	Clusters, networks, institutes	Korea Chamber of Commerce
2023	Startup Korea Fund announced as a fund of funds in which the public and the private sectors jointly invest over US$1.4 billion for four years from 2024 to 2027	Funding	MSS
	K-Tech College launched, which will offer training programs in software and provides job placement opportunities with Korean startups to talented students from developing economies	Education and training	MSS
	K-Scouter program to identify and nurture foreign startups with high potential in the Korean market	Attracting talent and investment	MSS

TABLE A3.   Taiwan's startup-centric innovation policies (1958–2023)

YEAR	INITIATIVE	INNOVATION POLICY TYPE	IMPLEMENTING ORGANIZATION
1958	Export-led growth support of SMEs initiated at the urging of US aid	Regulation	Executive Yuan
	Six-year science education program initiated to send Chinese scientists to the United States for advanced study	Education and training	Academia Sinica, US AID
1959	National Council for Scientific Development established	Regulation	Executive Yuan
1960	Nineteen-Point Economic and Fiscal Reform Program liberalized trade and encouraged export activity	Regulation	Executive Yuan
	Statute for the Encouragement of Investment (SEI) offered tax incentives for export-oriented activity in particular technological areas	Taxation	Ministry of Economic Affairs
1961	Third Four-Year Economic Plan (1961–1964) emphasized labor-intensive export activities	Regulation	Ministry of Economic Affairs
	Statute for the Encouragement of Technical Cooperation to foster technology transfer to Taiwan	Attracting talent and investment	Executive Yuan
1963	Council for International Economic Cooperation and Development established	Regulation	Executive Yuan
	Taiwan Stock Exchange launched (after being initially formed in 1961)	Stock market	Ministry of Finance
1964	Sino-American Committee on Science Cooperation was created to institutionalize US technology transfers	Attracting talent and investment	Academia Sinica, US National Science Foundation
1965	Statute for the Establishment and Management of Export Processing Zones	Infrastructure	Ministry of Economic Affairs
1966	Working Group for Planning and Development of the Electronics Industry	Clusters, networks, institutes	Council for International Economic Cooperation and Development
	Modern Engineering and Technology Seminars established to bring leading engineers and scientists to Taipei	Attracting talent and investment	Ministry of Communications
1973	Industrial Technology Research Institute (ITRI) established to support the hardware industry	Clusters, networks, institutes	Ministry of Economic Affairs

TABLE A3.

YEAR	INITIATIVE	INNOVATION POLICY TYPE	IMPLEMENTING ORGANIZATION
1974	Electronic Research Service Organization (ERSO) established to develop semiconductor industry capabilities	Clusters, networks, institutes	ITRI
	SME Credit Guarantee Fund established to boost financing available to SMEs	Funding	Executive Yuan and Ministry of Finance
1976	Very-Large-Scale Integration (VLSI) established	Clusters, networks, institutes	ITRI
1979	Institute for Information Industry (III) established at the urging of K. T. Li to support software firms	Clusters, networks, institutes	Ministry of Economic Affairs
	Science and Technology Development Program initiated efforts to attract and employ returnee overseas Chinese in R&D projects	Attracting talent and investment	Executive Yuan, Science and Technology Advisory Group[1]
1980	Ten Year Economic Development Project (1980–1989); a set of strategic industries was selected according to the *two-large* (large linkage effects, large market potential), *two-high* (high rate of value added, high technology intensity), and *two-low* (low energy intensity, low pollution) criteria	Clusters, networks, institutes	Ministry of Economic Affairs
	Hsinchu Park established, after being initiated by the 1979 Science and Technology Development Program, as a technology cluster	Clusters, networks, institutes	National Science Council
1981	Medium and Small Business Administration established to develop and coordinate policy efforts	Regulation	Ministry of Economic Affairs
1983	Regulations for the Administration of Venture Capital Enterprises passed to encourage market development	Regulation	Ministry of Finance
	US$72.5 million allocation to further VLSI capabilities to boost semiconductor capabilities	Funding	ITRI
1984	Tax incentives offered to manufacturers who allocate a percentage of revenues to R&D	Taxation	Ministry of Economic Affairs
1985	Development Fund and Chiao Tung Bank provide NT$50 million and NT$30 million, respectively, to the First VC Investment Program	Funding	National Development Fund

(continued)

TABLE A3. *(continued)*

YEAR	INITIATIVE	INNOVATION POLICY TYPE	IMPLEMENTING ORGANIZATION
1987	TSMC founded by ITRI, Philips, and private investors	Clusters, networks, institutes	ITRI, China Development Corporation
1990	Information and Communications Research Laboratories established to develop advanced and core technologies (for PCs and network communications)	Clusters, networks, institutes	ITRI
1991	Statute for Industrial Upgrading replaces the SEI as tax package for SME R&D incentives	Taxation	Ministry of Economic Affairs
	Liberalization of stock market to allow foreign institutional investors to invest in growth list of publicly traded technology firms	Regulation	Ministry of Finance
	Development Fund and Chiao Tung Bank provide NT$1 billion and NT$60 million, respectively, to the Second VC Investment Program	Funding	National Development Fund
1992	Banking Law liberalized the banking sector so that commercial banks were more able to lend to small firms	Regulation	Ministry of Finance
1993	Three-year stimulus comprised of US$1.5 billion in loans to SMEs and US$750 million for high-technology enterprises	Funding	Ministry of Economic Affairs
1994	Taipei Exchange (TPEx) established as a public-equities venue for smaller companies	Stock market access	Ministry of Finance
1995	Southern Taiwan Science Park in Tainan, inspired by the Hsinchu Science Park, site approved as part of New Establishment of Science Parks program in the Six-Year National Development Project; focus on optoelectronics and biotechnology	Clusters, networks, institutes	Executive Yuan
1999	Small Business Innovation Research (SBIR) launched to boost R&D spending among small firms	Funding	Ministry of Economic Affairs
2000	Venture capital investor tax credit discontinued on account of political changes and market's maturity	Taxation	Executive Yuan
2001	Development of the Kaohsiung Science Park and Tainan Science Park ratified	Clusters, networks institutes	ITRI

TABLE A3.

YEAR	INITIATIVE	INNOVATION POLICY TYPE	IMPLEMENTING ORGANIZATION
	Issuance of Regulations on the Scope and Guidance of Venture Capital Enterprises (hereafter referred to as "the Scope"); the Financial Holding Company Act in 2001 allowed financial holding companies to invest in venture capital	Regulation	Ministry of Economic Affairs
	Plans to strengthen the venture capital industry under the National Development Plan to be matched by the establishment of an NT$100 billion VC fund (NT$30 billion public and NT$70 billion private funding)	Funding	Executive Yuan
2002	Emerging Stock Board created within the Taipei Exchange to help emerging enterprises access the capital market	Stock market access	Ministry of Finance
	Six-Year Development Plan 2002–2007 offered incentives to R&D centers for Challenge 2008	Attracting talent and investment	Ministry of Economic Affairs
	Business Startup Award established to recognize outstanding startup performances annually	Clusters, networks, institutes	MoEA SME Administration
2003	Hsinchu Biomedical Science Park plans approved to foster a biomedicine-focused cluster	Clusters, networks, institutes	Executive Yuan
	SME Online University created to provide accessible business training	Education and training	MoEA SME Administration
2004	Amendment of Regulations on the Scope and Guidance of Venture Capital Enterprises to expand funding channels and ease restrictions on investment scope and fund utilization	Regulation	Ministry of Economic Affairs
2005	National Science and Technology Development Plan (2005–2008) names *startup* three times	Regulation	National Science Council
	Scope revisions require venture capital funds with capital commitments from banks, insurance companies, securities firms, financial holding companies, or pension funds to apply to the Industrial Development Bureau for approval	Regulation	Ministry of Economic Affairs

(continued)

TABLE A3. *(continued)*

YEAR	INITIATIVE	INNOVATION POLICY TYPE	IMPLEMENTING ORGANIZATION
2006	Relaxed Scope makes it easier for investors to exit their positions by decreasing the required holding time of company securities and lifting the limit on share sales	Stock market access	Ministry of Finance
2008	Challenge 2008 (passed in 2002) to invest NT$30 billion alongside private funding of NT$70 billion in VC	Funding	National Development Fund
2009	National Science and Technology Development Plan (2009–2012) specifies startup competitions and promoting entrepreneurial spirit as key elements	Regulation	National Science Council
2010	InvesTaiwan Service Center established to provide a one-stop shop for investors in the Taiwanese startup ecosystem	Attracting talent and investment	MoEA
2012	In bid to boost software-based gaming startups' capital markets access, the TPEx launched its online gaming sector index	Stock market access	Ministry of Finance
	Bilateral fund of VC fund (Strategic Cooperation on Joint Investments in Venture Capital Funds) with New Zealand created	Funding	National Development Fund
2013	National Science and Technology Development Plan (2013–2016) mentions *startup* eight times, and *entrepreneur** three times	Regulation	Executive Yuan
	Launch of From IP to IPO program to enable startups' scale-up abilities through the provision of mentorship on fundraising negotiations	Education and training	National Science Council
2014	Launch of HeadStart Taiwan, a startup funding program	Funding	National Development Council
	Innovation and Startups Taskforce launched to coordinate entrepreneurial capabilities across agencies	Clusters, networks, institutes	Executive Yuan
2015	Taiwan Startup Hub established to provide consulting and advisory services to entrepreneurs	Education and training	Executive Yuan
	Contact Taiwan Program approved with the aim of attracting global startup talent	Attracting talent and investment	National Development Council

TABLE A3.

YEAR	INITIATIVE	INNOVATION POLICY TYPE	IMPLEMENTING ORGANIZATION
	Taiwan Startup Stadium established as a global ecosystem builder	Attracting talent and investment	National Development Council
	Taiwan Rapid Innovation Prototyping League for Entrepreneurs platform activated to connect global hardware startups with partners in Taiwan	Technology infrastructure and government procurement	MoST
	The International Entrepreneur Initiative Taiwan established as a single-portal website for entrepreneurial activities	Technology infrastructure and government procurement	MoST
	Plans for Taiwan Innovation and Entrepreneurship Center, a state-sponsored innovation office in Silicon Valley, announced	Clusters, networks, institutes	MoST
2016	Launch of the Asia Silicon Valley Development Plan; the Asia Silicon Valley Development Agency is created to coordinate efforts	Clusters, networks, and institutes	National Development Council
	National S&T Development Plan (2017–2020) mentions *startup* eighteen times and *entrepreneur* eighty-two times and offers startups funding, accelerators, coworking spaces, websites, international links, and so on	Regulation	MoST
2017	5+2 Innovative Industries Plan to promote seven pillar industries, including Internet of Things (branded as Asia Silicon Valley), green energy, biomedicine, national defense and aerospace, new agriculture, and the circular economy	Cluster, networks, institutes	Executive Yuan
	Taiwania Capital is founded as a government-run VC fund	Funding	Executive Yuan's National Development Fund
	NT$2 billion Business Angel Investment Program established to extend the startup investment ecosystem	Funding	Executive Yuan's National Development Fund
2018	Action Plan for Enhancing Taiwan's Startup Ecosystem initiated	Cluster, networks, institutes	National Development Council

(continued)

TABLE A3. *(continued)*

YEAR	INITIATIVE	INNOVATION POLICY TYPE	IMPLEMENTING ORGANIZATION
	Launch of FinTechSpace, a fintech-focused coworking space in Taipei	Clusters, networks, institutes	Financial Supervisory Commission and Taiwan Financial Services Roundtable
	Taiwan Tech Arena established to provide training and international connections for technology startups	Attracting talent and investment	MoST
	Women Entrepreneurship Awards launched	Cluster, networks, institutes	MoEA SME Administration
2019	Linkou Startup Terrace established as an international startup-centric innovation hub in a university environment	Cluster, networks, institutes	Executive Yuan
	Act for the Recruitment and Employment of Foreign Professionals launches Entrepreneur Visa	Attracting talent and investment	MoST
2020	Taiwan Accelerator Plus creates Advanced Industry Strategic Implementation Plan	Attracting talent and investment	MoEA SME Administration
	Project on Promoting Innovative Financing and Commercialization offers a web-based platform to source prototyping manufactures and information on crowdfunding	Infrastructure	MoEA SME Administration
2021	TPEx creates Pioneer Stock Board to assist stock market access for companies operating in strategic industries	Stock market access	Ministry of Finance
	Women Entrepreneurship Program to encourage and train female founders	Clusters, networks, institutes	MoEA SME Administration
	Next Big program launches, to identify and promote startups internationally	Clusters, networks, institutes	MoEA and NDC
2022	500 Global Accelerator Taiwan run again, with twenty startups	Clusters, networks, institutes	Taiwan Tech Arena and 500 Startups
2023	Next Big startup initiative expanded, selecting 13 startups for backing as Taiwan's startup island brand ambassadors	Clusters, networks, institutes	MoEA and NDC

TABLE A4.   China's startup-centric innovation policies (1979–2023)

YEAR	INITIATIVE	INNOVATION POLICY TYPE	IMPLEMENTING ORGANIZATION
1980	State Patent Office of the PRC established	Regulation	State Council
1985	CPC Central Committee Decision on the Reform of the Science and Technology System	Regulation	CPC Central Committee
1986	China New Technology Start-Up Investment Company enables VC funding	Funding	State Science and Technology Commission (SSTC), MOF
1987	Wuhan East Lake Hi-Tech Innovation Center established	Clusters, networks, institutes	Wuhan Municipal Government
1988	Torch Program created, which included technology business incubators and equity funding components	Funding and clusters, networks, institutes	SSTC
	Beijing (Zhongguancun) New Technology Industry Experimental Zone approved	Clusters, networks, institutes	State Council
1989	China KZ High Technology Co. Ltd. established	Funding	SSTC, Commission for Science, Technology, and Industry for National Defense, China Merchants Group
1991	National High-Tech Industrial Development Zones established	Clusters, networks, institutes	State Council
	National Science and Technology Venture Capital Development Center established	Funding	SSTC, MOF, Industrial and Commercial Bank of China
1993	Law of the People's Republic of China on Progress of Science and Technology	Regulation	Standing Committee of the National People's Congress
1994	Nanjing Overseas Students Entrepreneurship Park established	Attracting talent and investment	Ministry of Education, Ministry of Personnel, State Administration of Foreign Experts Affairs, Nanjing Municipal Government
1995	Torch Program Industrial Base prioritization scheme	Clusters, networks, institutes	SSTC
1997	Opinion on Establishing International Enterprise Incubator	Clusters, networks, institutes	SSTC
1998	State Intellectual Property Office of the PRC established	Regulation	CPC Central Committee, State Council

(continued)

TABLE A4. *(continued)*

YEAR	INITIATIVE	INNOVATION POLICY TYPE	IMPLEMENTING ORGANIZATION
1999	Decision of the CPC Central Committee and the PRC State Council on Strengthening Technology Innovation, Developing High Technology, and Realizing Industrialization	Regulation	CPC Central Committee, State Council
	Opinions on Establishing a Venture Investment System	Regulation	MoST, State Development Planning Commission, State Economic and Trade Commission, People's Bank of China, SAT, China Securities Regulatory Commission (CSRC)
	Revision of the Company Law of the PRC	Regulation	Standing Committee of the NPC
	Innofund further advanced	Funding	MoST, MOFC
2000	Policies on Encouraging and Promoting the Development of SMEs	Regulation	State Economic and Trade Commission
	Opinions on Accelerating the Establishment and Development of High-Tech Entrepreneurship Service Centers	Clusters, networks, institutes	MoST
	Amendment to the Patent Law of the PRC	Regulation	Standing Committee of the NPC
	SME International Market Development Fund established Measures for the Administration of the SME International Market Development Fund (Provisional)	Attracting talent and investment	MOF, Ministry of Foreign Trade and Economic Cooperation
	(Beijing) Preferential Household Registry (*hukou*) policy for entrepreneurs	Attracting talent and investment	Beijing Municipal Government
2001	Provisions Concerning the Establishment of Foreign-Funded Venture Capital Enterprises	Regulation	MoST, State Administration for Industry and Commerce (SAIC)
	Measures for Administrating Overseas Students Entrepreneurship Parks	Attracting talent and investment	Ministry of Personnel
2002	Law of the PRC on the Promotion of Small and Medium-Sized Enterprises	Regulation	Standing Committee of the NPC
	Beijing Venture Award for Outstanding Overseas Returnees	Attracting talent and investment	Beijing Administration of Personnel

TABLE A4.

YEAR	INITIATIVE	INNOVATION POLICY TYPE	IMPLEMENTING ORGANIZATION
2003	Provisions Concerning the Administration of Foreign-Funded Venture Capital Enterprises	Attracting talent and investment	MOFTEC, MoST, SAIC, State Administration of Taxation (SAT), State Administration of Foreign Exchange
	Opinions on Further Improving the Operation of High-Tech Enterprise Incubators	Clusters, networks, institutes	MoST
	Special Subsidy for SME Service System	Clusters, networks, institutes	MoF
2004	SME Board created	Stock market access	CSRC
	Special Fund for SME Development	Funding	MoF, NDRC
	Roadmap Scheme for Growth of Tech-Based SMEs	Regulation	Innofund Administration Center, Shenzhen Stock Exchange (SZSE), China Development Bank, National Business Incubator Association, China VC Association
	Opinions concerning further promotion of the Establishment and Development of National University Technology Parks to encourage entrepreneurship among university students	Education and training	MoST, MOE
	Special Central Government Subsidy for the Establishment of Local SME Platform Service Systems	Clusters, networks, institutes	MoST
2005	Provisions on the Administration of Venture Capital Enterprises	Regulation	NDRC, MoST, MoF, Ministry of Commerce (MOFCOM) PBOC, SAT, SAIC, China Banking Regulatory Commission, CSRC, SAFE
	Guidance Opinions on Banks' Loan Business with Small Enterprises	Regulation	China Banking Regulatory Commission
	SME Information Technology Promotion Project	Education and training	NDRC, MIIT

(continued)

TABLE A4. *(continued)*

YEAR	INITIATIVE	INNOVATION POLICY TYPE	IMPLEMENTING ORGANIZATION
2006	Tax incentives for Technology Innovations by Enterprises	Taxation	MoF, SAT
	Opinions on Strengthening the SME Credit Guarantee System	Regulation	NDRC, MOFCOM , PBOC, SAT, China Banking Regulatory Commission
	11th Five-Year Plan on University Technology Parks	Education and training	MoST, Ministry of Education
	11th Five-Year Plan on Chinese Tech-Based Enterprise Incubators	Clusters, networks, institutes	MoST
	Measures for Accrediting and Administering Tech-Based Enterprise Incubators	Clusters, networks, institutes	MoST
2007	Tax incentives for Venture Capital Investments in High-Tech SMEs, for National University Technology Parks, and for Tech-Based Enterprise Incubators	Taxation	MoF, SAT
	Tax incentives for High-Tech Enterprises Newly Set Up in Special Economic Zones and in Pudong District of Shanghai[2]	Taxation	State Council
	Priority for independent innovation products in government procurement	Technology, infrastructure, and government procurement	MoST
	Venture Capital Guiding Fund for Tech-Based SMEs	Funding	MoF, MoST
	Several Opinions on Promoting Development Zone for New and High Technology Industries to Further Develop and to Increase Independent Innovation Capacity	Clusters, networks, institutes	MoST, NDRC, Ministry of Land Resources, Ministry of Construction
2008	Guiding Opinions on the Establishment and Operation of the Venture Capital Guiding Fund for Tech-Based SMEs	Regulation	NDRC, MoF, MOFCOM
	Thousand Talents Plan (Recruitment Program of Global Experts Directorate and Office)	Attracting talent and investment	CPC Organization Department
	Guiding Opinions on Promoting Employment through Entrepreneurship	Regulation	Ministry of Human Resources and Social Security (MOHRSS), NDRC, MOE, MIIT, MoF, Ministry of Land and Resources, Ministry of Housing and Urban-Rural Development, MOFCOM, PBOC, SAT, SAIC

TABLE A4.

YEAR	INITIATIVE	INNOVATION POLICY TYPE	IMPLEMENTING ORGANIZATION
	Creation of Government-Guided Investment Funds	Funding	State Council, MoF, NDRC
	Building of Entrepreneurial Cities	Clusters, networks, institutes	MOHRSS
2009	ChiNext	Stock market access	CSRC
	Youth Employment and Entrepreneurship Bases Program	Clusters, networks, institutes	Communist Youth League of China
	Emerging Industries Venture Capital Program	Funding	NDRC, MoF
	Chinese Overseas Students' Return and Entrepreneurship Support Program	Attracting talent and investment	MOHRSS
2010	China Innovation Relay Network	Clusters, networks, institutes	MoST
	Measures for Accrediting University Students' Technology Entrepreneurship and Internship Bases (Provisional)	Clusters, networks, institutes	Ministry of Education, MoST
	National Medium- to Long-Term Talent Development Plan Outline (2010–2020)	Regulation	Central Committee of the CPC, State Council
	University Students Entrepreneurship Guidance Program	Education	MOHRSS
2011	Provisional Measures for Promoting SME Development through Government Procurement	Technology infrastructure and government procurement	MoF, MIIT
	Innovative Talents Promotion Program	Clusters, networks, institutes	MoST, MoF, MOHRSS
	University Graduates Grassroots Nurturing Program	Clusters, networks, institutes	CPC Organization Department, Ministry of Education, MOHRSS, Central Committee of the Communist Youth League of China
	12th Five-Year Plan on Science and Technology Development	Regulation	State Planning Commission, MoST
	12th Five-Year Plan on SME Growth	Regulation	MIIT
	National Fund for Technology Transfer and Commercialization	Funding	MoF, MoST
	Opinion on Supporting Overseas Students to Return to China and Start Businesses	Attracting talent and investment	CPC Organization Department, MOHRSS
	China Innovation and Entrepreneurship Competition	Clusters, networks, institutes	Torch High Technology Industry Development Center of the MoST, Innovation Fund for Tech-Based SMEs Administrative Center

(continued)

TABLE A4. *(continued)*

YEAR	INITIATIVE	INNOVATION POLICY TYPE	IMPLEMENTING ORGANIZATION
2012	State Council Opinion on Further Support the Healthy Development of Micro and Small Enterprises, No. 14	Regulation	State Council
	Tax incentives for micro and small enterprises	Taxation	State Council
	Opinion on Deepening Technology System Reform and Accelerating the Establishment of National Innovation System, No.6	Regulation	CPC Central Committee, State Council
	China Innovation and Entrepreneur-ship Competition	Cluster, networks, institutes	Torch High Technology Industry Development Center of the MoST, Innovation Fund for Tech-Based SMEs Administrative Center
2013	Amendment to the Company Law of the People's Republic of China	Regulation	Standing Committee of the NPC
	Innovation-Based Industrial Clusters	Clusters, networks, institutes	MoST
	National Equities Exchange and Quotation	Stock market access	MoF
2014	Roadmap Scheme for Growth of Tech-Based SMEs 2.0	Clusters, networks, institutes	Torch High Technology Industry Development Center of the MoST, SZSE, National Equities Exchange and Quota-tions Co. Ltd., China Merchants Bank
	Notice on the Plan for Deepening the Reform of the Management of Centrally Financed S&T Projects	Funding	State Council
2015	Guiding Opinions of the General Office of the State Council on Expanding Mass Entrepreneurship Space and Promoting Mass Innovation and Entrepreneurship	Regulation	State Council
	Master Plan of the Startup Ecosystem Development Strategies	Regulation	State Council
	Model Cities for Micro and Small Businesses Entrepreneurship and Innovation	Clusters, networks, institutes	MoF, MIIT, MoST, MOFCOM, SAIC
	National Fund for SME Develop-ment and National Guiding Fund for Emerging Industries Venture Capital	Funding	State Council

TABLE A4.

YEAR	INITIATIVE	INNOVATION POLICY TYPE	IMPLEMENTING ORGANIZATION
	E-commerce Entrepreneurship and Innovation Service Project[3]	Technology infrastructure and government procurement	NDRC, MOFCOM, PBOC, SAT, SAIC, General Administration of Quality Supervision, Inspection, and Quarantine
	13th Five-Year Plan for the Development of National Enterprise S&T Enterprise Incubators	Clusters, networks, institutes	MoST
	Chinese Enterprises "Go Global" Innovation and Entrepreneurship Competition	Clusters, networks, institutes	MOFCOM
2016	E-commerce Entrepreneurship and Innovation Service Project	Technology infrastructure and government procurement	NDRC, MOFCOM, PBOC, General Administration of Customs, General Office of SAT, SATC
	China Innovation Challenge	Clusters, networks, institutes	Torch High Technology Industry Development Center of the MOST, Innovation Fund for Tech-Based SMEs Administrative Center'
	Tax incentives for Tech-Based Enterprise Incubators	Taxation	MoST, SAT
	Promoting Continuous and Healthy Development of Venture Capital, No. 53	Funding	State Council
2017	Several Measures for Promoting Innovation Development in Free-Trade Zones	Clusters, networks, institutes	MoST, MOFCOM
	Opinions on Promoting the High-Quality Development and the Establishment of an Upgraded Version of Mass Innovation and Entrepreneurship	Regulation	State Council
	National High-End Foreign Experts Recruitment Plan	Attracting talent and investment	MoST
	Guiding Opinions on Promoting the Development of National University S&T Parks	Clusters, networks, institutes	MoST, Ministry of Education
	2017 "Maker China" Small and Medium-Sized Enterprise Innovation and Entrepreneurship Competition (first year)	Clusters, networks, institutes	MIIT, MoF

(continued)

TABLE A4. *(continued)*

YEAR	INITIATIVE	INNOVATION POLICY TYPE	IMPLEMENTING ORGANIZATION
2018	Measures for the Administration of Technological Business Incubators	Clusters, networks, institutes	MoST
	Notice on Tax Policies for Technology Business Incubators, University Science Parks, and Maker Spaces	Taxation	MoF, SAT, MoST, Ministry of Education
	Negative List for Market Access established to restrict sectors for private investment; with 151 items	Regulation	NDRC, MOFCOM
2019	Launch of Science and Technology Innovation Board on Shanghai Stock Exchange	Stock market access	Shanghai Stock Exchange
	Issuing Several Policies and Measures to Support the Accelerating Innovation and Development of Technological SMEs in the New Era	Clusters, networks, institutes	MoST
	Organizing and Recommending National Technological Innovation Demonstration Enterprises, No. 97	Regulation	MIIT
	"Little Giants" named as high-growth startups in select industries, such as semiconductors, machinery, and pharmaceuticals	Clusters, networks, institutes	MIIT
	Preferential Startup Tax policies; VC investors receive a 70% deduction on taxable income	Taxation	SAT
	Issuing the Guiding Opinions on Promoting the Innovation and Development of National University Science Parks	Clusters, networks, institutes	MoST
2020	Foreign Investment Law to standardize corporate structure and governance	Regulation	State Council
	Draft rules on limiting monopolistic practices by internet platforms	Regulation	State Administration for Market Regulation
	Draft personal data protection plan	Regulation	Cybersecurity Administration
2021	Statement on labor laws' maximum of forty-four-hour work week	Regulation	Ministry of Labor, High Court
	Ban on cryptocurrency and for-profit companies in the Edtech industry (not-for-profit companies cannot go public nor raise foreign investment capital)	Regulation	CPC Central Committee, State Council, PBOC
	Plans for a negative list for Variable Interest Entities who list in overseas capital markets	Regulation	CSRC
	Creation of the Beijing Stock Exchange to cater to startups	Stock market access	CSRC

TABLE A4.

YEAR	INITIATIVE	INNOVATION POLICY TYPE	IMPLEMENTING ORGANIZATION
2022	Acceptance of Ant Financial application for financial holding company	Regulation	PBOC
2023	Special Provisions regarding Venture Capital Funds simplifies fund registration, offers less frequent inspections by the CRSC, and facilitating exits for qualifying VCs	Regulation	State Council
	Launch of US$40 billion state-backed fund to invest in the semiconductor industry, as part of the Big Fund	Funding	MoF

[1] The STAG was created by the premier's office, with K. T. Li leading the formation of the group in 1979.

[2] Tax relief from enterprise income tax for the first two years of operations; taxes to be levied at half of the statutory tax rate of 25 percent for the third to the fifth years.

[3] For policy details, see Notice from the National Development and Reform Commission and Seven Other Departments on Promoting the Development of e-commerce [in Chinese]. July 30, 2024, http://www.cac.gov.cn/2016-06/01/c_1118968390.htm.

Notes

INTRODUCTION

1. The attributes of the developmental state have been debated. We note that before the developmental state concept was articulated, neoclassical economists provided the dominant interpretation of East Asian economic success on the theme incentivized exports and getting the prices right (e.g., Balassa 1985). From the 1990s, "counter-revisionists" argued that accounts of the role of industrial policy making were overstated. These scholars asserted that ineffective policy leadership, a lack of cohesion, and the rise of politicization appeared by (at least) the 1980s (Friedman 1988; Kitschelt 1991; Callon 1995; Noble 1998; Cumings 1999; Keller and Samuels 2003). Scholars have also challenged the consistency of the model, noting that small firms were also driving technology-centric upgrading in some cases (Tsai 1999) and playing an important role, even in models led by large firms (e.g., Japan's keiretsu or Korea's chaebol) (Ibata-Arens 2005; Breznitz 2007; Greene 2008).

2. *Unicorn* is the widely used term to describe startups with valuations of US$1 billion or more. The term was coined in the context of high-growth startups—rather than mythical stories—in a 2013 *TechCrunch* article by venture capitalist Aileen Lee (see Lee 2013).

3. For a sample of the VoC literature, see Crouch (2005), Becker (2009), Carney et al. (2009), Carney (2016), Coates (2005), Hancke et al. (2007), and Hancke (2009).

4. Patient capital refers to long-term capital with societal aims and less emphasis on achieving a timely return. See Richard Deeg, Iain Hardie, and Sylvia Maxfield (2016) for a conceptualization of patient capital that takes engagement and time horizon into account; see also Albert O. Hirschman (1970) for essential framing of the choice of whether to exit (in the context of finance, to sell), use voice (actively engage management), and remain loyal (maintain investment position).

5. A cognate strand of this research delineates varieties of state capitalism, conceptualizing different roles of state-led development and governance modes (Kang 2010; Chen 2015; Naughton and Tsai 2015).

6. There has long been diversity in terms of the size of firms supported by the state. Notably, in Taiwan, it was SMEs rather than conglomerates that were to drive technology-centric upgrading (Breznitz 2007; Greene 2008). In the Chinese context, a combination of smaller "gladiatorial entrepreneurs" (Lee 2018) and bigger state-backed firms were essential to driving advances.

7. Astro Teller, "The Unexpected Benefit of Celebrating Failure," TED talk, May 9, 2016, YouTube video, 15:32, https://www.youtube.com/watch?v=2t13Rq4oc7A.

8. Mission-oriented or transformative policies are those that target a clearly articulated and society-wide outcome (Schot and Steinmueller 2018).

9. See literature on the instruments used in startup policy (Brown et al. 2013; Klingler-Vidra 2014; Blackburn and Schaper 2016).

10. This is not at the hand of creative destruction, though; big businesses have been challenged through regulatory crackdowns. The Chinese government has not threatened the position of other large companies, such as Tencent and ByteDance, which also operate platform business models (Rahman and Thelen 2019; Jia and Kenney 2022; McKnight et al. 2023).

1. ANALYTICAL FRAMEWORK

1. In addition to the LME and CME types, scholars debate the extent to which there are regional variations. Given this book's focus on East Asia, we note that some have depicted an Asian model of capitalism (see Hundt and Uttam 2017; Storz et al. 2013; Amable 2003). More state-specific depictions have been conceptualized across national innovation system (NIS) and East Asian business system literature (Chen and Hamilton 1996; Whitley 1999, 2007; Beeson and Liew 2002; Aoki et al. 2007; Globerman et al. 2011; Walter and Zhang 2012; Witt and Redding 2013; Lee et al. 2016; Chen 20019). In this book, we strive to contribute further to this line of work that distinguishes variation within the region.

2. Some scholars also point to a cultural element, noting Confucian traditions (Hofstede and Bond 1988; Kim and Park 2003).

3. In addition to studying how much change has occurred, research also explains why the change is happening. Some point to crises, such as the EAFC, as potential critical junctures capable of ushering in change (Capoccia 2015; Collier and Munck 2022).

4. The mechanisms by which large firms may engage governments, and vice versa, are not the focus of this book. According to recent research, incumbent firms exercising their political connections lobby for self-serving policies (Bombardini et al. 2023) and related means of asserting their power to impose barriers to creative destruction (Baslandze 2023). We do not strive to observe backroom dealings that may shape how, and why, incumbent firms enter startup initiatives. What we do strive to systematically observe is whether and how large firms appear in startup policies. We can then analyze how big company and startup interactions are expected to deliver socioeconomic value.

5. In China, the state has a mixed approach, sometimes watching "gladiatorial entrepreneurs" fight in nascent markets before offering access to state largess for those who emerge as winners (Lee 2018). In other cases, state-owned enterprises lead in developing a critical technology, such as the partially state-owned SMIC and its attempts to lead China's semiconductor abilities since it was established in 2000.

6. There is growing evidence that entrepreneurship tax incentives can be unproductive forms of government initiatives (IMF 2016, 40). Zoltan Acs and coauthors (2016) conclude that tax incentives are ineffective in boosting innovative startups, instead propping up lifestyle entrepreneurs who do not go on to employ others and do not advance innovative products.

7. Accelerators and incubators differ in their expectation of participants' business ideas, their length, and their selection process. Accelerators can be highly selective in striving to identify individuals or teams with concrete business ideas and then run as cohort-based programs over the course of months, whereas incubators tend to be more open to would-be entrepreneurs at the idea generation stage (Bone et al. 2017, 12–13).

8. Patient capital is defined as finance from providers that "aim to capture benefits (both financial and otherwise) specific to long-term investments and who do not exit their investment or loan if non-financial company (NFC) managers do not respond to short-term market pressures" (Klingler-Vidra 2016, 692; Deeg et al. 2016).

9. One of the central challenges around the advance of startup-friendly stock exchanges is the balance of governance (prudent listing requirements) and accessibility (ease of listing) with public protection concerns (e.g., potential for fraud and excessive risk).

10. What is considered radical innovation changes over time. To give an example, in the evolution of the semiconductor industry, the 1950s and 1960s were periods of radical innovation in which the technology was being defined; then, from the 1970s and especially the 1980s, advances in manufacturing became ever more important to the industry's commercialization (Miller 2022).

11. Input legitimacy has to do with the substance or the process, whereas output legitimacy refers to the initiative's impact or performance (see Scharpf 1999).

2. JAPAN

1. Scholars have contested the validity of the keiretsu-centric developmental state for different reasons; for instance, Ibata-Arens (2005) argues that all along it was small firms that powered national innovation prowess, not the keiretsu themselves. Bob Johnstone (1999) similarly points to the long-standing presence of Japan's entrepreneurs, even in the developmental state era. Steven K. Vogel (2018, 107) details government assistance for small businesses, beginning with MITI's provision of subsidized loans in the 1960s. David Friedman asserts in *The Misunderstood Miracle* that the mainstream account of the Japanese postwar model overlooked what he argues is the fundamental role that SME manufacturers played (1988, 2). There are three primary types of Japanese conglomerates (keiretsu): horizontal keiretsu have large firms in different industries and receive finance from a major city bank, or "main bank"; vertical keiretsu refer to subcontracting relationships between large industrial firms and SMEs; and distribution keiretsu guarantee sales and marketing channels. Japan's "big six" horizontal keiretsu are Fuyo, Sanwa, Sumitomo, Mitsubishi, Mitsui, and DKB Group. DKB was delisted in 2000, and then the combined Mizuho Holdings was formed (also combining Fuji and the Industrial Bank of Japan). The vertical keiretsu are Toyota, Toshiba, and Nissan.

2. In a contemporary setting, the three Japanese mega banks are Mitsubishi UFJ Financial Group, Sumitomo Mitsui Financial Group, and Mizuho Financial Group.

3. Japan's reforms in 2006 saw the creation of the Government Pension Investment Fund (GPIF), which is the world's largest pension fund at the time of writing. The GPIF, because of this twenty-first-century restructuring, only enters the analytical lens later in the story.

4. For more details on the J-Startup Initiative, see J-Startup, accessed June 13, 2024, https://www.j-startup.go.jp/en/about/docs/J-Startup_EN_181009.pdf.

5. This move was hoped to enhance labor mobility, but labor market flexibility did not proliferate quickly.

6. The keiretsu still offered welfare programs that were more generous than the National Pension offering. In this sense, the incentive to stay and grow with a firm remained—though you could move from one keiretsu to another.

7. For an example of SoftBank announcements of stock option issuance in this period, see SoftBank Group, accessed June 13, 2024, https://group.softbank/en/news/press/20040527.

8. In 1982, the first VC fund was launched in Japan, with the Japan Associated Finance Co. Ltd. (JAFCO) partnering with Nomura Securities, Sanwa Bank, and Nippon Life Insurance Company to establish a VC fund structured as a limited liability company (Hata et al. 2007, 158).

9. The program aims to "promote corporate investments in startups" by allowing "existing companies to deduct from their taxable income 25% of the value of their investments in startups" (*Japan Times* 2021).

10. Corporate VC–backed deals accounted for 24 percent of all global VC transactions in 2019 (and also 2020), which was up from an average of 20 percent a few years before (CB Insights 2021).

11. Son has made waves in Europe and Silicon Valley, where he has been said to have "massively disrupted" startup investments as he has deployed the world's largest VC fund (de Leon 2019). SoftBank made headlines in Europe in 2016 in the context of the acquisition of Arm, a leading semiconductor design firm based in the United Kingdom, as Arm was seen as a critical asset for British technology (Farrell and Kollewe 2016). SoftBank's

investment in Arm was again a big news story in 2023 (*Nikkei* Staff Writers 2023c). Son's big-ticket VC model has been questioned, given a decline in tech company valuations (Pesek 2023). In that context, Son's 2018 remark that SoftBank's Vision Fund was not "just recklessly making investments" has been retrospectively criticized as having "little to show," as the massive fund seemed to miss out on the big winners in artificial intelligence—their core theme (Brown 2023).

12. While these American-styled policies were employed, some evidence suggests that they have had lackluster results (Mowery and Sampat 2004; Vogel 2018).

13. The Bank of Japan drove interest rate hikes in 1989 to counter the pressures but ultimately failed, and the bubble burst in 1991. The recession caused corporate bankruptcies, bank failures, and a relatively large increase in unemployment. Beyond the immediate causes of the recession, its fallout was worsened due to its coinciding with a generational shift and an industrial hollowing out (Ibata-Arens 2005, 63).

14. Scholars note that Japan did not wholly succumb to pressures to converge on an American system (Amyx 2004). Jonathan Zeitlin and Gary Herrigel (2000) conceive the shifts in technology and management as selectively adopted and modified elements of the US system. Leonard J. Schoppa (2006) argues that pressure for reform (Hirschman's concept of "voice") to Japan's system of "convoy capitalism" did not fully materialize in the 1990s due, in part, to the low costs incurred by large firms in moving operations and financial transactions offshore ("exit"). Kent E. Calder (2017, 43–44) asserts that while some American initiatives and practices have been adopted into the Japanese context, there remains "deep resistance to Anglo-American-style market practices." Fumihito Gotoh and Timothy J. Sinclair (2017) detail limits to adopting American practices in the Japanese financial system. Ulrike Schaede (2020) speaks of Japan's business reinvention but notes the persistence of its large firms.

15. SoftBank's Masayoshi Son had become a household name, synonymous with a new breed of brash technology entrepreneurs in Japan. Son was challenging Japan Inc. after bringing Yahoo to Japan in 1996.

16. While these policies aimed to boost rates of women active in entrepreneurship, we note that by the end of his term, Abe's "Womenomics" push (which ran from 2013 to 2020) fell short of its targets (Crawford 2021).

3. KOREA

1. Some of Korea's new chaebol—Coupang, Kakao, and Naver, for instance—are among the world's most active corporate VC investors. Some long-established chaebol, especially Samsung, are prolific actors in startup accelerators and VC activities in Korea and across world regions. However, we acknowledge varying levels of startup engagement among the approximately seventy companies identified by the Korean Foreign Trade Commission as chaebol each year.

2. Revisionists to the Korean developmental state model assert that SMEs played a role as well as the chaebol. Chang-Yong Sung and colleagues (2016) explain that SMEs had long been nurtured by the government. Others note that the chaebol were, after all, fledgling entrepreneurial firms at earlier historical eras (Hemmert and Kim 2021).

3. We note that the government passed the Support for Small and Medium Enterprises Establishment Act and launched twelve VC firms in 1986. The act and these early VC firms provided the first infrastructure for US-style VC to exist. By 1995, there were forty-nine VC firms (Ko and Shin 1999). Also, at the tail end of the antecedent period (1996), the state established KOSDAQ to promote access to equity financing for high-growth firms (Sung et al. 2016). However, these early VC activities were marginal relative to the thrust of the bank-based system.

4. Park was involved in a scandal in which Samsung and other chaebol were accused of providing donations to a close confidant of the president in exchange for political favors, further eroding the image of large corporations (Chung 2018). Ultimately, this culminated in Park's impeachment and subsequent prison sentence (Chung 2018).

5. Yoon Suk-yeol, New Year address to nation, January 1, 2023.

6. A KRW25 billion FoF for Industrial Technology Commercialization was created in 2013 to promote the commercialization of technologies by startups with little experience in this area. This was followed shortly after by a Foreign VC Investment Fund. Also launched in 2013, this KRW135.4 billion fund focused on enabling the entry of startups in foreign markets. A second such fund, worth KRW170.7 billion, was launched in 2016 (KVIC 2024c). Furthermore, a KRW41.6 billion Angel FoF was created in 2015 to invest in private investment associations making investments in early-stage startups (KVIC 2024a).

7. The first venture boom was said to have taken place in the late 1990s and early 2000s.

8. Korea liberalized capital controls (Chinn and Ito 2006; Gallagher 2015), which led to short-term foreign borrowing by the chaebol ballooning to 67 percent of all foreign debt and 300 percent of foreign reserves by mid-1997 (Wang 2007, 1093). Korea's inability to service this debt was the immediate cause of the EAFC hitting the country.

9. However, only a few months after taking office, he faced large protests due to his decision to reverse a ban, in place since 2003, on US beef imports, as Korea and the United States negotiated the KORUS trade agreement. The so-called US beef protests made Lee take a more cautious and less laissez-faire approach (Moon 2009).

10. Lee Myung-bak, New Year's message to the nation, January 3, 2012.

11. Park Geun-hye, "Opening a New Era of Hope," February 25, 2013.

12. Government of the Republic of Korea, "The Park Geun-hye Administration's Creative Economy Blueprint: Creative Economy Action Plan and Measures to Establish a Creative Economic Ecosystem," June 5, 2013.

13. Moon Jae-in, congratulatory remarks by President Moon Jae-in at the second annual meeting of the Board of Governors of the Asian Infrastructure Investment Bank, June 16, 2017.

4. TAIWAN

1. Like revisionist work on other developmental states, there is debate as to whether the state was *the* central protagonist in the story of Taiwan's economic miracle. Some argue that the Taiwanese state was not as instrumental as has been construed, nor as coherent as portrayed (Chu 1989, 2007; Haggard and Zheng 2013). Instead, they argue that outperformance should be primarily attributed to the "strategies and abilities of entrepreneurs, engineers and managers" (Hobday 1995, 98). Others emphasize the relative decline in the role of the state, especially from the 1980s (Yeung 2016; Fuller 2020), while still others point to sectoral variability in the state's performance (Fuller 2013b).

2. We note that state-led import substitution industrialization, which prioritized large public firms, was pursued in Taiwan from 1952 to 1958. Major corporations (e.g., Taiyuen Textile and Far Eastern Textile) and even conglomerates (e.g., Formosa Plastics) emanate from the early years, when large firms played a crucial role. In terms of the motivations for entrepreneurial support, scholars such as Richard Whitley (1992) note that the KMT leadership (who had fled from mainland China) desired to limit the power of ethnic Taiwanese in particular, rather than all private-sector actors.

3. Taiwan's democratization advanced following the death of Chiang Kai-shek in 1975. Political parties were legalized later, in 1987, along with the end of Martial Law.

4. The Nineteen-Point Program liberalized the market by establishing "permanent economic institutions like the central banking system and capital market; and it provided preferential treatment to private business" (Tsai 1999, 73). The SEI introduced the provision of tax rebates on products that were exported and simplified investment licensing procedures. It provided for a five-year tax holiday as well as a tax deduction for annual export proceeds (Kuo 1982, 301) and delineated "encouraged enterprises" as types of companies on a list of categories, which was under constant revision (Haggard 1990, 96).

5. Policy "sought to maximize the benefits from FDI [foreign direct investment] for local firms by promoting local sourcing and subcontracting" (Lall 1996, 73), which helped facilitate significant technology transfer to Taiwan's small suppliers.

6. Taiwan Startup Stadium, "Our Story," accessed June 16, 2024, https://www.start upstadium.tw/ourstory.

7. The two universities are National Chiao-Tung University and National Tsing-Hua University.

8. Martin Kenney and colleagues (2013) debate this centrality of returnees to the Taiwanese technology industry around Hsinchu. They detail the transnational experience of the founders of the first cohort of very successful companies, showing that the first cohort primarily drew from local education and experience. It was a later group of returnees that boosted what was an already exciting technology cluster.

9. To do this, global links have been sought to build the capacity of domestic startups to expand to world markets. For instance, the MoST announced the launch of the Taiwan Innovation and Entrepreneurship Center in 2015, which provides high-growth startups with grants of up to US$20,000 as well as mentorship while based at the center to boost their scaling up. The National Science Council was reorganized as the MoST in 2014 and given the responsibility of delivering on the Executive Yuan's Innovation and Entrepreneur initiative.

10. For more on the Taiwan Accelerator Plus and its different programs, see https://taccplus.com/en/accelerator-2/. (Accessed July 26, 2024).

11. Two of the industry leaders were Dr. Ta-Lin Hsu and Morris Chang. Hsu was a senior manager at IBM and a VC investor in California who is said to have brought Silicon Valley–style venture capital to Taiwan by setting up H&Q in Taiwan and by initially educating policy makers—especially K. T. Li and the Executive Yuan—about VC (Klingler-Vidra 2018). Morris Chang, who worked in the United States, including at Texas Instruments, for more than twenty-five years, was recruited to Taiwan by Li to be the head of ITRI. In 1987, he founded Taiwan Semiconductor Manufacturing Company at the behest of Li (Saxenian 2006).

12. According to the Taiwan Venture Capital Association, the tax credit had been essential in boosting the number of VC funds as well as the money under management. The number of VC funds grew from 1996 to 2000 alone, and there was an increase from 47 to 170 VC managers, with the assets under management growing from US$820 million to US$4 billion (Fulco 2015).

13. Taiwania Capital, "About Us," accessed June 16, 2024, https://en.taiwaniacapital .com/#.

14. TSMC was founded in a similar way to how UMC had been. The Taiwanese state organized a group of investors to establish the privatization of the very large scale integration (VLSI) fabrication facility segment of ERSO in 1986. Initial investors included Philips and China Development Corporation.

15. We note that while ITRI and state support for the hardware sector is widely seen as effective, policy to boost innovation capacity in the software industry, with the Institute for Information Industry (III) as its primary promoter, is viewed as a relative failure (Fuller 2002). The explanation given for the divergent experiences of hardware and soft-

ware has centered around ITRI's role in conducting R&D that enabled "world-leading capabilities" for hardware firms, while III was effectively competing with software firms (Breznitz 2007, 100).

16. Biotechnology was on the science and technology agenda as early as the 1980s. However, Joseph Wong (2005, 173) notes that it was only in 1995 that resources began flowing toward the area with the creation of the Promotion Program for Biotechnology and the 1996 Biotechnology and Pharmaceutical Industries Promotion Office (BPIPO) within the jurisdiction of the Industrial Development Bureau.

17. In 1979, the United States and the PRC established formal diplomatic relations. While the Taiwan Relations Act in March 1979, afforded implicit support, the explicit security alliance, via the US-ROC Mutual Defense Treaty, expired in January 1980.

18. Taiwan did pursue an Import Substitution Industrialization strategy until 1958.

5. CHINA

1. Daniel Zhang stepped down as CEO in September 2023 in a planned leadership transition as the company continued its spin-off efforts (Qu and Cao 2023).

2. Debate persists on whether the state is a driver or inhibitor of the country's ability to escape the middle-income trap (Huang 2008; Ang 2016). For some, there is the counterintuitively positive role of weak institutions in enabling China's development (Ang 2020), while others emphasize the inability of innovation to continue to thrive given this institutional environment (Fuller 2016). Still others emphasize the role of local governments, such as those in Shanghai and Shenzhen, rather than a monolithic central government (Breznitz and Murphree 2011).

3. The Torch Program strove to boost Silicon Valley–like activities, in terms of technology incubators, science parks, and equity funding. Zhongguancun Science Park, for many, is the first science and industrial park in China, given its importance to the ecosystem and the extent to which it has acted as the model for startup-centric innovation clusters in China (Blank 2013). Zhongguancun quickly came to be known as "China's Silicon Valley" (Segal 2003, 57–59). Indeed, some of its biggest technology firms, including search portal Baidu, TikTok owner ByteDance, ride-hailing app DiDi Chuxing, e-commerce platform JD.com, IT firm Lenovo, or food delivery app Meituan-Dianping, were all set up in this cluster (Jing 2018).

4. We note the vibrant scholarship (such as Tsai 2002) that argues that these early interventions were not largely (or even peripherally) responsible for the performance of startups in this era. Yasheng Huang (2008, ix) asserts that "as late as 1998 much of the Chinese officialdom held private entrepreneurship in utter contempt."

5. The 1985 CPC Central Committee Decision on the Reform of the Science and Technology System allowed for the establishment of VC investment.

6. While the China Venturetech Investment Corporation has been referred to as a VC firm, it was more of an investment vehicle that allowed the central government to invest in a variety of assets, such as real estate and financial securities. After that initial use of the term VC, more than twenty provincial governments eventually designed, funded, and ran VC funds (Wang and Wang 2011).

7. The 863 Program listed seven key technological fields: biotechnology, space, IT, laser technology, automation, energy, and new materials; telecommunications and marine technology would be added to the list in 1992 and 1996, respectively.

8. There was not widespread agreement on this direction among the leading coalition (Shih 2022). Instead, key figures like Deng and Zhu Rongji advocated for the reduction of the planned economy. Chen Yun, who was the head of the national Economic and Financial Commission from 1979 and then the chairman of the Central Advisory Commission for Deng's government from 1981 until 1987, had advocated for a "bird cage economy"

in which the plan is the cage and the economy (the bird) can fly freely within that. Chen opposed more liberal openings, particularly as advocated by Deng, throughout the 1980s and is said to have slowed China's shift to a market economy (Tyler 1995).

9. The mass entrepreneurship and innovation initiative targeted the public, but two groups were singled out. The first was the migrant worker population. In general, rural migrants moving to the cities have higher entrepreneurship rates than urban and rural residents, in sectors such as wholesale, retail, or food (Liu et al. 2019, 681). The initiative sought to tap into their entrepreneurial mindset to boost employment.

10. At this point in time, two types of VC firms coexisted, according to Douglas Fuller (2010, 452–453). The first type included foreign firms invested in technology-light deals, such as internet startups. These firms leveraged the Chinese government's decision to largely exclude foreign firms such as Google, Yahoo!, Facebook, and Twitter from its market, providing the market space for equivalents such as Baidu, Sina, Tencent, 51jobs, and so on. The second type invested in more technology-intensive deals, such as semiconductor design firms.

11. While startup financing increased, following protests in 1994, state direction of credit had also recentralized (Su et al. 2018). These two trends—fiscal centralization and increased startup funding—continued to advance concomitantly in the early 2000s.

12. We note that research has shown that access to Innofund is dependent on other factors, such as political connections (Wang et al. 2017). As a result, there is an ongoing debate about the extent to which Innofund has offered widespread support for startup prowess (Chen and Xu 2020).

13. There were differences between Chinese VC professionals who did and did not have overseas experience. On the individual level, Manhong Mannie Liu (2015, 117) explains that, historically, there were "two tracks" of domestic VC firms in China: "ground beetles" and "sea turtles." Ground beetles referred to Chinese VCs with little overseas experience and most often referred to private VCs who had prior government experience and were new to VC. These ground beetles became active in 1999, when regulations were changed so that nongovernmental venture capitalists were allowed to operate (Kenney et al. 2002). Sea turtles, on the other hand, are Chinese professionals who returned from living overseas, often gleaning experience in VC firms while abroad.

14. Liu Xinlian, "A New Gold Rush," Beijing Review, August 15, 2011.

15. While a welcome development, government approval for firms to be listed in ChiNext was considered opaque in the first few years after the stock exchange's launch (Zhang et al. 2017, 400). Indeed, larger Chinese tech firms are said to have preferred to list in Nasdaq or the New York Stock Exchange (Gucbilmez 2014, 180).

16. The State Council issued the "Notice on the Plan for Deepening the Reform of Management of Centrally Financed S&T Projects." Under the new system, the Inter-Ministerial Joint Council was introduced to coordinate priorities and budgeting while preventing overlap across and within ministries. MoST was put in charge of the council.

17. The Technology Innovation Guiding Fund(s) was divided into three funds: the Venture Capital Guidance Fund for Emerging Industries, launched in 2015; the National Fund for Technology Transfer and Commercialization, which had been established in 2011 but became more active from 2015; and the National Fund for SME Development, also launched in 2015. By the end of 2017, these three funds oversaw sixty-five funds of funds managing RMB114.1 billion, with plans to eventually reach RMB300 billion. Therefore, government funding disbursement was decentralized. The funds had to adhere to the priorities outlined by the Xi government, but once in operation, they were free to decide which startups to support and how to manage their own programs. Furthermore, the central government provided funds along with local governments, SOEs, banks, and other actors (China Innovation Funding 2020b).

18. The government wanted to support startups that were finding it more difficult to be listed in the United States. Furthermore, more established (former) startups, such as Alibaba, JD.com, or Xiaomi, were opting to list in Hong Kong as an insurance policy in case they were asked to leave US stock exchanges (Lockett 2020).

19. We note that scholars like Huang (2008) contest the gradualist reform narrative and instead depict the 1980s as an era of radical reforms and the 1990s as a reversal of those efforts. The share of China's SOEs over time is a fraught measurement, as one needs to count their numerous subsidiaries (Pettis 2013). According to the *Economist's* (2013) measurements, in 2001, Chinese SOEs still accounted for around 65 percent of assets and 50 percent of profits and sales; by 2008, the figures were down to around 45 percent of assets and 30 percent of profits and sales. Meanwhile, the number of private firms, especially in the technology sector, continued to grow exponentially throughout this period. The SOEs were largely in sectors such as petroleum (Sinopec or China National Petroleum), utilities (State Grid Corporation), banking (Industrial and Commercial Bank of China, or Bank of China), telecommunications (China Mobile), or chemicals (Sinochem) (Fortune 2020).

20. The local governments did not, though, get to retain the corporate taxes paid by startups in HIDZs (Su et al. 2018). Revenue for local government coffers came through the broader activity—consumption, land development, and more—that the clusters represented.

CONCLUSION

1. We do note that, outside of startup policy, there are government efforts to ensure sufficient talent and infrastructure to aid the ongoing competitiveness of the Silicon Shield.

2. We say that "the story goes" because this account of the origin of the phrase is contested. See Gautam Mukunda (2020), who details that what Wilson said was the opposite—that what was good for the country was good for General Motors.

References

Acemoglu, Daron, Philippe Aghion, and Fabrizio Zilibotti. 2006. "Distance to Frontier, Selection, and Economic Growth." *Journal of European Economic Association* 4, no. 1: 37–74. https://doi.org/10.1162/jeea.2006.4.1.37.

Acemoglu, Daron, Georgy Egorov, and Konstantin Sonin. 2021. "Institutional Change and Institutional Persistence." In *The Handbook of Historical Economics*, edited by Alberto Bisin and Giovanni Federico. Elsevier Science and Technology, 365–389. Cambridge, MA: Academic Press.

Acemoglu, Daron, and Simon Johnson. 2023. "Big Tech Is Bad. AI Will Be Worse." *New York Times*, June 9, 2023.

Acemoglu, Daron, and James A. Robinson. 2006. *Economic Origins of Dictatorship and Democracy*. Cambridge, UK: Cambridge University Press.

Acs, Zoltan J., Thomas Åstebro, David B. Audretsch, and David T. Robinson. 2016. "Public Policy to Promote Entrepreneurship: A Call to Arms." *Small Business Economics* 47, no. 1: 35–51. https://doi.org/10.1007/s11187-016-9712-2.

Aggarwal, Vinod K., and Andrew W. Reddie. 2021. "Economic Statecraft in the 21st Century: Implications for the Future of the Global Trade Regime." *World Trade Review* 20, no. 2: 137–151.

Aghion, Philippe, Céline Antonin, and Simon Brunel. 2021. *The Power of Creative Destruction: Economic Upheaval and the Wealth of Nations*. Cambridge, MA: Harvard Belknap.

Aghion, Philippe, and Peter Howitt. 1992. "A Model of Growth through Creative Destruction." *Econometrica* 60, no. 2: 323–351. https://doi.org/10.2307/2951599.

Ahlstrom, David, and Garry D. Bruton. 2006. "Venture Capital in Emerging Economies: Networks and Institutional Change." *Entrepreneurship Theory and Practice* 30, no. 2: 299–320. https://doi.org/10.1111/j.1540-6520.2006.00122.x.

Ahmadjian, Christina L., and Patricia Robinson. 2001. "Safety in Numbers: Downsizing and Deinstitutionalization of Permanent Employment in Japan." *Administrative Science Quarterly* 12: 622–654. https://doi.org/10.2307/309482.

Aiginger, Karl, and Dani Rodrik. 2020. "Rebirth of Industrial Policy and an Agenda for the Twenty-First Century." *Journal of Industry, Competition and Trade* 20, 189–207.

Aizenman, Joshua. 2015. "Internationalization of the RMB, Capital Market Openness and Financial Reform in China." *Pacific Economic Review* 20, no. 3: 444–460. https://doi.org/10.1111/1468-0106.12116.

Akcigit, Ufuk, Salome Baslandze, and Francesca Lotti. 2023. "Connecting to Power: Political Connections, Innovation, and Firm Dynamics." *Econometrica* 91, no. 2: 529–564. https://doi.org/10.3982/ECTA18338.

Akcigit, Ufuk, and John Van Reenen. 2023. "Introduction." In *The Economics of Creative Destruction: New Research Themes from Aghion and Howitt*, edited by Ufuk Akcigit and John Van Reenen, 1–14. Cambridge, MA: Harvard University Press.

Aldrich, Howard E., and Martin Ruef. 2018. "Unicorns, Gazelles, and Other Distractions on the Way to Understanding Real Entrepreneurship in the United States." *Academy of Management Perspectives* 32, no. 4. https://doi.org/10.5465/amp.2017.0123.

Alemany, Luisa, and Job. J. Andreoli. 2018. *Entrepreneurial Finance: The Art and Science of Growing Ventures*. Cambridge, UK: Cambridge University Press.

Allison, Graham, and Eric Schmidt. 2022. "China's 5G Soars Over America's." *Wall Street Journal*, February 16, 2022.

Alperovych, Yan, Alexander Groh, and Anita Quas. 2020. "Bridging the Equity Gap for Young Innovative Companies: The Design of Effective Government Venture Capital Fund Programs." *Research Policy* 49, no. 10. https://doi.org/10.1016/j.res pol.2020.104051.

Alvarez-Garrido, Elisa, and Gary Dushnitsky. 2016. "Are Entrepreneurial Venture's Innovation Rates Sensitive to Investor Complementary Assets? Comparing Biotech Ventures Backed by Corporate and Independent VCs." *Strategic Management Journal* 37, no. 5: 819–834. https://doi.org/10.1002/smj.2359.

Amable, Bruno. 2003. *The Diversity of Modern Capitalism*. Oxford: Oxford University Press.

Amazon Web Services. 2023. "Startup Loft Accelerator." Accessed June 24, 2024. https://aws-startup-lofts.com/emea/program/accelerator.

American Institute in Taiwan. 2022. "SelectUSA." Accessed June 24, 2024. https://www.ait.org.tw/selectusa/.

Amsden, Alice. 1979. "Taiwan's Economic History: A Case of Étatisme and a Challenge to Dependency Theory." *Modern China* 5, no. 3: 341–379. https://www.jstor.org/stable/188893.

Amsden, Alice. 1985. "The State and Taiwan's Economic Development." In *Bringing the State Back In*, edited by Peter B. Evans, Dana Rueschemeyer, and Theda Skocpol, 78–106. Cambridge, UK: Cambridge University Press.

Amsden, Alice. 1989. *Asia's Next Giant: South Korea and Late Industrialization*. Oxford: Oxford University Press.

Amsden, Alice. 2001. *The Rise of "The Rest": Challenges to the West from Late-Industrializing Economies*. Oxford: Oxford University Press.

Amyx, Jennifer. 2004. *Japan's Financial Crisis: Institutional Rigidity and Reluctant Change*. Princeton, NJ: Princeton University Press.

Anchordoguy, Marie. 1989. *Computers Inc.: Japan's Challenge to IBM*. Cambridge, MA: Harvard University Press.

Anchordoguy, Marie. 2005. *Reprogramming Japan: The High-Tech Crisis under Communitarian Capitalism*. Ithaca, NY: Cornell University Press.

Anderson, Mark, David Elgar, Kevin Grant, Keith Halcro, Julio Mario Rodriguez Devis, and Lautaro Guera Genskowsky, eds. 2014. *Innovation Support in Latin America and Europe: Theory, Practice and Policy Innovation in Innovation Systems*. London: Routledge.

Andreas, Joel. 2009. *Rise of the Red Engineers: The Cultural Revolution and the Origins of China's New Class*. Stanford: Stanford University Press.

Ang, Yuen Yuen. 2016. *How China Escaped the Poverty Trap*. Ithaca, NY: Cornell University Press.

Ang, Yuen Yuen. 2020. *China's Gilded Age: The Paradox of Economic Boom and Vast Corruption*. Cambridge, UK: Cambridge University Press.

Aoki, Masahiko. 1988. *Information, Incentives, and Bargaining in the Japanese Economy*. Cambridge, UK: Cambridge University Press.

Aoki, Masahiko. 2000. *Information, Corporate Governance and Institutional Diversity: Competitiveness in Japan, the USA, and the Transitional Economies*. Oxford: Oxford University Press.

Aoki, Masahiko, and Ronald Dore. 1994. *The Japanese Firm: The Sources of Competitive Strength*. Oxford: Oxford University Press.

Aoki, Masahiko, Gregory Jackson, and Hideaki Miyajima. 2007. *Corporate Governance in Japan: Institutional Change and Organizational Diversity.* Oxford: Oxford University Press.

Aoki, Masahiko, Hyung-Ki Kim, and Masahiro Okuno-Fujiwara. 1998. *The Role of Government in East Asian Economic Development: Comparative Institutional Analysis.* Oxford: Oxford University Press.

Aoki, Masahiko, and Hugh T. Patrick, eds. 1994. *The Japanese Main Bank System: Its Relevance for Developing and Transforming Economies.* Oxford: Oxford University Press.

Appelbaum, Richard P., Rachel Parker, Cong Cao, and Gary Gereffi. 2011. "China's (Not So Hidden) Developmental State: Becoming a Leading Nanotechnology Innovator in the Twenty-First Century." In *State of Innovation: The U.S. Government's Role in Technology Development,* edited by Fred L. Block and Matthew R. Keller, 217–235. London: Routledge.

Asia Silicon Valley Development Agency. 2024. "Origins and Pillars. Accessed July 26, 2024. https://www.ndc.gov.tw/en/Content_List.aspx?n=5B40E2CED6E6DB42.

Atkinson, Robert, and Michael Lind. 2018. "Belittled: How Small Became Beautiful." In *Big Is Beautiful: Debunking the Myth of Small Business,* 3–17. Cambridge, MA: MIT Press.

Audretsch, David B., Alessandra Colombelli, Luca Grilli, Tommaso Minola, and Einar Rasmussen. 2020. "Innovative Start-Ups and Policy Initiatives." *Research Policy* 49, no. 10: 104027. https://doi.org/10.1016/j.respol.2020.104027.

Autio, Erkko, and Heikki Rannikko. 2016. "Retaining Winners: Can Policy Boost High-Growth Entrepreneurship?" *Research Policy* 45, no. 1: 42–55. https://doi.org/10.1016/j.respol.2015.06.002.

AVCJ (Asian Venture Capital Journal). 2005 Asian Private Equity Guide 300 Guide. Hong Kong: Incisive Media.

Avnimelech, Gil, and Morris Teubal. 2006. "Creating Venture Capital Industries That Co-evolve with High Tech: Insights from an Extended Industry Life Cycle Perspective of the Israeli Experience." *Research Policy* 35, no. 10: 1477–1498. https://doi.org/10.1016/j.respol.2006.09.017.

Baark, Erik. 2016. "The Chinese State and Its Role in Shaping China's Innovation System." In *The Asian Developmental State: Reexamination and New Departures,* edited by Yin-wah Chu, 159–174. London: Palgrave Macmillan.

Bae, Hannah. 2011. "Can Korea Become a True Startup Powerhouse?" *IDG Connect,* June 9, 2011.

Bae, Jeong-Cheol. 2023. "Lotte to Open Silicon Valley Corporate Venture Capital Unit." *Korea Economic Daily,* May 23, 2023. https://amp-kedglobal-com.cdn.ampproject.org/c/s/amp.kedglobal.com/newsAmp/ked202305260020.

Bai, Jessica, Shai Bernstein, Abhishek Dev, and Josh Lerner. 2022. "The Dance between Government and Private Investors: Public Entrepreneurial Finance around the Globe." National Bureau for Economic Research Working Paper 28744.

Balassa, Bela. 1985. "Exports, Policy Choices, and Economic Growth in Developing Countries after the 1973 Oil Shock." *Journal of Development Economics* 18, no. 1: 23–35. https://doi.org/10.1016/0304-3878(85)90004-5.

Banasevic, Nicholas, and Zuzanna Boboweic. 2023. "SEP-Based Injunctions: How Much Has the Huawei v ZTE Judgment Achieved in Practice?" *Journal of European Competition Law & Practice* 14, no. 2: 121–133. https://doi.org/10.1093/jeclap/lpad012.

Baslandze, Salome. 2023. "Barriers to Creative Destruction: Large Firms and Nonproductive Strategies." In *The Economics of Creative Destruction: New Research on*

Themes from Aghion and Howitt, edited by Ufuk Akcigit and John Van Reenen, 558–584. Cambridge, MA: Harvard University Press.

Batjargal, Bat. 2007. "Internet Entrepreneurship: Social Capital, Human Capital, and Performance of Internet Ventures in China." *Research Policy* 36: 605–618. https://doi.org/10.1016/j.respol.2006.09.029.

Baygan, Günseli. 2003. "Venture Capital Policies in Israel." OECD STI Working Paper 2003/3, Industry Issues.

Beck, Peter M. 1998. "Revitalizing Korea's Chaebol." *Asian Survey* 38, no. 11: 1018–1035. https://doi.org/10.2307/2645683.

Becker, Uwe. 2009. *Open Varieties of Capitalism: Continuity, Change and Performance.* Basingstoke, UK: Palgrave Macmillan.

Beeson, Mark, and Leong Liew. 2002. "Capitalism in East Asia: The Political Economy of Business Organization in Japan, Korea and China." In *Reconfiguring East Asia: Regional Institutions and Organizations After the Crisis*, edited by Mark Beeson, 139–158. London: Routledge.

Bell, Stephen, and Hui Feng. 2013. *The Rise of the People's Bank of China: The Politics of Institutional Change.* Cambridge, MA: Harvard University Press.

Blackburn, Robert A., and Michael T. Schaper. 2016. "Introduction." In *Government, SMEs and Entrepreneurship Development: Policy, Practice and Challenges*, 1–13. London: Routledge.

Blanchard, Ben, and Thomas Escritt. 2023. "Germany Spends Big to Win $11 Billion TSMC Chip Plant." Reuters, August 8, 2023. https://www.reuters.com/technology/taiwan-chipmaker-tsmc-approves-38-bln-germany-factory-plan-2023-08-08/.

Blank, Steve. 2013. "China's Torch Program: The Glow That Can Light the World (part 2 of 5)." *UC Berkeley Blog*, April 11, 2013. https://blogs.berkeley.edu/2013/04/11/chinas-torch-program-the-glow-that-can-light-the-world-part-2-of-5/.

Blank, Steve. 2019. "Why Companies Do 'Innovation Theater' Instead of Actual Innovation." *Harvard Business Review*, October 7, 2019. https://hbr.org/2019/10/why-companies-do-innovation-theater-instead-of-actual-innovation.

Block, Fred. 2008. "Swimming Against the Current: The Rise of a Hidden Developmental State in the United States." *Politics & Society* 36, no. 2: 169–206.

Block, Fred L., and Matthew R. Keller. 2010. *State of Innovation: The U.S. Government's Role in Technology Development.* London: Routledge.

Bloomberg News. 2022. "China Weighs Reviving Jack Ma's Ant IPO as Crackdown Eases." June 9, 2022. https://www.bloomberg.com/news/articles/2022-06-09/china-considers-reviving-jack-ma-s-ant-ipo-as-crackdown-eases.

Bombardini, Matilde, Olimpia Cutinelli-Rendina, and Francesco Trebbi. 2023. "Lobbying behind the Frontier." In *The Economics of Creative Destruction: New Research on Themes from Aghion and Howitt*, edited by Ufuk Akcigit and John Van Reenen, 533–557. Cambridge, MA: Harvard University Press.

Bone, Jonathan, Olivia Allen, and Christopher Haley. 2017. *Business Incubators and Accelerators: The National Picture.* BEIS Research Paper no. 7. London: BEIS.

Boyer, Robert. 2003. "The Embedded Innovation Systems of Germany and Japan: Distinctive Features and Future." In *The End of Diversity? Prospects for German and Japanese Capitalism*, edited by Kozo Yamamura and Wolfgang Streeck, 147–182. Ithaca, NY: Cornell University Press.

Boyer, Robert. 2005. "How and Why Capitalisms Differ." *Economy and Society* 34, no. 4: 509–557. https://doi.org/10.1080/03085140500277070.

Boyer, Robert. 2022. "Platform Capitalism: A Socio-Economic Analysis." *Socio-Economic Review* 20, no. 4: 1857–1879. https://doi.org/10.1093/ser/mwaa055.

Brandt, Loren, and Eric Thun. 2016. "Constructing a Ladder for Growth: Policy, Markets, and Industrial Upgrading in China." *World Development* 80: 78–95. https://doi.org/10.1016/j.worlddev.2015.11.001.

Brazinsky, Gregg. 2007. *Nation Building in South Korea: Koreans, Americans, and the Making of Democracy.* Chapel Hill: University of North Carolina Press.

Breznitz, Dan. 2007. *Innovation and the State: Political Choices and Strategies for Growth in Israel, Taiwan and Ireland.* New Haven, CT: Yale University Press.

Breznitz, Dan, and Michael Murphree. 2011. *Run of the Red Queen: Government, Innovation, Globalization, and Economic Growth in China.* New Haven, CT: Yale University Press.

Brown, Eliot. 2023. "He Spent $140 Billion on AI With Little to Show. Now He Is Trying Again." *Wall Street Journal*, July 3, 2023. https://www.wsj.com/articles/he-spent-140-billion-on-ai-with-little-to-show-now-he-is-trying-again-dbcca17?mod=tech_lead_pos1.

Brown, James R., Gustav Martinsson, and Bruce C. Petersen. 2013. "Law, Stock Markets and Innovation." *Journal of Finance* 68, no. 4: 1517–1549. https://doi.org/10.1111/jofi.12040.

Bugl, Benjamin M., Frank P. Balz, and Dominik K. Kanbach. 2022. "Leveraging Smart Capital through Corporate Venture Capital: A Typology of Value Creation for New Venture Firms." *Journal of Business Venturing Insights*, 17. https://doi.org/10.1016/j.jbvi.2021.e00292.

Business Times. 2019. "South-east Asia's First Korean Startup Centre to Be Set Up in Singapore." November 25, 2019. https://www.businesstimes.com.sg/garage/south-east-asias-first-korean-startup-centre-to-be-set-up-in-singapore.

Cabinet Secretariat (Japan). 2022. "Startup Development Five-Year Plan." Accessed June 24, 2024. https://www.cas.go.jp/jp/seisaku/atarashii_sihonsyugi/pdf/sdfyplan2022en.pdf.

Cai, Hongbin, and Daniel Treisman. 2006. "Did Government Decentralization Cause China's Economic Miracle?" *World Politics* 58, no. 4: 505–535. https://doi.org/10.1353/wp.2007.0005.

Cai, Kevin G. 2008. *The Political Economy of East Asia: Regional and National Dimensions.* New York: Palgrave Macmillan.

Calder, Kent E. 1990. "Linking Welfare and the Developmental State: Postal Savings in Japan." *Journal of Japanese Studies* 16, no. 1: 31–59. https://doi.org/10.2307/132493.

Calder, Kent E. 2017. *Circles of Compensation: Economic Growth and the Globalization of Japan.* Stanford: Stanford University Press.

Callon, Scott. 1995. *Divided Sun: MITI and the Breakdown of Japanese High-Tech Industrial Policy.* Redwood City, CA: Stanford University Press.

Campbell, Stefan. 2022. "TikTok vs Instagram—Users and Stats Compared for 2022." *Small Business Blog*, April 24, 2022. https://thesmallbusinessblog.net/tiktok-vs-instagram/.

Cao, Ann. 2023. "China Gave 190 Chip Firms US$1.75 Billion in Subsidies in 2022 as It Seeks Semiconductor Self-Sufficiency." *South China Morning Post*, May 7, 2023. https://www.scmp.com/tech/tech-war/article/3219697/china-gave-190-chip-firms-us175-billion-subsidies-2022-it-seeks-semiconductor-self-sufficiency.

Cao, Cong. 2004. *China's Scientific Elite.* London: Routledge.

Cao, Yuanzhang, Yingyi Qian, and Barry R. Weingast. 1999. "From Federalism, Chinese Style to Privatization, Chinese Style." *Economics of Transition and Institutional Change* 7, no. 1 (March): 103–131.

Capoccia, Giovanni. 2015. "Critical Junctures and Institutional Change." In *Advances in Comparative Historical Analysis,* edited by James Mahoney and Kathleen Thelen, 147–117. Cambridge, UK: Cambridge University Press.

Carney, Michael, Eric Gedajlovic, and Xiaohua Yang. 2009. "Varieties of Asian Capitalism: Toward and Institutional Theory of Asian Enterprise." *Asia Pacific Journal of Management* 26, no. 3: 361–380. https://doi.org/10.1007/s10490-009-9139-2.

Carney, Richard W. 2016. "Varieties of Hierarchical Capitalism: Family and State Market Economies in East Asia." *Pacific Review* 29, no. 2: 137–163. https://doi.org/10.10 80/09512748.2015.1020963.

CB Insights. 2017. "The History Of CVC: From Exxon And DuPont To Xerox And Microsoft, How Corporates Began Chasing 'The Future.'" March 7, 2017. https://www.cbinsights.com/research/report/corporate-venture-capital-history/.

CB Insights. 2019. "The Most Active Corporate VC Firms Globally." March 28, 2019. https://www.cbinsights.com/research/corporate-venture-capital-active-2014/.

CB Insights. 2021. "The 2020 Global CVC Report." March 16, 2021. https://www.cbin sights.com/research/report/corporate-venture-capital-trends-2020/.

CCEI. 2019. "Available Space." [In Korean.] Accessed June 24, 2024. https://ccei.cre ativekorea.or.kr/service/reserve_place.do.

Central People's Government of the PRC. 2009. "Chinese Overseas Students' Return and Entrepreneurship Support Program." [In Chinese.] Accessed June 24, 2024. http://www.gov.cn/zwgk/2009-10/29/content_1451729.htm.

Central People's Government of the PRC. 2010. "National Medium- to Long-Term Talent Development Plan Outline (2010–2020)." [In Chinese.] Accessed June 24, 2024. http://www.gov.cn/jrzg/2010-06/06/content_1621777.htm.

Central People's Government of the PRC. 2011. "Opinion on Supporting Overseas Students to Return to China and Start Businesses." [In Chinese.] Accessed June 24, 2024. http://www.gov.cn/zwgk/2011-04/14/content_1843836.htm.

Cha, Victor T., and Ramon Pacheco Pardo. 2023. *Korea: A New History of South and North.* New Haven, CT: Yale University Press.

Chang, Ching-Wen. 2017. "Why Morris Chang Opposed? Three Reasons That 5+2 Industrial Innovation Plan Cannot Deliver the Next TSMC." *CM Media,* September 27, 2017. https://www.cmmedia.com.tw/home/articles/5810.

Chang, Chun-Yen, and Po-Lung Yu, eds. 2001. *Made by Taiwan: Booming in the Information Technology Era.* Singapore: World Scientific.

Chang, Ha-Joon. 2010. *Institutions and Economic Development: Theory, Policy and History.* Cambridge, UK: Cambridge University Press.

Chang, Sea-Jin. 2003. *Financial Crisis and Transformation of Korean Business Groups: The Rise and Fall of Chaebols.* Cambridge, UK: Cambridge University Press.

Chazan, Guy. 2019. "Germany Acts to Stop Sale of Tech Companies to Non-EU Investors." *Financial Times,* November 29, 2019.

Chen, Chengfeng, and Peiyan Xu. 2020. "Did Government R&D Subsidies Increase Chinese Firms' Trade Margins? Evidence from Innofund Program." *Applied Economic Letters.* https://doi.org/10.1080/13504851.2020.1757608.

Chen, Christopher. 2019. "Taiwan." In *Corporate Governance in Asia: A Comparative Approach,* edited by Bruce Aronson and Joongi Kim, 325–352. Cambridge, UK: Cambridge University Press.

Chen, Edward, and Gary G. Hamilton. 1996. "Introduction: Business Groups and Economic Development." In *Asian Business Networks,* edited by Gary G. Hamilton, 1–6. Berlin: De Gruyter.

Chen, Jun. 2023. "Venture Capital Research in China: Data and Institutional Details." *Journal of Corporate Finance* 81. https://doi.org/10.1016/j.jcorpfin.2022.102239.

Chen, Lulu Yilun. 2022a. *Influence Empire: The Story of Tencent and China's Tech Ambition*. London: Hodder & Stoughton.

Chen, Lulu Yilun. 2022b. "What It Would Take for Jack Ma's Ant to Reboot an IPO." Bloomberg, June 16, 2022. https://www.bloomberg.com/news/articles/2022-06-16/what-it-would-take-for-jack-ma-s-ant-to-reboot-an-ipo-quicktake?leadSource=uverify%20wall.

Chen, Zhongshi. 2015. *The Revival, Legitimization, and Development of Private Enterprise in China Empowering State Capitalism*. Basingstoke, UK: Palgrave Macmillan.

Cheng, Evelyn. 2019. "China Kicks Off New Shanghai Tech Board as It Tests New Ways to Improve Volatile Stock Market." *CNBC Markets*, July 21, 2019. https://www.cnbc.com/2019/07/22/china-star-market-shanghai-kicks-off-new-nasdaq-style-tech-board.html.

Cheng, Ting-Fang, and Lauly Li. 2021. "TSMC's Morris Chang Calls on Taiwan to Defend Its Chip Industry." *Nikkei Asia*, April 21, 2021. https://asia.nikkei.com/Business/Tech/Semiconductors/TSMC-s-Morris-Chang-calls-on-Taiwan-to-defend-its-chip-industry#:~:text=%22It's%20very%20difficult%20to%20create,bring%20vital%20semiconductor%20manufacturing%20onshore.

Cherry, Judith. 2005. "Big Deal or Big Disappointment? The Continuing Evolution of the South Korean Developmental State." *Pacific Review* 18, no. 3: 327–354. https://doi.org/10.1080/09512740500188977.

Chesbrough, Henry William. 2003. *Open Innovation: The New Imperative for Creating and Profiting from Technology*. Cambridge, MA: Harvard Business Review.

Chesbrough, Henry William. 2012. "Open Innovation: Where We've Been and Where We're Going." *Research-Technology Management* 55, no. 4: 20–27. https://doi.org/10.5437/08956308X5504085.

Chesbrough, Henry, and Marcel Bogers. 2014. "Explicating Open Innovation." In *New Frontiers in Open Innovation*, edited by Henry Chesbrough, Wim Vanhaverbeke, and Joel West, 3–28. Oxford: Oxford University Press.

Cheung, Gordon. 2018. *China in the Global Political Economy: From Developmental to Entrepreneurial*. Cheltenham, UK: Edward Elgar.

Cheung, Tai Ming. 2022. *Innovate to Dominate: The Rise of the Chinese Techno-Security State*. Ithaca, NY: Cornell University Press.

Child, John. 2016. "Building the Innovative Capacity of SMEs in China." In *China's Innovation Challenge: Overcoming the Middle-Income Trap*, edited by Arie Y. Lewin, Martin Kenney, and Johann Peter Murmann, 189–218. Cambridge, UK: Cambridge University Press.

China Daily. 2014. "Entrepreneurs, Scientists Call for Innovation." December 17, 2014. http://www.chinadaily.com.cn/m/fujian/2014-12/17/content_19106199.htm.

China Innovation and Entrepreneurship Competition. 2024. "China Innovation and Entrepreneurship Competition." [In Chinese.] http://www.cxcyds.com. Accessed July 19, 2024.

China Policy. 2017. *China Going Global: Between Ambiguity and Capacity*. Beijing: China Policy.

Chinn, Menzie D., and Hiro Ito. 2006. "What Matters for Financial Development? Capital Controls, Institutions, and Interactions." *Journal of Development Economics* 81, no. 1: 163–192. https://doi.org/10.1016/j.jdeveco.2005.05.010.

Cho, EunYoung. 2021. "The Role of a State in Technology Innovation: A New Authoritarian Developmental State." *Asia Review* 11, no. 1: 357–400. https://doi.org/10.24987/SNUACAR.2021.4.11.1.357.

Choe, Sang-Hun. 1998. "South Korea's Social Contract Being Torn Up." *Seattle Times*, January 2, 1998.

Choi, Si-young. 2022. "Yoon Eyes Plan to Raise More Unicorns." *Korea Herald*, April 26, 2022. https://www.koreaherald.com/view.php?ud=20220426000766.

Chou, Jyo, and Kenjiro Suzuki. 2024. "Japan VC Association Sets 30% Diversity Target for Senior Leadership." *Nikkei Asia*, January 6, 2024. https://asia.nikkei.com/Business /Finance/Japan-VC-association-sets-30-diversity-target-for-senior-leadership.

Choung, Jae-Yong, Hye-Ran Hwang, and Wichin Song. 2014. "Transitions of Innovation Activities in Latecomer Countries: An Explanatory Case Study of South Korea." *World Development* 54: 156–167. https://doi.org/10.1016/j.worlddev.2013.07.013.

Chu, Yun-han. 1989. "State Structure and Economic Adjustment of the East Asian Newly Industrializing Countries." *International Organization* 43: 647–672. https://doi .org/10.1017/S0020818300034470.

Chu, Yun-han. 1999. "Surviving the East Asian Financial Storm: The Political Foundation of Taiwan's Economic Resilience." In *The Politics of the Asian Economic Crisis*, edited by T. J. Pempel, 184–202. Ithaca, NY: Cornell University Press.

Chu, Yun-han. 2007. "Re-engineering the Developmental State in an Age of Globalization: Taiwan's Quest for High-Tech Industries." In *Taiwan in the 21st Century*, edited by Robert Ash and J. Megan Greene, 154–176. London: Routledge.

Chuma, A. Hiroyuki. 2002. "Employment Adjustment in Japanese Firms during the Current Crisis." *Industrial Relations* 41: 653–682. https://doi.org/10.1111/1468 -232X.00268.

Chung, Esther. 2018. "Former President Park Sentenced to 24 Years in Prison." *JoongAng Daily*, April 6, 2018. https://koreajoongangdaily.joins.com/2018/04/06/politics /Former-President-Park-sentenced-to-24-years-in-prison/3046606.html.

Cioffi, John W., Martin F. Kenney, and John Zysman. 2022. "Platform Power and Regulatory Politics: Polanyi for the Twenty-First Century." *New Political Economy* 27, no. 5: 820–836. https://doi.org/10.1080/13563467.2022.2027355.

Clover, Charles, Emily Feng, and Sherry Fei Ju. 2017. "China Enlists Startups in High-Tech Arms Race." *Financial Times*, July 9, 2017. https://www.ft.com/content/5883 d3d2-62cd-11e7-91a7-502f7ee26895.

Coates, David, ed. 2005. *Varieties of Capitalism, Varieties of Approaches*. Basingstoke, UK: Palgrave Macmillan.

Collier, David, and Gerardo L. Munck, eds. 2022. *Critical Junctures and Historical Legacies: Insights and Methods for Comparative Social Science*. Lanham, MD: Rowman & Littlefield.

Committee on the History of Japan's Trade and Industry Policy. 2020. *Dynamics of Japan's Trade and Industrial Policy in the Post Rapid Growth Era (1980–2000)*. Tokyo: Springer.

Contact Taiwan. 2018. "Innovation & Startup: Entrepreneur Visa." January 31, 2018. https:// www.contacttaiwan.tw/main/docdetail.aspx?uid=634&pid=34&docid=258.

Corning, Gregory P. 2003. *Japan and the Politics of Techno-globalism*. London: Routledge.

Crawford, Mark. 2021. "Abe's Womenomics Policy, 2013–2020: Tokenism, Gradualism, or Failed Strategy?" *Asia Pacific Journal* 19, no. 4: 1–16. https://apjjf.org/2021/4 /crawford.

Crouch, Colin. 2005. "Models of Capitalism." *New Political Economy* 10, no. 4: 439–456. https://doi.org/10.1080=13563460500344336.

Crunchbase. 2020. "China Artificial Intelligence Companies." Accessed June 25, 2024. https://www.crunchbase.com/hub/china-artificial-intelligence-companies.

Culpepper, Pepper D., and Kathleen Thelen. 2020. "Are We All Amazon Primed? Consumers and the Politics of Platform Power." *Comparative Political Studies* 53, no. 2: 288–318. https://doi.org/10.1177/0010414019852687.

Cumings, Bruce. 1999. "Web with No Spider, Spider with No Web: The Genealogy of the Developmental State." In *The Developmental State*, edited by Meredith Woo-Cumings, 61–92. Ithaca, NY: Cornell University Press.

Dabic, Marina, Tugrul Daim, Marcel L. A. M. Bogers, and Anne-Laure Menton. 2023. "The Limits of Open Innovation: Failures, Risks, and the Costs of Open Innovation Practice and Theory." *Technovation* 126. https://doi.org/10.1016/j.tech novation.2023.102786.

Dahlander, Linus, and David M. Gann. 2010. "How Open Is Innovation?" *Research Policy* 39: 699–709. https://doi.org/10.1016/j.respol.2010.01.013.

Dahlander, Linus, David M. Gann, and Martin W. Wallin. 2021. "How Open Is Innovation? A Retrospective and Ideas Forward." *Research Policy* 50, no. 4. https://doi .org/10.1016/j.respol.2021.104218.

Dai, Sarah, and Li Tao. 2019. "China's Work Ethic Stretches Beyond '996' as Tech Companies Feel the Impact of Slowdown." *South China Morning Post*, January 29, 2019. https://www.scmp.com/tech/start-ups/article/2183950/chinas-work-ethic -stretches-beyond-996-tech-companies-feel-impact.

Da Rin, Marco, Giovanna Nicodano, and Alessandro Sembenelli. 2005. "Public Policy and the Creation of Active Venture Capital Markets." European Central Bank Working Paper Series 430.

Dave, Aditi. 2023. "Korean Ministry Launches Women's Venture Fostering Project to Support Female Entrepreneurs." *Korea Tech Desk*, March 8, 2023. https://www .koreatechdesk.com/korean-ministry-launches-womens-venture-fostering-proj ect-to-support-female-entrepreneurs/.

Debanes, Pauline. 2017. "Layering the Developmental State Away? The Knock-On Effect of Startup Promotion Policies on the Innovation Bureaucracy in South Korea." *Technology Governance* 78 (November).

Decker, Ryan A., John Haltiwanger, Ron S. Jarmin, and Javier Miranda. 2016a. "Declining Business Dynamism: What We Know and The Way Forward." *American Economic Review* 106, no. 5: 203–207. https://doi.org/10.1257/aer.p20161050.

Decker, Ryan A., John Haltiwanger, Ron S. Jarmin, and Javier Miranda. 2016b. "Where Has All the Skewness Gone? The Decline in High-Growth (Young) Firms in the U.S." *European Economic Review* 86: 4–23. https://doi.org/10.1016/j.euroeco rev.2015.12.013.

Deeg, Richard, Iain Hardie, and Sylvia Maxfield. 2016. "What Is Patient Capital, and Where Does It Exist?" *Socio-Economic Review* 14, no. 4: 615–625. https://doi.org /10.1093/ser/mww030.

de Leon, Riley. 2019. "How SoftBank and its $100 Billion Vision Fund Has Become a Global Start-Up Machine." *CNBC*, May 17, 2019. https://www.cnbc.com/2019 /05/17/softbanks-100-billion-vision-fund-reshapes-world-of-venture-capital .html.

Deng, Iris. 2023. "China Wants Metaverse Firms with 'Global Influence' and Plans for Up to 5 Industrial Clusters by 2025." *South China Morning Post*, September 10, 2023. https://www.scmp.com/tech/policy/article/3233933/china-wants-metaverse-firms -global-influence-and-plans-five-industrial-clusters-2025.

Deng, Jet. 2022. "The Alibaba Case: An Open Sesame to China's Antitrust Regulation on the Internet Platforms." *Journal of Antitrust Enforcement* 10: 230–238. https:// doi.org/10.1093/jaenfo/jnab021.

Dent, Christopher M. 2003. "Taiwan's Foreign Economic Policy: The 'Liberalization Plus' Approach of an Evolving Developmental State." *Modern Asian Studies* 37, no. 2: 461–483. https://doi.org/10.1017/S0026749X03002087.

Dore, Ronald. 1986. *Flexible Rigidities: Industrial Policy and Structural Adjustment in the Japanese Economy 1970–80*. Stanford: Stanford University Press.

Dore, Ronald. 1987. *Taking Japan Seriously: A Confucian Perspective on Leading Economic Issues*. Stanford: Stanford University Press.

Dore, Ronald. 2000. *Stock Market Capitalism, Welfare Capitalism: Japan and Germany versus the Anglo-Saxons*. Oxford: Oxford University Press.

Dunsby, Megan. 2021. "25 Best Corporate Brands for Start-Ups to Work with Revealed." *Startups*, May 12, 2021. https://startups.co.uk/news/european-ranking-reveals-scale-of-corporate-startup-collaboration/.

Economist. 2013. "The Long Weekend." November 2, 2013.

Economist. 2018a. "American Tech Giants Are Making Life Tough for Startups." June 2, 2018.

Economist. 2018b. "Feeding Frenzy: Alibaba and Tencent Have Become China's Most Formidable Investors." August 2, 2018.

Economist. 2018c. "The Impact of Masayoshi Son's $100bn Tech Fund Will Be Profound." May 10, 2018.

Economist. 2020. "Can Zoom Be Trusted with Users' Secrets?" June 20, 2020.

Economist. 2023a. "Beneath France's Revolts, Hidden Success." July 27, 2023.

Economist. 2023b. "Foreign Investment in South Korea: Too Close for Comfort." July 1, 2023.

Economist. 2023c. "How to Make It Big in Xi Jinping's China." April 29, 2023.

Economist. 2023d. "Is Big Business Really Getting Too Big?" July 12, 2023.

Economist. 2024a. "The Chinese Communist Party Wants (a Bit) Less Consumer Internet." January 4, 2024.

Economist. 2024b. "An Influx of Chinese Cars Is Terrifying the West." January 11, 2024.

Edler, Jakob, and Jan Fagerberg. 2017. "Innovation Policy: What, Why and How." *Oxford Review of Economic Policy* 33, no. 1: 2–23. https://doi.org/10.1093/oxrep/grx001.

Edmondson, Duncan L., Florian Kern, and Karoline S. Rogge. 2019. "The Co-evolution of Policy Mixes and Socio-technical Systems: Toward a Conceptual Framework of Policy Mix Feedback in Sustainability Transitions." *Research Policy* 48, no. 10: 103555. https://doi.org/10.1016/j.respol.2018.03.010.

Engel, Jerome S. 2014. *Global Clusters of Innovation: Entrepreneurial Engines of Economic Growth around the World*. London: Edward Elgar.

Ergas, Henry. 1986. "Does Technology Policy Matter?" In *Technology and Global Industry: Companies and Nations in the World Economy*, edited by B. R. Guile and H. Brooks. 191–245. Washington, DC; National Academy.

European Commission. 1995. "Green Paper on Innovation." European Union. Accessed June 25, 2024. http://europa.eu/documents/comm/green_papers/pdf/com95_688_en.pdf.

European Commission. 2020. "EU and Japan Step Up Cooperation in Science, Technology and Innovation." European Commission, May 26, 2020. https://ec.europa.eu/info/news/eu-and-japan-step-cooperation-science-technology-and-innovation-2020-may-26_en.

European Venture Capital Association (EVCA). 2013. Tax Benchmark Study 2012 (June).

Evans, Peter. 1995. *Embedded Autonomy: States and Industrial Transformation*. Princeton, NJ: Princeton University Press.

Executive Yuan. 2001. Abstract of National Science and Development Plan (FY 2001 to FY 2004). Available at: https://www.nstc.gov.tw/nstc/attachments/defdb55d-7dda-4ef6-bac6-fc9c2a36e2a4. Accessed July 19, 2024.

Executive Yuan. 2005. National Science and Technology Development Plan (2005 to 2008). June 29, 2005. Taipei, National Science Council, Executive Yuan.

Executive Yuan. 2009. National Science and Technology Development Plan (2009–2012). July 2, 2009. Taipei, National Science Council, Executive Yuan.

Executive Yuan. 2019a. "Startup Terrace—Building an Innovative Future." November 22, 2019. https://english.ey.gov.tw/News3/9E5540D592A5FECD/558487e2-6280-43a0-a01a-19ebc033d0b1.

Executive Yuan. 2019b. "Taiwan Collaborates with Amazon Web Services to Aid SMEs and Startups." March 26, 2019. https://english.ey.gov.tw/Page/61BF20C3E89B856/e4085872-eeee-41d1-af7a-bad6f3624823.

Fahey, Rob. 2018. "Japan by the Numbers: Permanent Employment." *Tokyo Review*, April 6, 2018.

Fairlie, Robert W., Zachary Kroff, Javier Miranda, and Nikolas Zolas. 2023. *The Promise and Peril of Entrepreneurship: Job Creation and Survival among US Startups.* Cambridge, MA: MIT Press.

Falke, Mike. 2007. "China's New Law on Enterprise Bankruptcy: A Story with a Happy End?" *International Solvency Review* 16, no. 1: 63–74. https://doi.org/10.1002/iir.146.

Fannin, Rebecca A. 2008. *Silicon Dragon: How China Is Winning the Tech Race.* New York: McGraw Hill.

Farrell, Sean, and Julia Kollewe. 2016. "ARM Shareholders Approve SoftBank Takeover." *Guardian*, August 30, 2016. https://www.theguardian.com/business/2016/aug/30/arm-shareholders-softbank-takeover-tech-lord-myners.

Feld, Brad, and Jason Mendelson. 2013. *Venture Deals: Be Smarter Than Your Lawyer and Venture Capitalist.* New York: John Wiley.

Fields, Karl J. 1995. *Enterprise and the State in Korea and Taiwan.* Ithaca, NY: Cornell University Press.

Fields, Karl J. 1997. "Strong States and Business Organization in Korea and Taiwan." In *Business and the State in Developing Countries*, edited by Sylvia Maxfield and Ben Ross Schneider, 122–151. Ithaca, NY: Cornell University Press.

Fields, Karl J. 2012. "Not of a Piece: Developmental States, Industrial Policy, and Evolving Patterns of Capitalism in Japan, Korea, and Taiwan." In *East Asian Capitalism: Diversity, Continuity and Change*, edited by Andrew Walter and Xiaoke Zhang, 46–67. Oxford: Oxford University Press.

Fisher, Lucy. 2020a. "Approval for £1b Huawei Hub Triggers Washington Backlash." *The Times*, June 26, 2020. https://www.thetimes.co.uk/article/approval-for-1bn-huawei-hub-triggers-washington-backlash-52n57dw90.

Fisher, Lucy. 2020b. "Ministers Poised to Ban Huawei from 5G Network." *The Times*, July 10, 2020. https://www.thetimes.co.uk/article/decision-on-huaweis-role-in-5g-network-set-for-tuesday-j5ztpwz7b.

Fleckenstein, Timo, and Soohyun Christine Lee. 2017. "Democratization, Post-industrialization, and East Asian Welfare Capitalism: The Politics of Welfare State Reform in Japan, South Korea, and Taiwan." *Journal of International and Comparative Social Policy* 33, no. 1: 36–54. https://doi.org/10.1080/21699763.2017.1288158.

Fontana, Roberto, Arianna Martinelli, and Alessandro Nuvolari. 2021. "Regimes Reloaded! A Reappraisal of Schumpeterian Patterns of Innovation, 1977–2011." *Journal of Evolutionary Economics* 31: 1495–1519. https://doi.org/10.1007/s00191-021-00735-6.

Forbes Japan. 2018. "What Is the Ideal Startup that Will Support Japan in the Future? To Create Unicorns for 20 Companies by 2023." November 22, 2018. https://forbesjapan.com/articles/detail/24038/3/1/1.

Fortune. 2020. "Global 500." Accessed June 25, 2024. https://fortune.com/global500/.

Friedman, David. 1988. *The Misunderstood Miracle: Industrial Development and Political Change in Japan.* Ithaca, NY: Cornell University Press.

Fujisaki, Kotari. 2017. "Entrepreneurship Support That the Tokyo Metropolitan Government Will Also Focus On. Visit to TOKYO Founding Station." August 12, 2017.

Fulco, Matthew. 2015. "Taiwanese Startups: Making up for Lost Time." *AmCham Taiwan*, March 8, 2015. https://topics.amcham.com.tw/2015/03/taiwanese-startups-making-up-for-lost-time/.

Fuller, Douglas B. 2002. "Globalization for Nation Building: Industrial Policy for High-Technology Products in Taiwan." MIT Japan Working Paper 02.02.

Fuller, Douglas B., ed. 2010. *Innovation Policy and The Limits of Laissez-Faire*. New York: Palgrave MacMillan.

Fuller, Douglas B. 2013a. "Building Ladders Out of Chains: China's Hybrid-Led Technological Development in Disaggregated Value Chains." *Journal of Development Studies* 49, no. 4: 547–563. https://doi.org/10.1080/00220388.2012.733370.

Fuller, Douglas B., ed. 2013b. *Technology Transfer Between the US, China and Taiwan: Moving Knowledge*. London: Routledge.

Fuller, Douglas B. 2016. *Paper Tigers, Hidden Dragons: Firms and the Political Economy of China's Technology Development*. Oxford: Oxford University Press.

Fuller, Douglas B. 2019. "Growth, Upgrading, and Limited Catch-Up in China's Semiconductor Industry." In *Policy, Regulation and Innovation in China's Electricity and Telecom Industries*, edited by Loren Brandt and Thomas G. Rawski, 262–303. Cambridge, UK: Cambridge University Press.

Fuller, Douglas B. 2020. "The Increasing Irrelevance of Industrial Policy in Taiwan, 2016–2020." In *Taiwan during the first Administration of Tsai Ing-wen: Navigating in Stormy Waters*, edited by Gunter Schubert and Chun-yi Lee. 128–141. London: Routledge.

FutureWard. 2019. "What is TITAN? FutureWard's Involvement." August 13, 2019. https://futureward.com/en/what-is-titan/.

Gage, Deborah. 2012. "The Venture Capital Secret: 3 out of 4 Startups Fail." *Wall Street Journal*, September 20, 2012. https://www.wsj.com/articles/SB10000872396390443720204578004980476429190.

Gagne, Nana Okura. 2018. "'Correcting Capitalism': Changing Metrics and Meanings of Work Among Japanese Employees." *Journal of Contemporary Asia* 48, no. 1: 67–87. https://doi.org/10.1080/00472336.2017.1381984.

Gallagher, Kevin J. 2015. *Ruling Capital: Emerging Markets and the Reregulation of Cross-border Finance*. Ithaca, NY: Cornell University Press.

Garon, Sheldon. 1997. *Molding Japanese Minds: The State in Everyday Life*. Princeton, NJ: Princeton University Press.

Gerlach, Michael L. 1992. *Alliance Capitalism: The Social Organization of Japanese Business*. Berkeley: University of California Press.

Gilson, Ronald J., and Bernard S. Black. 1998. "Venture Capital and the Structure of Capital Markets: Banks Versus Stock Markets." *Journal of Financial Economics* 47: 243–277. https://doi.org/10.1016/S0304-405X(97)00045-7.

GIO (Government Information Office). 1986. *Republic of China: A Reference Book*. Taipei: Hilit Publishing Company Ltd.

Global Entrepreneurship Monitor (GEM). 2019. *Global Entrepreneurship Monitor 2019/ 2020 Global Report*. Accessed June 25, 2024. https://www.gemconsortium.org/file/open?fileId=50443.

Globerman, Steven, Mike W. Peng, and Daniel M. Shapiro. 2011. "Corporate Governance and Asian Companies." *Asia Pacific Journal of Management* 28, no. 1: 1–14. https://doi.org/10.1007/s10490-010-9240-6.

Gold, Thomas B. 1986. *State and Society in the Taiwan Miracle*. Armonk, NY: M. E. Sharpe.

Gonzalez-Uribe, Juanita, and Michael Leatherbee. 2018. "The Effects of Business Accelerators on Venture Performance: Evidence from Start-Up Chile." *Review of Financial Studies* 31, no. 4: 1566–1603. https://doi.org/10.1093/rfs/hhx103.

Goto, Akira. 2009. "Technology Policies in Japan: 1990 to the Present." In *21st Century Innovation Systems for Japan and the United States: Lessons from a Decade of Change*, edited by Sadao Nagaoka, Masayuki Kondo, Kenneth Flamm, and Charles Wessner. 29–39. Washington, DC: National Academies.

Goto, Yasuo, and Scott Wilbur. 2019. "Unfinished Business: Zombie Firms among SME in Japan's Lost Decades." *Japan and the World Economy* 49: 105–112. https://doi.org/10.1016/j.japwor.2018.09.007.

Gotoh, Fumihito, and Timothy J. Sinclair. 2017. "Social Norms Strike Back: Why American Financial Practices Failed in Japan." *Review of International Political Economy* 24, no. 6: 1030–1051. https://doi.org/10.1080/09692290.2017.1381983.

Graham, Edward M. 2003. *Reforming Korea's Industrial Conglomerates*. Washington, DC: Peterson Institute for International Economics.

Greene, J. Megan. 2008. *The Origins of the Developmental State in Taiwan*. Cambridge, MA: Harvard University Press.

Grimes, William W. 2001. *Unmaking the Japanese Miracle: Macroeconomic Politics 1985–2000*. Ithaca, NY: Cornell University Press.

Grove, Andy. 2010. "How American Can Create Jobs." July 1, 2010. https://www.bloomberg.com/news/articles/2010-07-01/andy-grove-how-america-can-create-jobs.

Gucbilmez, Ufuk. 2014. "Why Do Some Chinese Technology Firms Avoid ChiNext and Go Public in the US?" *International Review of Financial Analysis* 36: 179–194. https://doi.org/10.1016/j.irfa.2014.02.010.

Gulinello, Christopher. 2005. "Engineering a Venture Capital Market and the Effects of Government Control on Private Ordering: Lessons from the Taiwan Experience." *George Washington International Law Review* 37, no. 4: 845–883.

Haggard, Stephan. 1990. *Pathways from the Periphery: The Politics of Growth in the Newly Industrializing Countries*. Ithaca, NY: Cornell University Press.

Haggard, Stephan, and Yu Zheng. 2013. "Institutional Innovation and Investment in Taiwan." *Business and Politics* 15, no. 4: 435–466. https://doi.org/10.1515/bap-2012-0010.

Hahm, Seung Deuk, and L. Christopher Plein. 1995. "Institutions and Technological Development in Korea: The Role of the Presidency." *Comparative Politics* 28, no. 1: 55–76. https://doi.org/10.2307/421997.

Hai, Steven Jiawei, and Robyn Klingler-Vidra. 2022. "Chinese Blockchain: Convergence around a Beijing-Aligned Model." *Global Policy*, August 4, 2022. https://www.globalpolicyjournal.com/articles/science-and-technology/chinese-blockchain-convergence-around-beijing-aligned-strategy.

Hall, Peter. 1993. "Policy Paradigms, Social Learning, and the State: The Case of Economic Policymaking in Britain." *Comparative Politics* 25, no. 3: 275–296. https://doi.org/10.2307/422246.

Hall, Peter A., and David Soskice. 2001. "An Introduction to Varieties of Capitalism." In *Varieties of Capitalism: The Institutional Foundations of Comparative Advantage*, edited by Peter A. Hall and David Soskice, 1–71. Oxford: Oxford University Press.

Han, Heejin. 2015. "Korea's Pursuit of Low-Carbon Green Growth: A Middle-Power State's Dream of Becoming a Green Pioneer." *Pacific Review* 28, no. 5: 731–754. https://doi.org/10.1080/09512748.2015.1013491.

Hancke, Bob, ed. 2009. *Debating Varieties of Capitalism: A Reader*. Oxford: Oxford University Press.

Hancke, Bob, Martin Rhodes, and Mark Thatcher. 2007. "Introduction: Beyond Varieties of Capitalism." In *Beyond Varieties of Capitalism: Conflict, Contradictions, and Complementarities in the European Economy*, edited by Bob Hancke, Martin Rhodes, and Mark Thatcher, 3–38. Oxford: Oxford University Press.

Hanusch, Horst, and Andreas Pyka. 2007. "Principles of Neo-Schumpeterian Economics." *Cambridge Journal of Economics* 31, no. 2: 275–289. https://www.jstor.org/stable/23601693.

Harris, Bryan. 2019. "South Korea Pins Hopes on Startups to Power Economic Growth." *Financial Times*, January 31, 2019. https://www.ft.com/content/89875374-f6be-11e8-af46-2022a0b02a6c.

Harris, Mark. 2016. "Japan's Silicon Valley? Osaka Hopes Hi-tech Startups Will Reverse Economic Woes." *Guardian*, March 31, 2016. https://www.theguardian.com/sustainable-business/2016/mar/31/japan-silicon-valley-osaka-hi-tech-startups-reverse-economic-woes.

Hata, Nobuyuki, Haruhiko Ando, and Yoshiaki Ishii. 2007. "Venture Capital and Its Governance: The Emergence of Equity Financing Conduits in Japan." In *Corporate Governance in Japan: Institutional Change and Organizational Diversity*, edited by Masahiko Aoki, Gregory Jackson, and Hideaki Miyajima, 151–178. Oxford: Oxford University Press.

Hausman, Angela, and Wesley J. Johnston. 2014. "The Role of Innovation in Driving the Economy: Lessons from the Global Financial Crisis." *Journal of Business Research*, 67, no. 1: 2720–2726. https://doi.org/10.1016/j.jbusres.2013.03.021.

Hawksford. 2019. "Launch of the Science and Technology Innovation Board—STAR Market." September 5, 2019. https://www.hawksford.com/knowledge-hub/china-business-guides/launch-of-star-market.

Heberer, Thomas. 2016. "The Chinese 'Developmental State 3.0' and the Resilience of Authoritarianism." *Journal of Chinese Governance* 1, no. 4: 611–632. https://doi.org/10.1080/23812346.2016.1243905.

Hemmert, Martin, and Jae-Jin Kim. 2021. *Entrepreneurship in Korea: From Chaebols to Startups*. London: Routledge.

Heo, Uk, and Terrence Roehrig. 2014. *South Korea's Rise: Economic Development, Power, and Foreign Relations*. Cambridge, UK: Cambridge University Press.

Hirschman, Albert O. 1970. *Exit, Voice, and Loyalty: Responses to Decline in Firms, Organizations, and States*. Cambridge, MA: Harvard University Press.

Hirsh, Michael. 2023. "Does Japan's Economy Prove That Neoliberalism Lost?" *Foreign Policy*, September 14, 2023. https://foreignpolicy.com/2023/09/14/japan-economy-neoliberalism-east-asia-washington-consensus-imf/?tpcc=recirc_latest062921#cookie_message_anchor.

Hobday, Michael. 1995. *Innovation in East Asia: The Challenge to Japan*. Aldershot, UK: Edward Elgar.

Hofstede, Geert, and Michael Harris Bond. 1988. "The Confucius Connection: From Cultural Roots to Economic Growth." *Organizational Dynamics* 16, no. 4: 5–21. https://doi.org/10.1016/0090-2616(88)90009-5.

Holroyd, Carin. 2022. "Technological Innovation and Building a 'Super Smart' Society: Japan's Vision of Society 5.0." *Journal of Asian Public Policy* 15, no. 1: 18–31. https://doi.org/10.1080/17516234.2020.1749340.

Holzhausen, Arne. 2000. "Japanese Employment Practices in Transition: Promotion Policy and Compensation Schemes in the 1990s." *Social Sciences Japan Journal* 3: 221–235.

Horowitz, Jeremy. 2018. "South Korean Carriers Agree to Build Single 5G Network, Saving Money and Time." *Venture Beat*, April 11, 2018. https://venturebeat.com/mobile/korean-carriers-agree-to-build-single-5g-network-saving-money-and-time/.

Horwitz, Josh. 2015. "Taiwan Government to Invest in over $80 Million in Four VC Funds, Including 500 Startups." *TechinAsia*, January 26, 2015.

Horwitz, Josh. 2023. "China's Alibaba to Break Up Empire into Six Units, as Jack Ma Returns Home." *Financial Management*, March 29, 2023.

Hsieh, Michelle F. 2018. "South Korean SMEs and the Quest for an Innovation Economy." In *Strategic, Policy, and Social Innovation for a Post-Industrial Korea*, edited by Joon Nak Choi, Yong Suk Lee, and Gi-Wook Shin. 66–82. London: Routledge.

Hu, Krystal, and Jane Lee. 2023. "Exclusive: Kleiner Perkins Partner Wen Hsieh to Launch TSMC-Backed New Fund." Reuters, May 1, 2023. https://www.reuters.com/business/finance/kleiner-perkins-partner-wen-hsieh-launch-tsmc-backed-new-fund-sources-2023-05-01/.

Huang, Yasheng. 2008. *Capitalism with Chinese Characteristics: Entrepreneurship and the State*. Cambridge, UK: Cambridge University Press.

Huang, Yasheng. 2023. *The Rise and the Fall of the EAST: Examination, Autocracy, Stability, and Technology in Chinese History and Today*. New Haven, CT: Yale University Press.

Huang, Zhaojun, and Xuan Tian. 2020. "China's Venture Capital Market." In *The Handbook of China's Financial System*, edited by Amstad, Marlene, Guofeng Sun, and Wei Xiong, 383–420. Princeton, NJ: Princeton University Press.

Huergo, Elena, and Lourdes Moreno. 2017. "Subsidies or Loans? Evaluating the Impact of R&D Support Programs." *Research Policy* 46, no. 7: 1198–1214.

Hsu, Sara. 2021. "Introducing the New Beijing Stock Exchange China's Third Stock Exchange Is Geared Toward Financing Start-ups, but It Is Unlikely to Prevent Overseas Listings." *Diplomat*, November 8, 2021.

Huld, Arendse. 2021. "The New Beijing Stock Exchange for SMEs—What You Need to Know." *China Briefing*, November 18, 2021.

Huld, Arendse. 2023. "China's Start-up Landscape—Industries, Investment, and Incentive Policies." *China Briefing*, May 12, 2023.

Hundt, David. 2005. "A Legitimate Paradox: Neo-liberal Reform and the Return of the State in Korea." *Journal of Development Studies* 21, no. 2: 242–260.

Hundt, David. 2008. *Korea's Developmental Alliance: State, Capital, and the Politics of Rapid Development*. London: Routledge.

Hundt, David. 2014. "Economic Crisis in Korea and the Degraded Developmental State." *Australian Journal of International Affairs* 68, no. 5: 499–514.

Hundt, David, and Jitendra Uttam. 2017. *Varieties of Capitalism in Asia: Beyond the Developmental State*. London: Palgrave Macmillan.

Hwang, Kelley K. 1996. "South Korea's Bureaucracy and the Informal Politics of Economic Development." *Asian Survey* 36, no. 3: 306–319.

Hwang, Seunghyun. 2023. "Signs MOU on K-Bio Lab Hub." March 28, 2023. https://www.mss.go.kr/site/eng/ex/bbs/View.do?cbIdx=273&bcIdx=1040491.

Ibata-Arens, Kathryn. 2005. *Innovation and Entrepreneurship in Japan: Politics, Organizations, and High Technology Firms*. Cambridge, UK: Cambridge University Press.

Ibata-Arens, Kathryn. 2019. *Beyond Technonationalism: Biomedical Innovation and Entrepreneurship in Asia*. Redwood City, CA: Stanford University Press.

Ikeda, Masaru. 2018. "Japanese Government Unveils Action Plan to Create More Global Startup Unicorns." *Bridge*, June 21, 2018.

Im, Eun-byel. 2023. "10 Specialized Industrial Zones to be Designated to Spur Innovation." *Korea Herald*, May 8, 2023.

Inagaki, Kana. 2018. "Japanese Venture Capital Investment Hits Record Levels." *Financial Times*, March 1, 2018.

Inagaki, Kana. 2023. "Japan Seeks Revival as a Semiconductor Powerhouse." *Financial Times*, September 6, 2023.

Inagami, Takeshi. 2001. "From Industrial Relations to Investor Relations? Persistence and Change in Japanese Corporate Governance, Employment Practices, and Industrial Relations." *Social Science Japan Journal* 4: 225–241.

Incubate Fund. 2020. "A Future in which Venture Capital Plays a Leading Role in Reviving Japan. Why Akaura Wants to Increase the Number of Capitalists in Japan." *Zero to Impact Magazine*, April 16, 2020. https://m.incubatefund.com/media/why_more_vc_in_japan.

Intel. 2023. "Intel Ignite Launches First London Cohort." September 7, 2023. https://www.intel.com/content/www/us/en/newsroom/news/intel-ignite-first-london-cohort.html.

International Monetary Fund (IMF). 2016. *Chapter 2: Fiscal Policies for Innovation and Growth*. In *Fiscal Monitor*, April 2016. USA: International Monetary Fund. Accessed July 19, 2024, from https://doi.org/10.5089/9781513510590.089.ch002.

Itami, Hiroyuki. 2005. "Revision of the Commercial Code and Reform of the Japanese Corporate Governance." RIETI Discussion Papers. https://www.jil.go.jp/english/JLR/documents/2005/JLR05_itami.pdf. Accessed July 19, 2024.

ITRI. 2021. "ITRI Provides Resources for Innovative IC Design Startups in Taiwan with Arm." Accessed June 25, 2024. https://www.itri.org.tw/english/ListStyle.aspx?DisplayStyle=01_content&SiteID=1&MmmID=1037333533651512530&MGID=1127601230422570431.

Iwamoto, Kentaro. 2017. "ASEAN and Japan Aim to Foster Startups in Southeast Asia." *Nikkei Asian Review*, April 13, 2017.

Iwasaki, Kaori. 2016. "The Rising of Japanese Startups in Southeast Asia." *Pacific Business and Industries* 16, no. 62: 2–20.

Jackson, Gregory. 2003. "Corporate Governance in Germany and Japan: Liberalization Pressures and Responses during the 1990s." In *The End of Diversity? Prospects for German and Japanese Capitalism*, edited by Kozo Yamamura and Wolfgang Streeck, 261–305. Ithaca, NY: Cornell University Press.

Japan Cabinet Secretariat. 2022. "Startup Development Five-Year Plan." Accessed June 25, 2024. https://www.cas.go.jp/jp/seisaku/atarashii_sihonsyugi/pdf/sdfyplan2022en.pdf.

Japan Exchange Group. 2020. "History." Accessed June 25, 2024. https://www.jpx.co.jp/english/corporate/about-jpx/history/01-01.html.

Japan Times. 2021. "Japan to Extend Startup Investment Tax Break Program." https://www.japantimes.co.jp/news/2021/12/02/business/startup-tax-break/.

Jayasuriya, Kanishka. 2005. "Beyond Institutional Fetishism: From Developmental to the Regulatory State." *New Political Economy* 10, no. 3: 381–387.

Jeon, Yongil, and Stephen M. Miller. 2005. "Performance of Domestic and Foreign Banks: The Case of Korea and the Asian Financial Crisis." *Global Economic Review* 24, no. 2: 145–165.

JETRO. 2019. "Japan Ranked First in the Number of Innovation Outposts in Silicon Valley." October 15, 2019. https://www.jetro.go.jp/en/jgc/reports/2020/94ac3ce88d2518de.html.

JETRO. 2023. "Key Players in Japanese Innovation Ecosystem." March 27, 2023. https://www.jetro.go.jp/en/jgc/keyplayers.html.

Jia, Jepeng. 2018. "China's Plan to Recruit Talented Researchers." *Nature*, January 17, 2018.

Jia, Kai, and Martin Kenney. 2022. "The Chinese Platform Business Group: An Alternative to the Silicon Valley Model?" *Journal of Chinese Governance* 7, no. 1: 58–80.

Jing, Men. 2018. "Zhongguancun: Beijing's Innovation Hub Is at the Centre of China's Aim to Become a Tech Powerhouse." *South China Morning Post*, November 13, 2018.

Jinju, Jeon. 2020. "'TIPSX beSUCCESS Korean Startup Showcase @Silicon Valley' 2020 edition to be held on February 4 & 5." *Korea Tech Desk*, February 6, 2020. https://www.koreatechdesk.com/tipsx-besuccess-korean-startup-showcase-silicon-valley-2020-edition-to-be-held-on-february-4-5/.

Joh, Sung Wook. 2015. "Chaebols as Korean Entrepreneurship." In *Handbook of East Asian Entrepreneurship*, edited by Fu-Lai Tony Yu and Ho-Don Yan, 157–168. London: Routledge.

Johnson, Chalmers. 1982. *MITI and the Japanese Miracle: The Growth of Industrial Policy 1925–1975*. Palo Alto, CA: Stanford University Press.

Johnstone, Bob. 1999. *We Were Burning: Japanese Entrepreneurs and The Forging of The Electronic Age.*

Jones, Randall S., and Myungkyoo Kim. 2014. Promoting the Finance of SMEs and Startups in Korea. OECD Economics Department Working Paper 1162.

Jones, Randall S., and Jae Wan Lee. 2018. "Enhancing Dynamism in SMEs and Entrepreneurship in Korea." OECD Economics Department Working Paper 1510.

JST. 2019. "START: Program for Creating Startups from Advanced Research and Technology." [In Japanese]. https://www.jst.go.jp/start/index.html.

JST. 2020. "Industry-Academia Collaborative R&D Programs: Center of Innovation (CoI) Program." [In Japanese]. https://www.jst.go.jp/EN/programs/funding.html.

Juhász, Réka, Nathan Lane, and Dani Rodrik. 2023. "The New Economics of Industrial Policy." National Bureau of Economic Research Working Paper 31538. August.

Juhász, Réka, Shogo Sakabe, and David Weinstein. 2024. "Codification, Technology Absorption, and the Globalization of the Industrial Revolution." National Bureau of Economic Research Working Paper 32667. July.

Jung, Suk-yee. 2020. "Shinhan Financial Group Rapidly Expanding in Southeast Asia." *Business Korea*, January 31, 2020.

Jwa, Sung-Hee. 2002. *The Evolution of Large Corporations in Korea: A New Institutional Economics Perspective of the Chaebol*. Cheltenham, UK: Edward Elgar.

Kahn, Herman. 1979. *World Economic Development: 1979 and Beyond*. New York: William Morrow.

Kalinowski, Thomas. 1999. "The Politics of Market Reforms: Korea's Path from Chaebol Republic to Market Democracy and Back." *Contemporary Politics* 15, no. 3: 287–304.

Kalinowski, Thomas. 2008. "Korea's Recovery since the 1997/98 Financial Crisis: The Last Stage of the Developmental State." *New Political Economy* 13, no. 4: 447–462.

Kaneko, Ryoichi. 2022. "Japan: Insight and Pointers on Startup and Venture Investment in Japan for Foreign Investors." *Mondaq*, January 6, 2022. https://www.mondaq.com/shareholders/1147746/insight-and-pointers-on-startup-and-venture-investment-in-japan-for-foreign-investors.

Kang, Nahee. 2010. "Globalization and Institutional Change in the State-Led Model: The Case of Corporate Governance in South Korea." *New Political Economy* 15, no. 4: 519–542.

Kania, Elsa B. 2019. "Chinese Military Innovation in the AI Revolution." *RUSI Journal* 164, no. 5–6: 26–34.

Kantei. 2014. "Revision of Japan Revitalization Strategy: 10 Key Reforms." Accessed July 25, 2024. https://japan.kantei.go.jp/ongoingtopics/pdf/2014/1406242000_revision_jpn_revitalization.pdf.

Kato, Takao. 2001. "The End of Lifetime Employment in Japan? Evidence from National Surveys and Field Research." *Journal of the Japanese and International Economies* 15: 489–514.

Katz, Richard. 1998. *Japan, the System that Soured: The Rise and Fall of the Japanese Economic Miracle*. London: Routledge.

Kaur, Dashveenjit. 2021. "Chip Wars: Here's How China's SMIC Plans to Challenge Taiwan's TSMC." *Techwire Asia*, September 9, 2021.

Kawashima, Yutaka. 2005. *Japanese Foreign Policy at the Crossroads: Challenges and Options for the Twenty-First Century*. Washington, DC: Brookings Institution.

Kay, John. 2012. *The Kay Review of UK Equity Markets and Long-Term Decision Making*. London: UK Department of Business Innovation and Skills.

Keller, William W., and Richard J. Samuels. 2003. *Crisis and Innovation in Asian Technology*. Cambridge, UK: Cambridge University Press.

Ken, Ning. 2022. *Zhong Guan Village: Tales from the Heart of China's Silicon Valley*. London: ACA.

Kenney, Martin, Dan Breznitz, and Michael Murphree. 2013. "Coming Back Home after the Sun Rises: Returnee Entrepreneurs and Growth of High Tech Industries." *Research Policy* 42, no. 2: 391–407.

Kenney, Martin, Kyonghee Han, and Shoko Tanaka. 2002. "Scattering Geese: The Venture Capital Industries of East Asia, A Report to the World Bank." BRIE Working Paper, September 17, 2002, 100–105.

Kenney, Martin, Kyonghee Han, and Shoko Tanaka. 2004. "The Globalization of Venture Capital: The Cases of Taiwan and Japan." In *Financial Systems, Corporate Investment in Innovation, and Venture Capital*, edited by Anthony Bartzokas and Sunil Mani, chapter 4. Cheltenham, UK: Edward Elgar.

Kenney, Martin, John Zysman, and Dafna Bearson. 2020. "Transformation or Structural Change? What Polanyi Can Teach Us About the Platform Economy." *Sociologica* 14, no. 3: 227–240.

K-Growth. 2020. "Key Figures of K-Growth." https://eng.kgrowth.or.kr/main.asp. Accessed July 19, 2024.

Kim, Andrew Eungi, and Gil-sung Park. 2003. "Nationalism, Confucianism, Work Ethic and Industrialization in South Korea." *Journal of Contemporary Asia* 33, no. 1: 37–49.

Kim, Byung-Kook. 1992. "Economic Policy and the Economic Planning Board (EPB) in Korea." *Asian Affairs: An American Review* 18, no. 4: 197–213.

Kim, Chan-hyuk. 2020. "Drugmakers in Active Open Innovation with Startups." *Korea Biomedical Review*, August 25, 2020.

Kim, Dae-jung. 2019. *Conscience in Action: The Autobiography of Kim Dae-jung*. Translated by Seung-hee Jeon. London: Palgrave Macmillan.

Kim, Dong-Won, and Stuart W. Leslie. 1998. "Winning Markets of Winning Nobel Prizes? KAIST and the Challenges of Late Industrialization." *Osiris* 13: 154–185.

Kim, Eun Mee. 1988. "From Dominance to Symbiosis: State and Chaebol in Korea." *Pacific Focus* 3, no. 2: 105–121.

Kim, Eun Mee. 1997. *Big Business, Strong State: Collusion and Conflict in South Korean Development 1960–1990*. Albany: State University of New York Press.

Kim, Eun Mee, and Jiyoung Kim. 2005. "Developmental State vs. Globalization: South Korea's Developmental State in the Aftermath of the Asian Financial Crisis of 1997–98." *Korean Social Science Journal* 32, no. 2: 43–70.

Kim, Eunyoung. 2016. "Japanese Policy and Programs for the Fostering of Global Entrepreneurs." *STI Policy Review* 7, no. 1: 40–65.

Kim, Hyungjoo, Yong-Sook Lee, and Hye-Ran Hwang. 2014. "Regionalization of Planned S&T Parks: The Case of Daedeok S&T Park in Daejeon, South Korea." *Environment and Planning C: Government and Policy* 32, no. 5: 843–862.

Kim, Jae-fu. 2021. "NPS Selects Four Korean VCs to Invest 150 Bn Won." *Korea Economic Daily*, November 9, 2021.

Kim, Jae-heun. 2020. "Coupang Employes Third-Largest Number of Workers after Samsung, Hyungai." *Korea Times*, November 18, 2020.

Kim, Jaewon. 2020. "Startups vs Chaebol: Inside South Korea's Delivery Wars." *Nikkei Asian Review*, September 3, 2020.

Kim, Linsu, and Jeffrey B. Nugent. 1994. "The Republic of Korea's Small and Medium-Size Enterprises and Their Support Systems." World Bank Policy Research Working Paper 1404.

Kim, S. Ran. 1996. "The Korean System of Innovation and the Semiconductor Industry: A Governance Perspective." SPRU/SEI-Working Paper (December).

Kim, Sungwoong. 2010. "From Brain Drain to Brain Competition: Changing Opportunities and the Career Patterns of US-Trained Korean Academics." In *American Universities in a Global Market*, edited by Charles T. Clotfelter, 335–369. Chicago: University of Chicago Press.

Kim, Sung-Young. 2012. "Transitioning from Fast-Follower to Innovator: The Institutional Foundations of the Korean Telecommunications Sector." *Review of International Political Economy* 19, no. 1: 140–168.

Kim, Yujeong. 2023. "The Largest Festival of Women Entrepreneurs, with 2.95 Million Participants." July 10, 2023. https://www.korea.net/Government/Briefing-Room/Press-Releases/view?articleId=1043004&insttCode=A260117&type=N.

Kimura, Yui. 1997. "Technological Innovation and Competition in the Japanese Semiconductor Industry." In *Innovation in Japan*, edited by Akira Goto and Hiroyuki Odagiri, 121–158. Oxford: Oxford University Press.

King, Michael R. 2001. "Who Triggered the Asian Financial Crisis?" *Review of International Political Economy* 8, no. 3: 438–466.

Kirby, Carrie. 2002. "Q & A: STAN SHIH OF ACER Computing Success: Taiwanese Exec Discusses PC Industry, Links to Bay Area." *San Francisco Chronicle*, March 25, 2002.

KISED. 2021. "The Future of Korean Start-up Global Unicorn." https://www.k-unicorn.or.kr/eng/index.php.

Kitschelt, Herbert. 1991. "Industrial Governance Structures, Innovation Strategies and the Case of Japan: Sectoral or Cross-National Comparative Analysis." *International Organization* 45: 453–493.

Klingler-Vidra, Robyn. 2014. "The Public Venture Policy Menu: Policies Public Authorities Can Take." *Venture Findings* 1, no. 1: 36–42.

Klingler-Vidra, Robyn. 2016. "When Venture Capital is Patient Capital: Seed Funding as a Source of Patient Capital for High-Growth Companies." *Socio-Economic Review* 14, no. 4: 691–708. https://doi.org/10.1093/ser/mww022.

Klingler-Vidra, Robyn. 2018. *The Venture Capital State: The Silicon Valley Model in East Asia*. Ithaca, NY: Cornell University Press.

Klingler-Vidra, Robyn. 2023. "The Microchip Industry Would Implode if China Invaded Taiwan, and It Would Affect Everyone." *Conversation*, June 9, 2023. https://theconversation.com/the-microchip-industry-would-implode-if-china-invaded-taiwan-and-it-would-affect-everyone-206335.

Klingler-Vidra, Robyn and Steve Jiawei Hai. 2024. "China's Chip Industry Is Gaining Momentum—It Could Alter the Global Economic and Security Landscape." *Conversation,* February 13, 2024. https://theconversation.com/chinas-chip-industry

-is-gaining-momentum-it-could-alter-the-global-economic-and-security-landscape
-222958.

Klingler-Vidra, Robyn, and Adam W. Chalmers. 2023. "The Entrepreneurial University's Impact on Regional Socioeconomic Development: The 'Alumni Policymaker' Mechanism." *Business and Politics* 25, no. 3: 251–292. https://doi.org/10.1017/bap.2023.9.

Klingler-Vidra, Robyn, and Yu Ching Kuo. 2021. "Brexit, Supply Chains and the Contest for Supremacy: The Case of Taiwan and the Semiconductor Industry." In *Taiwan in an Age of Uncertainty*, edited by Chun-yi Lee and Michael Reilly, 183–203. Singapore: Springer.

Klingler-Vidra, Robyn, Alex Glennie, and Courtney Savie Lawrence. 2022. *Inclusive Innovation*. London: Routledge.

Klingler-Vidra, Robyn, Steven Jiawei Hai, Ye Liu, and Adam W. Chalmers. 2021. "Is the Jack Ma trajectory Unique? Assessing the Place-Based Hypothesis on Entrepreneurial Success." *Journal of Small Business & Entrepreneurship* 34, no. 4: 419–442. https://doi.org/10.1080/08276331.2021.1974236.

Klingler-Vidra, Robyn, Martin Kenney, and Dan Breznitz. 2016. "Policies for Financing Entrepreneurship through Venture Capital: Learning from the Successes of Israel and Taiwan." *International Journal of Innovation & Regional Development* 7, no. 3: 203–221.

Klingler-Vidra, Robyn, and Ye Liu. 2020. "Inclusive Innovation Policy as Social Capital Accumulation Strategy." *International Affairs* 96, no. 4: 1033–1050. https://doi.org/10.1093/ia/iiaa091.

Klingler-Vidra, Robyn, and Ramon Pacheco Pardo. 2019. "Beyond the *Chaebol*? The Social Purpose of Entrepreneurship Promotion in South Korea." *Asian Studies Review* 43, no. 4: 637–656. https://doi.org/10.1080/10357823.2019.1663576.

Klingler-Vidra, Robyn, and Ramon Pacheco Pardo. 2020. "Legitimate Social Purpose and South Korea's Support for Entrepreneurial Finance Since the Asian Financial Crisis." *New Political Economy* 25, no. 3: 337–353. https://doi.org/10.1080/13563467.2018.1563058.

Klingler-Vidra, Robyn, and Ramon Pacheco Pardo. 2022. "Bridging Developmental State and Entrepreneurial State Theory: A Typology of Startup Policies' Incumbent Firm Benefits." *Journal of Asian Public Policy* 1–17. https://doi.org/10.1080/17516234.2022.2132584.

Klingler-Vidra, Robyn, and Ramon Pacheco Pardo. 2024. "David Meets Goliath: Japan and Korea Make Startups Work with Large Conglomerates in a Twist on the Silicon Valley Model." *Fortune*, June 30, 2024. https://fortune.com/asia/2024/06/30/david-meets-goliath-japan-korea-make-startups-work-large-conglomerates-twist-silicon-valley/.

Klingler-Vidra, Robyn, and Robert H. Wade. 2020. "Science and Technology Policies and the Middle-Income Trap: Lessons from Vietnam." *Journal of Development Studies* 56, no. 4: 717–731. https://doi.org/10.1080/00220388.2019.1595598.

Kneller, Robert. 2007. *Bridging Islands: Venture Companies and the Future of Japanese and American Industry*. Oxford: Oxford University Press.

Knight, John B. 2014. "China as a Developmental State." *World Economy* 37, no. 10: 1335–1347.

Ko, Haksoo, and Hyun Young Shin. 1999. "Venture Capital in Korea? Special Law to Promote Venture Capital Companies." *American University International Law Review* 15, no. 2: 457–480.

Koh, Gillian. 1997. "Bureaucratic Rationality in an Evolving Developmental State: Challenges to Governance in Singapore." *Asian Journal of Political Science* 5, no. 2: 114–141. https://doi.org/10.1080/02185379708434108.

Koh, Winston T. H., and Poh Kam Wong. 2005. "The Venture Capital Industry in Singapore: A Comparative Study with Taiwan and Israel on the Government's Role." NUS Entrepreneurship Centre Working Paper, WP2005–09.

Kohli, Atul. 2004. *State-Directed Development: Political Power and Industrialization in the Global Periphery*. Cambridge, UK: Cambridge University Press.

KONEX. 2020. "Introduction to KONEX Market." Accessed June 25, 2024. http://konex.krx.co.kr/contents/OPN/01/01010301/OPN01010301.jsp.

Kong, Tat Yan. 2013. "Between Late-Industrialisation and Globalisation: The Hybridisation of Labor Relations among Leading South Korean Firms." *New Political Economy* 18, no. 5: 625–652.

Kong, Xavier. 2022. "500 Global Opens Doors for 2022 Taiwan Accelerator." *Tech in Asia*, June 1, 2022.

Kono, Shohei. 2023. "Japan Post Bank to Spend $7bn on Turning Startups into Unicorns." *Nikkei Asia*, June 20, 2023. https://asia.nikkei.com/Business/Startups/Japan-Post-Bank-to-spend-7bn-on-turning-startups-into-unicorns.

Koo, Richard C. 2009. *The Holy Grail of Macroeconomics: Lessons from Japan's Great Recession*. Singapore: John Wiley.

Korean Law Information Center. 2008. "Guarantee of Workers' Retirement Benefits Act." March 28, 2008. https://www.law.go.kr/LSW/lsInfoP.do?lsiSeq=86562&urlMode=engLsInfoR&viewCls=engLsInfoR#0000.

Korean Startup Ecosystem Forum. 2016. Korean Startup Ecosystem Forum White Paper Seoul, Korean Startup Ecosystem Forum.

KOSME. 2017. "School Introduction." [In Korean]. Accessed July 19, 2024. https://start.kosmes.or.kr/yh_ysi001_001.do.

KOSME. 2018. "Human Resource Development." Accessed July 19, 2024. https://www.kosmes.or.kr/sbc/SH/EHP/SHEHP012M0.do.

Kroeber, Arthur R. 2020. *China's Economy: What Everyone Needs to Know*. Oxford: Oxford University Press.

Krupp, Jason. 2012. "Private Equity Deal Signed with Taiwan." *Business Day*, October 17, 2012.

Kruppa, Miles, and Yuan Yang. 2020. "Alibaba Leads Chinese Retreat from Silicon Valley." *Financial Times*, February 10, 2020.

K-Startup. 2018. "Business Introduction." [In Korean]. Accessed July 19, 2024. https://www.k-startup.go.kr/.

Kume, Ikuo. 1998. *Disparaged Success: Labor Politics in Postwar Japan*. Ithaca, NY: Cornell University Press.

Kuo, Shirley W. Y. 1983. *The Taiwan Economy in Transition*. New York: Routledge.

Kuo, Tai-Chun, and Ramon H. Myers. 2011. *Taiwan's Economic Transformation: Leadership, Property Rights and Institutional Change 1949–1965*. London: Routledge.

Kuo, Yu-Ching, and Xiao Han. 2017. "Continuity and Change: Looking into the Future of Taiwan's Innovation and Entrepreneurship Policy." Paper presented at the Joint-Research Symposium on Smart Cities, Innovation and Entrepreneurship in Asia: Challenges and Opportunities, Hong Kong, April 20, 2017.

Kung, Shiann-Far and Yung-Chih Yen. 2018. "The Promotion of Startups in Tainan Technopolis." *World Technopolis Review* 7: 59–70.

Kushida, Kenji E. 2011. "Leading without Followers: How Politics and Market Dynamics Trapped Innovations in Japan's Domestic 'Galapagos' Telecommunications Sector." *Journal of Industry, Competition and Trade* 11, no. 3: 279–307.

Kushida, Kenji. 2018. "Departing from Silicon Valley: Japan's New Startup Ecosystem." In *Reinventing Japan: New Directions in Global Leadership*, edited by Martin Fackler and Yoichi Funabashi. Santa Barbara, CA: Praeger.

Kushida, Kenji. 2023. *The People Powering Japan's Startup Ecosystem*. Washington, DC: Carnegie Endowment for International Peace.

Kuzina, Viktoriya. 2018. "J-Startup Aims to Create Unicorns. *SME Japan*. Accessed July 22, 2024. https://www.smejapan.com/business-news/j-startup-aims-to-create-uni corns/.

KVIC. 2019. *KVIC MarketWatch. International Edition*, vol 1. Seoul: KVIC.

KVIC. 2024a. "Angel Fund of Funds." Accessed July 22, 2024. https://kvic.or.kr/en/busi ness/business5_1.

KVIC. 2024b. "Angel Investment Matching Fund." Accessed July 22, 2024. https://kvic .or.kr/en/matchingFund/matching1_1.

KVIC. 2024c. "Foreign VC Investment Fund." Accessed July 22, 2024. https://kvic.or.kr /en/business/business2_1.

KVIC. 2024d. "History." Accessed July 22, 2024. https://kvic.or.kr/en/company/com pany2_1.

KVIC. 2024e. "Job Creation Fund." Accessed July 22, 2024. https://kvic.or.kr/en/business /business3_1.

KVIC. 2024f. "Korea Fund of Funds." Accessed July 22, 2024. https://kvic.or.kr/en/busi ness/business1_1.

KVIC. 2023. "K-Unicorn Supporters." Accessed July 22, 2024. https://kvic.or.kr/k-uni corn/en/supporters/supporters1.

Kwong, Kai-Sun, Chau Leung-Chuen, Francis T. Lui, and Larry D. Qiu. 2001. *Industrial Development in Singapore, Taiwan and South Korea*. Singapore: World Scientific.

Kwong, Robin. 2009. "TSMC's Open Innovation Platform." *Financial Times*, June 21, 2009.

Lall, Sanjaya. 1996. *Learning from the Asian Tigers: Studies in Technology and Industrial Policy*. London: Macmillan.

Lall, Sanjaya. 1999. *Promoting Industrial Competitiveness in Developing Countries: Lessons from Asia*. London: Commonwealth Secretariat.

Lardy, Nicholas R. 2014. *Markets Over Mao: The Rise of Private Business in China*. New York: Columbia University Press.

Lardy, Nicholas R. 2019. *The State Strikes Back: The End of Economic Reform in China?* Washington, DC: Peterson Institute.

Larson, James F., and Jaemin Park. 2014. "From Developmental to Network State: Government Restructuring and ICT-Led Innovation in Korea." *Telecommunications Policy* 38, no. 4: 344–359.

Lee, Aileen. 2013. "Welcome to the Unicorn Club: Learning from Billion-Dollar Startups." *TechCrunch*, November 2, 2013. https://techcrunch.com/2013/11/02/welcome -to-the-unicorn-club.

Lee, David D. 2019. "US, Chinese Unicorns May Lead, but South Korea Shows It's Not a Two-Horse Race." *South China Morning Post*, June 3, 2019. https://www.scmp .com/week-asia/economics/article/3012681/us-chinese-unicorns-may-lead -south-korea-shows-its-not-two.

Lee, Ji-yoon. 2022. "Chaebol Groups, Startups Join Hands to Reshape Corporate Culture." *Korea Herald*, May 24, 2022.

Lee, Jong Won. 2006. "Industrial Policies, Chaebols, and Market Reform in Korea." *Journal of East Asian Affairs* 20, no. 1: 117–154.

Lee, Joonkoo, Jong-Cheol Kim, and Jinho Lim. 2016. "Globalization and Divergent Paths of Industrial Development: Mobile Phone Manufacturing in China, Japan, South Korea and Taiwan." *Journal of Contemporary Asia* 46, no. 2: 222–246.

Lee, June Y., and Jane Yeonjae Lee. 2020. "Female Transnational Entrepreneurs (FTEs): A Case Study of Korean American Female Entrepreneurs in Silicon Valley." *Journal of Entrepreneurship and Innovation in Emerging Economies* 6, no. 1: 67–83.

Lee, Kai-fu. 2018. *AI Superpowers: Silicon Valley, China and the New World Order*. Houghton Mifflin.

Lee, Keun. 2013. *Schumepterian Analysis of Economic Catch-up: Knowledge, Path-Creation, and the Middle-Income Trap*. Cambridge, UK: Cambridge University Press.

Lee, Keun. 2024. *Innovation-Development Detours for Latecomers: Managing Global-Local Interfaces in the De-Globalization Era*. Cambridge: Cambridge University Press.

Lee, Keun, Donghoon Hahn, and Justin Lin. 2002. "Is China Following the East Asian Model? A 'Comparative Institutional Analysis' Perspective." *China Review* 2, no. 1: 85–120.

Lee, Keun, and Hochul Shin. 2021. "Varieties of Capitalism and East Asia: Long-Term Evolution, Structural Change, and the End of East Asian Capitalism." *Structural Change and Economic Dynamics* 56: 431–437.

Lee, Kyung-min. 2020. "Chaebol to Own Corporate Venture Capital." *Korea Times*, July 30, 2020. https://www.koreatimes.co.kr/www/biz/2020/12/367_293651.html.

Lee, Lung-Sheng, and Chun-Chin Lai. 2005. "Technology Entrepreneurship Promoted by Universities' Incubation Centers in Taiwan: Its Successes and Challenges." Paper presented at the International Conference on Engineering Education 2005 (ICEE 2005), Gliwice, Poland, July 25–29, 2005.

Lee, Shin-Hyung. 2019. "Korean Shipbuilders Reclaim Global Top Spot." *Asia Times*, September 12, 2019.

Lee, Sung-eun. 2023. "Seoul Bets Big to Become Global 'Top 5' Startup City." *Korea JoongAng Daily*, June 21, 2023.

Lee, Wei-chen, and I-min Chang. 2014. "US Aid and Taiwan." *Asian Review of World Histories* 2, no. 1: 47–80.

Lehdonvirta, Vili. 2022. *Cloud Empires: How Digital Platforms Are Overtaking the State and How We Can Regain Control*. Cambridge, MA: MIT Press.

Lenschow, Andrea, Duncan Liefferink, and Sietske Veenman. 2005. "When the Birds Sing: A Framework for Analysing Domestic Factors behind Policy Convergence." *Journal of European Public Policy* 12, no. 5: 797–816.

Lerner, Josh. 2009. *Boulevard of Broken Dreams: Why Public Efforts to Boost Entrepreneurship and Venture Capital Have Failed—and What to Do About It*. Princeton, NJ: Princeton University Press.

Lerner, Josh, and Ramana Nanda. 2020. "Venture Capital's Role in Financing Innovation: What We Know and How Much We Still Need to Learn." *Journal of Economic Perspectives* 34, no. 3: 237–60.

Levy, Joaquim. 2000. "9 Reforms of Japan's Insolvency Laws." In *Post-Bubble Blues: How Japan Responded to Asset Price Collapse*, edited by Tamim Bayoumi and Charles Collyns. 200–227. Washington, DC: IMF.

Lewin, Arie Y., Martin Kenney, and Johann Peter Murmann. 2016. "China's Innovation Challenge: An Introduction." In *China's Innovation Challenge: Overcoming the Middle-Income Trap*, edited by Arie Y. Lewin, Martin Kenney, and Johann Peter Murmann, 1–31. Cambridge, UK: Cambridge University Press.

Li, Anthony Ho-fai. 2017. "E-commerce and Taobao Villages. A Promise for China's Rural Development." *China Perspectives* 3, no. 1: 57–62.

Li, Ji. 2018. *The Clash of Capitalisms? Chinese Companies in the United States*. Cambridge, UK: Cambridge University Press.

Li, Jizhen, Chengcheng Liu, and Elisabetta Gentile. 2020. *The Effects of the Innofund Program on Technology-Based SME's Performance: Evidence from Zhongguancun National Innovation Demonstration Zone (ZNID)*. Manila: Asian Development Bank.

Lie, John. 1998. *Han Unbound: The Political Economy of South Korea*. Stanford: Stanford University Press.

Lim, Harean. 2010. "The Transformation of the Developmental State and Economic Reform in Korea." *Journal of Contemporary Asia* 40, no. 2: 188–210.

Lim, Hyun-Chin, and Jin-Ho Jang. 2006. "Neo-liberalism in Post Crisis South Korea: Social Conditions and Outcomes." *Journal of Contemporary Asia* 36, no. 4: 442–463.

Lin, Justin Yifu, and Zhiqiang Liu. 2000. "Fiscal Decentralization and Economic Growth in China." *Economic Development and Cultural Change* 49, no. 1: 1–21.

Lin, Shu-yuan, and Frances Huang. 2010. "Service Center to Woo Foreign Investors to Begin Operations." *Taiwan News*, August 7, 2010. https://www.taiwannews.com.tw/en/news/1340946.

Lin, Syaru Shirley. 2021. "Taiwan in the High-Income Trap and Its Implications for Cross-Strait Relations." In *Taiwan's Economic and Diplomatic Challenges and Opportunities*, edited by Maria Thornton, Robert Ash, and Dafydd Fell, chapter 4. London: Routledge.

Liu, Cathy Yang, Lin Ye, and Bo Feng. 2019. "Migrant Entrepreneurship in China: Entrepreneurial Transition and Firm Performance." *Small Business Economics* 52, no. 3: 681–696.

Liu, Coco. 2022. "China Venture Funding Hits Record $131 Billion Despite Crackdown." Bloomberg, January 9, 2022. https://www.bloomberg.com/news/articles/2022-01-09/china-venture-funding-hits-record-131-billion-despite-crackdown.

Liu, Feng-chao, Denis Fred Simon, Yu-tao Sun, and Cong Gao. 2011. "China's Innovation Policies: Evolution, Institutional Structure, and Trajectory." *Research Policy* 40: 917–931.

Liu, Hong, and Els van Dongen. 2016. "China's Diaspora Policies as a New Mode of Transnational Governance." *Journal of Contemporary China* 25, no. 102: 805–821.

Liu, Luoyan, and Andrew Galbraith. 2020. "China Finalizes IPO Rules for Shenzhen's ChiNext Startup Board." Reuters, June 13, 2020.

Liu, Manhong Mannie. 2015. "Growing the Venture Dragon: China." *Coller Venture Review* 2: 112–122.

Liu, Zongyuan Zoe. 2023. "China's Pensions System Is Buckling Under an Aging Population." *Foreign Policy*, June 29, 2023. https://foreignpolicy.com/2023/06/29/china-pensions-aging-demographics-economy/.

Lockett, Hudson. 2019. "'China's Nasdaq': Shanghai's New Tech Trading Venue Explained." *Financial Times*, July 19, 2019.

Lockett, Hudson. 2020. "Alibaba Joins HK Stocks Benchmark in Changing of the Guard." *Financial Times*, August 14, 2020.

Lockett, Hudson. 2022. "How Xi Jingping Is Reshaping China's Capital Markets." *Financial Times*, June 12, 2022.

Lowery, Joseph, Johnny Jackson, and Marcia Layton Turner. 1998. *Netrepreneur: The Dimensions of Transferring Your Business Model to the Internet*. Indianapolis, IN: Que Publishing.

Lu, Hui. 2018. "China Focus: 40 Years On, Beijing's High-Tech Hub Remains Hotbed for Entrepreneurs." *Xinhua*, May 26, 2018.

Lu, Shen. 2022. "Didi Says It Will Proceed with Delisting From NYSE." *Wall Street Journal*, May 23, 2022.

Lucas, Louise. 2019. "New Wave of Chinese Tech Startups Focus on Overseas Markets." *Financial Times*, February 4, 2019.

Lundvall, Bengt-Ake. 1992. *National Systems of Innovation: Toward a Theory of Innovation and Interactive Learning*. London: Pinter.

Lynskey, Michael, and Seiichiro Yonekura. 2001. "Softbank: An Internet Keiretsu and Its Leveraging of Information Asymmetries." *European Management Journal* 19: 1–15.

Ma, Josephine. 2020. "What's It Like Working for Huawei? Employees Speak and Founder Ren Zhengfei Offers Some Metaphors." *South China Morning Post*, April 23, 2020.

Ma, Yuping, and Suyan Pan. 2015. "Chinese Returnees from Overseas Study: An Understanding of Brain Gain and Brain Circulation in the Age of Globalization." *Frontiers of Education in China* 10, no. 2: 306–329.

Mahoney, James, and Kathleen Thelen. 2010. "A Theory of Gradual Institutional Change." In *Explaining Institutional Change: Ambiguity, Agency and Power*, edited by James Mahoney and Kathleen Thelen, 1–37. Cambridge, UK: Cambridge University Press.

Malerba, Franco, and Luigi Orsenigo. 1995. "Schumpeterian Patterns of Innovation." *Cambridge Journal of Economics* 19, no. 1: 47–65.

Malerba, Franco, and Luigi Orsenigo. 1996. "Schumpeterian Patterns of Innovation Are Technology Specific." *Research Policy* 25, no. 3: 451–478.

Mallaby, Sebastian. 2022. *The Power Law: Venture Capital and the Art of Disruption*. New York: Penguin Random House.

Marr, Bernard. 2021. "China Poised To Dominate The Artificial Intelligence (AI) Market." *Forbes*, March 15, 2021.

Massoudi, Arash. 2017. "SoftBank Deals Held Up Before US Security Regulator." *Financial Times*, October 18, 2017.

Massoudi, Arash, James Fontanella-Khan, and Richard Waters. 2016. "SoftBank to acquire UK's Arm Holdings for £24.3bn." *Financial Times*, July 18, 2016.

Mathews, John A. 1997. "A Silicon Valley of the East: Creating Taiwan's Semiconductor Industry." *California Management Review* 39, no. 4: 26–54.

Matsugae, Yuka. 2018. "What Do Japanese Startups Need Now?" *JBpress Digital Innovation Review*, November 26, 2018. https://jbpress.ismedia.jp/articles/-/54733?page=2.

Mayer, Jorg. 2009. "Policy Space: What, for What and Where?" *Development Policy Review* 27, no. 4: 373–395.

Mazzucato, Mariana. 2013. *The Entrepreneurial State*. London: Anthem.

McCabe, David. 2023. "U.S. Accuses Amazon of Illegally Protecting Monopoly in Online Retail." *New York Times*, September 26, 2023.

McKnight, Scott, Martin Kenney, and Dan Breznitz. 2023. "Regulating the Platform Giants: Building and Governing China's Online Economy." *Policy & Internet*, March 13, 2023.

McMorrow, Ryan. 2020a. "Alibaba and Pinduoduo Surpass Sales Growth Expectations." *Financial Times*, May 22, 2020.

McMorrow, Ryan. 2020b. "China Startups Go Bust in 2019 'Capital Winter.'" *Financial Times*, January 6, 2020.

McMorrow, Ryan, George Hammond, Eleanor Olcott, and Kaye Wiggins. 2023. "Neil Shen Goes It Alone in China after Sequoia Split." *Financial Times*, June 9, 2023.

McMorrow, Ryan, and Joe Leahy. 2023. "China's Billionaires Back Xi Jinping's Plan to Restore Economy." *Financial Times*, July 20, 2023.

McMorrow, Ryan, and Nian Liu. 2020. "China Mobile Picks Huawei and ZTE to Build Its 5G Network." *Financial Times*, April 5, 2020.

McMorrow, Ryan, and Henny Sender. 2019. "Chinese Tech Startups Pursue Growth in Indian Market." *Financial Times*, December 1, 2019.

McMorrow, Ryan, Sun Yu, and Demetri Sevastopulo. 2023. "Dollar Funding for Chinese Start-ups Dries Up." *Financial Times*, February 18, 2023.

McNally, Christopher A. 2012. "Sino-Capitalism: China's Reemergence and the International Political Economy." *World Politics* 64, no. 4: 741–776.

Mendez, Andrew. 2023. "What Sony's Semiconductor Division Is Up To in San Jose." *Bay Area Inno*, October 6, 2023. https://www.bizjournals.com/sanfrancisco/inno/stories/news/2023/10/06/sony-semiconductor-san-jose-mark-hanson.html.

MEST. 2008. *Becoming an S&T Power Nation through the 577 Initiative. Science and Technology Basic Plan of the Lee Myung-bak Administration.* Seoul: MEST.

METI. 2003. "Supin Ofu Kenkyukai Hokoku-sho [Spin-Off Study Team Report]." Japan (April).

METI. 2014. "Venture Business Creation Council to be Established." Accessed October 24, 2020. https://www.meti.go.jp/english/press/2014/0917_02.html.

METI. 2018. "METI Launches New Initiative, "J-Startup" Program." Accessed May 14, 2020. https://www.meti.go.jp/english/press/2018/0611_003.html.

METI. 2020a. "First Steps in Asia DX Program—Meet Ups with Upcoming Indonesian Companies." February 3, 2020. https://www.meti.go.jp/english/press/2020/0203_004.html.

METI. 2020b. "Third Edition of the White Paper on Open Innovation Compiled." May 29, 2020. https://www.meti.go.jp/english/press/2020/0529_007.html.

METI. 2022. "Decision on Support for Four Temporary-Secondment Start-Ups." Accessed June 25, 2024. https://www.meti.go.jp/english/press/2022/0722_001.html.

METI. 2023. "METI Minister Nishimura Attends Meeting to Exchange Views with the Senior Executives of Global Semiconductor Companies." May 18, 2023. https://www.meti.go.jp/english/press/2023/0518_002.html.

METI. 2024. "Japan Startup Ecosystem." June 2024. Accessed July 25, 2024. https://www.meti.go.jp/policy/newbusiness/global_promotion.pdf.

METI Journal. 2020. "Growth Path Diversity Needed as Startup Ecosystem Takes Off." *Japan Times*, August 28, 2020. https://meti-journal.japantimes.co.jp/2020-08-28/.

MIIT. 2011. "12th Five-Year Plan on SME Growth." [In Chinese]. Accessed September 23, 2020. http://www.miit.gov.cn/n1146285/n1146352/n3054355/n3057267/n3057273/c3522119/content.html.

MIIT. 2022. "Development Results of Industry and Information Technology since the 18th CPC National Congress." China Internet Information Center, June 17, 2022.

Miller, Chris. 2022. *Chip War: The Fight for the World's Most Critical Technology.* New York: Simon & Schuster.

Mims, Christopher. 2023. "Is Big Tech's R&D Spending Actually Hurting Innovation in the U.S.?" *Wall Street Journal*, April 8, 2023. https://www.wsj.com/articles/is-big-techs-r-d-spending-actually-hurting-innovation-in-the-u-s-acfa004e.

Mind the Bridge. 2020. "Japanese Corporate Innovation in Silicon Valley: 2020 Report." Accessed June 25, 2024. https://mindthebridge.com/japanese-corporate-innovation-in-silicon-valley/.

Ministry of Education. 2010. "Measures for Accrediting University Students' Technology Entrepreneurship and Internship." http://www.moe.gov.cn/srcsite/A16/s3336/201004/t20100415_91770.html.

Ministry of Education. 2011. "CPC Organization Department, Ministry of Education, Ministry of Human Resources and Social Security and Central Committee of the Communist Youth League of China Regarding the Issuance of 'University Graduates Grassroots Nurturing Program Implementation Plan.'" http://www.moe.gov.cn/jyb_xxgk/moe_1777/moe_1779/201105/t20110530_124093.html.

Ministry of Finance. 2015. "Model Cities for Micro and Small Businesses Entrepreneurship and Innovation." Accessed September 9, 2020. http://www.mof.gov.cn/gp/xxgkml/jjjss/201505/t20150506_2512155.html.

Ministry of Human Resources and Social Security. 2001. "Measures for Administrating Overseas Students Entrepreneurship Parks." Accessed September 23, 2020. http://www.mohrss.gov.cn/gkml/zcfg/gfxwj/201407/t20140717_136319.html.

Ministry of Human Resources and Social Security. 2010. "University Students Entrepreneurship Guidance Program." Accessed September 23, 2020. http://www.mohrss.gov.cn/SYrlzyhshbzb/jiuye/zcwj/gaoxiaobiyesheng/201005/t20100505_86362.html.

Ministry of Labor and Employment of the Republic of Korea. 2013. [In Korean]. Access July 22, 2024. "What Is a Retirement Pension?" https://www.moel.go.kr/retirementpay.do.

Ministry of Science and Technology of Vietnam. 2017. "Regulation on Organization and Operation of Vietnam—Korea Institute of Science and Technology." March 22, 2017. https://www.most.gov.vn/en/pages/OrganDetail.aspx?tochucID=2749.

Minzer, Carl. 2018. *End of an Era: How China's Authoritarian Revival Is Undermining Its Rise*. Oxford: Oxford University Press.

Mitchell, Tom. 2022. "Why Xi Jinping Changed Tack in His Crackdown on Didi." *Financial Times*, July 21, 2022.

MoEA (Ministry of Economic Affairs) of the Republic of China. 2012. "Taiwan Signs Venture Capital Cooperation Agreement with New Zealand." March 14, 2012.

MoEA. 2014. "HeadStart Taiwan Project." National Development Council (August).

MoEA SME Administration. 2019a. "SME Online University." December 11, 2019. https://www.moeasmea.gov.tw/article-en-2618-4480.

MoEA SME Administration. 2019b. "Taiwan Entrepreneurship Ecosystem Foundational Service Integration Platform." Accessed January 27, 2022. https://www.moeasmea.gov.tw/article-en-2618-4479.

MoEA SME Administration. 2020. "Startup and Social Innovation." Accessed July 22, 2024. https://www.moeasmea.gov.tw/category-en-2459.

MoEA SME Administration. 2021. "Women Entrepreneurship Program." April 20, 2021. https://www.moeasmea.gov.tw/article-en-2618-4482.

MoEA SME Administration. 2023. "Taiwan Entrepreneur Visa." Ministry of Economic Affairs, May 10, 2023. https://www.moeasmea.gov.tw/article-en-2618-7911.

Mok, Ka Ho. 2013. "Promotion of Innovation and Knowledge Transfer: South Korean Experiences." In *The Quest for Entrepreneurial Universities in East Asia*, edited by Ka Ho Mok, 47–58. Basingstoke, UK: Palgrave Macmillan.

Mok, Ka Ho, and Xiao Fang Wu. 2013. "Dual Decentralization in China's Transition Economy: Welfare Regionalism and Policy Implications for Central-Local Relationship." *Policy and Society* 32, no. 1: 61–75.

Moon, Chung-in. 2009. "South Korea in 2008: From Crisis to Crisis." *Asian Survey* 49, no. 1: 120–128.

Moon, Mugyeong, and Ki-Seok Kim. 2001. "A Case of Korean Higher Education Reform: The Brain Korea 21 Project." *Asia Pacific Education Review* 2, no. 2: 96–105.

Moore, Martin, and Damian Tambini. 2021. *Regulating Big Tech: Policy Responses to Digital Dominance*. Oxford: Oxford University Press.

Morikawa, Hidemasa. 1992. *Zaibatsu: The Rise and Fall of the Family Enterprise Group in Japan*. Tokyo: University of Tokyo Press.

MoST (PRC). 2003. "Opinions on Further Improving the Operation of High-Tech Enterprise Incubators." Accessed September 9, 2020. http://www.most.gov.cn/fggw/zfwj/zfwj2003/200512/t20051214_54925.htm.

MoST (PRC). 2004. "Special Fund for SME Development." Accessed September 9, 2020. http://www.most.gov.cn/tjcw/tczcwj/200708/t20070813_52391.htm.

MoST (PRC). 2006a. "11th Five-Year Plan on Chinese Tech-Based Enterprise Incuba-tors." Accessed September 9, 2020. http://www.most.gov.cn/kjgh/kjfzgh/200708/t20070824_52686.htm.

MoST (PRC). 2006b. "11th Five-Year Plan on University Technology Parks." Accessed September 9, 2020. http://www.most.gov.cn/kjgh/kjfzgh/200708/t20070824_52688.htm.

MoST (PRC). 2006c. "Measures for Accrediting and Administering Tech-Based Enter-prise Incubators." Accessed September 23, 2020. http://www.most.gov.cn/ztzl/gjzctx/ptzckjcx/200802/t20080222_59218.htm.

MoST (PRC). 2017. "13th Five-Year Plan for the Development of National Enterprise S&T Enterprise Incubators." Accessed August 28, 2020. http://chinainnovationfunding.eu/dt_testimonials/13th-five-year-plan-for-the-development-of-national-st-enterprise-incubators/.

MoST and MOFCOM (PRC). 2017. "Several Measures for Promoting Innovation Development in Free-Trade Zones." Accessed August 29, 2020. http://chinainnovationfunding.eu/dt_testimonials/several-measures-for-promoting-innovation-development-in-free-trade-zones/.

MoST (ROC). 2017. "National Science and Technology Development Plan (2017–2020)." September 7, 2017. https://www.most.gov.tw/most/attachments/d29a7951-3e61-4bf8-bdbd-ebff3ddb9494.

MoST (ROC). 2021. "Taiwan's Ministry of Science and Technology Introduces Mentors from Silicon Valley, Paving the Way for Startups to Go Global." Accessed January 24, 2022. https://www.most.gov.tw/folksonomy/detail?subSite=&l=en&article_uid=7817c3ab-2af5-49fe-87f4-53abe7f21fde&menu_id=eb9eb136-4319-40d6-abd3-0788bea0d3a8.

Mowery, David C., and Bhaven N. Sampat. 2004. "The Bayh-Dole Act of 1980 and Uni-versity–Industry Technology Transfer: A Model for Other OECD Governments?" *Journal of Technology Transfer* 30: 115–127.

Mozur, Paul. 2016. "Obama Moves to Block Chinese Acquisition of a German Chip Maker." *New York Times DealBook*, December 2, 2016.

MSS. 2018. "Actively Foster Local SMEs in Non-metropolitan Areas." June 11, 2018. https://www.mss.go.kr/site/eng/mss/ex/bbs/View.do?cbIdx=244&bcIdx=1006824.

MSS. 2019a. "'Fund of Funds (FOF),' a Firm Assistant Leading the Innovative Growth of Startups and Ventures." May 27, 2019. https://www.mss.go.kr/site/eng/mss/ex/bbs/View.do?cbIdx=244&bcIdx=1012414&parentSeq=0.

MSS. 2019b. "Launch of 'SME Policy Deliberation Committee,' a Pan-Governmental Body to Manage SME Policies Comprehensively." https://www.mss.go.kr/site/eng/mss/ex/bbs/View.do?cbIdx=244&bcIdx=1011724&parentSeq=1011724.

MSS. 2019c. "To Expand Support for More StartUps and Solid Enterprises Led by Women." July 9, 2019. https://www.mss.go.kr/site/eng/mss/ex/bbs/View.do?cbIdx=244&bcIdx=1013127&parentSeq=1013127.

MSS. 2020. "Status of Korean SMEs." Accessed January 10, 2020. https://www.mss.go.kr/site/eng/02/10202000000002016111504.jsp.

Mukunda, Gautam. 2020. "'What's Good For GM Is Good For America'—What Should You Do During A National Crisis?" *Forbes*, June 5, 2020. https://www.forbes.com/sites/gautammukunda/2020/06/05/whats-good-for-gm-is-good-for-americawhat-should-you-do-during-a-national-crisis/.

Mulia, Khamila. 2021. "Taiwan Sets Sights to Become AI Hub, with Southeast Asia as Primary Market." *KrAsia*, February 25, 2021. https://kr-asia.com/taiwan-sets-sights-to-become-ai-hub-with-southeast-asia-as-primary-market.

Nagata, Kazuaki. 2023. "Japan Ramps Up Support for Startups Venturing Overseas." *Japan Times*, July 17, 2023. https://www.japantimes.co.jp/news/2023/07/17/busi ness/startups-overseas-success-initiatives/.

Nakabayashi, Yusuke. 2017. "Innovation Experience and Recommendation from Japan." Nomura Research Institute (NRI), June 1, 2017. https://boi.gov.ph/wp-content /uploads/2018/03/StartUps-and-the-Internet-of-Things-in-Japan-by-Yusuke -Nakabayashi.pdf.

National Bureau of Statistics of China. 2001. *China Statistical Yearbook 2001*. Beijing: China Statistics.

National Bureau of Statistics of China. 2013. *China Statistical Yearbook 2013*. Beijing: China Statistics.

National Bureau of Statistics of China. 2019. *China Statistical Yearbook 2019*. Beijing: China Statistics.

National Development Council (ROC). 2013. National Science and Technology Development Plan (2013–2016).

National Development Council (ROC). 2014. "HeadStart Taiwan: Regaining the Economic Momentum."

National Development Council (ROC). 2015. "Executive Yuan Approves the 'Contact Taiwan Program,' Redoubling the Effort to Attract Global Talent." September 14, 2015.

National Development Council (ROC). 2016. "Asia Silicon Valley Development Plan: From IT to IoT—Engineering a New Industrial Transformation for Taiwan."

National Development Council (ROC). 2017. "National Investment Company." Accessed June 25, 2024. https://www.ndc.gov.tw/en/cp.aspx?n=4BEEF51EB5F1EC40&s=2 54B0D7FCF14547D.

National Development Council (ROC). 2018. "Taiwan National Startup Brand." Accessed June 25, 2024. https://www.ndc.gov.tw/en/Content_List.aspx?n=7D09AF77A125 9036.

National Development Council (ROC). 2019. "Business Angel Investment Program National Development Fund, Executive Yuan." September 2, 2019.

National Research Council (US). 2013. *21st Century Manufacturing: The Role of Manufacturing Extension Partnership Program*. Washington, DC: National Academies.

National Research Foundation of Korea. 2017. "Business Introduction." Accessed January 13, 2020. https://bkplus.nrf.re.kr/sub01/sub101/list.do.

Naughton, Barry, and Kellee S. Tsai, eds. 2015. *State Capitalism, Institutional Adaptation, and the Chinese Miracle*. Cambridge, UK: Cambridge University Press.

NDRC. 2016. Notice of the Development and Reform Commission and Other Seven Departments on Promoting the Development of E-commerce." Accessed September 25, 2020. http://www.cac.gov.cn/2016-06/01/c_1118968390.htm.

NDRC and MoST. 2006. "National 'Eleventh Five-Year' Science and Technology Development Plan." Accessed September 25, 2020. http://most.gov.cn/kjgh/kjfzgh/200610 /t20061031_55485.htm.

Neate, Rupert. 2021. "AstraZeneca Vaccine Scientists Set for £22m Payday in New York Float." *Guardian*, April 7, 2021.

Nee, Victor, and Sonya Opper. 2012. *Capitalism from Below: Markets and Institutional Change in China*. Cambridge, MA: Harvard University Press.

Nelson, Richard R. 1988. "Institutions Supporting Technical Change in the United States." In *Technical Change and Economic Theory*, edited by Giovanni Dosi et al., 312–329. London: Pinter.

Nelson, Richard R., and Sidney G. Winter. 1982. *An Evolutionary Theory of Economic Change*. Cambridge, MA: Harvard University Press.

Newswitch. 2018. "The Current Location of Japanese Startups and Support Icons Talk." December 16, 2018. https://newswitch.jp/p/15681.

Nicholas, Tom. 2019. *VC: An American History*. Cambridge, MA: Harvard University Press.

Nicolas, Francoise. 2014. "China's Direct Investment in the European Union: Challenges and Policy Responses." *China Economic Journal* 7, no. 1: 103–125.

Nightingale, Paul, and Alex Coad. 2014. "Muppets and Gazelles: Political and Methodological Bases in Entrepreneurship Research." *Industrial and Corporate Change* 23, no. 1: 113–143.

Niiler, Eric. 2002. "US Wary of South Korean Plans for Californian Biocenter." *Nature Biotechnology* 20, no. 4: 321.

Nikkei Asia. 2022. "Japan to Subsidize TSMC's Kumamoto Plant by up to $3.5bn." June 17, 2022.

Nikkei Staff Writers. 2022. "Pension Giant GPIF to Invest in Japanese Startups for First Time." July 4, 2022.

Nikkei Staff Writers. 2023a. "On Topic: Japan Joins Asia Race for Global Talent." June 17, 2023.

Nikkei Staff Writers. 2023b. "Japan to Ease Stock-Option Tax Rules to Help Startups Gain Talent." August 28, 2023. https://asia.nikkei.com/Business/Startups/Japan-to-ease-stock-option-tax-rules-to-help-startups-gain-talent.

Nikkei Staff Writers. 2023c. "SoftBank Seeks Arm Valuation up to $52bn with Nasdaq Listing." September 5, 2023. https://asia.nikkei.com/Business/Markets/IPO/Soft Bank-seeks-Arm-valuation-up-to-52bn-with-Nasdaq-listing.

Niosi, Jorge. 2008. "Technology, Development and Innovation Systems: An Introduction." *Journal of Development Studies* 44, no. 5: 613–621.

Nishino, Anna. 2023. "Japan to Relax Rules for Startup Visas, Seeking Foreign Talent." May 17, 2023.

Nissan. 2018. "Nissan Joins Forces with Plug and Play Japan to Support Open Innovation." February 1, 2018. https://global.nissannews.com/en/releases/180201-03-e.

Njos, Rune, and Stig-Erik Jakobsen. 2016. "Cluster Policy and Regional Development: Scale, Scope and Renewal." *Regional Studies, Regional Science* 3, no. 1: 146–169.

Noble, Gregory W. 1998. *Collective Action in East Asia: How Ruling Parties Shape Industrial Policy*. Ithaca, NY: Cornell University Press.

Nolan, Jane, Chris Rowley, and Malcolm Warner. 2016. "Key Developments in Business Networks in East Asian Capitalisms: An Introduction." In *Business Networks in East Asian Capitalisms: Enduring Trends, Emerging Patterns*, edited by Jane Nolan, Chris Rowley, and Malcolm Warner, 1–14. London: Elsevier.

North, Douglass. 1990. *Institutions, Institutional Change and Economic Performance*. Cambridge, UK: Cambridge University Press.

Nystedt, Dan. 2010. "Taiwan Earthquake May Send LCD, Chip Prices Higher." *Computer World*, March 5, 2010. https://www.computerworld.com/article/2762847/taiwan-earthquake-may-send-lcd--chip-prices-higher.html.

Obe, Mitsuru. 2023a. "Japan Investor Group to Launch $14bn Toshiba Takeover Bid Tuesday." *Nikkei Asia*, August 7, 2023. https://asia.nikkei.com/Business/Business-deals/Japan-investor-group-to-launch-14bn-Toshiba-takeover-bid-Tuesday.

Obe, Mitsuru. 2023b. "As Toshiba Exits Market, Japan's Governance Reforms Remain Unfinished." *Nikkei Asia*, December 15, 2023. https://asia.nikkei.com/Business/Business-Spotlight/As-Toshiba-exits-market-Japan-s-governance-reforms-remain-unfinished.

OECD (Organization for Economic Co-operation and Development). 1997. *National Innovation Systems*. Paris: OECD.

OECD. 2007. *Innovation and Growth: Rationale for Innovation Strategy.* Paris: OECD.

OECD. 2010. *OECD Factbook 2010.* Paris: OECD.

OECD. 2014. *OECD Reviews of Innovation Policy. Industry and Technology Policies in Korea.* Paris: OECD.

OECD. 2020. "Gross Domestic Spending on R&D." Accessed June 25, 2024. https://data .oecd.org/rd/gross-domestic-spending-on-r-d.htm.

Oh, Seung-Youn. 2013. "Fragmented Liberalization in the Chinese Automotive Industry: The Political Logic of behind Beijing Hyundai's Success in the Chinese Market." *China Quarterly* 216: 920–945.

Okada, Yoshitaka. 2006. "Decline of the Japanese Semiconductor Industry: Institutional Restrictions and the Disintegration of Techno-Governance." In *Struggles for Survival,* edited by Y. Okada, 39–103. Tokyo: Springer.

O'Keeffe, Kate, Berber Jin, and Aruna Viswanatha. 2023. "Sequoia Made a Fortune Investing in the U.S. and China. Then It Had To Pick One." *Wall Street Journal,* June 27, 2023. https://www.wsj.com/articles/sequoia-made-a-fortune-investing -in-the-u-s-and-china-then-it-had-to-pick-one-f13e7b91.

Okimoto, Daniel. 1989. *Between MITI and the Market: Japanese Industrial Policy for High-Technology.* Stanford: Stanford University Press.

Okimoto, Daniel, Takuo Sugano, and Franklin B. Weinstein, eds. 1984. *The Competitive Edge: The Semiconductor Industry in the U.S. and Japan.* Stanford: Stanford University Press.

Ornston, Darius. 2018. *Good Governance Gone Bad: How Nordic Adaptability Leads to Excess.* Ithaca, NY: Cornell University Press.

Osaka Innovation Hub. 2020. "Startup Ecosystem: Osaka." Accessed June 25, 2024. https://www.innovation-osaka.jp/startup-ecosystem/.

Pacheco Pardo, Ramon. 2022. *Shrimp to Whale: South Korea from the Forgotten War to K-Pop.* London: C. Hurst.

Pacheco Pardo, Ramon, and Robyn Klingler-Vidra. 2019. "The Entrepreneurial Developmental State: What Is the Perceived Impact of South Korea's Creative Economy Action Plan on Entrepreneurial Activity?" *Asian Studies Review* 43, no. 2: 313–331.

Pacheco Pardo, Ramon, and Robyn Klingler-Vidra. 2024. "The Secret to Japanese and South Korean Innovation: How Tokyo and Seoul Partner with Startups—and What Silicon Valley Can Learn." *Foreign Affairs,* May 7, 2024. https://www.for eignaffairs.com/japan/secret-japanese-and-south-korean-innovation.

Pacheco Pardo, Ramon, Jan Knoerich, and Yuanfang Li. 2019. "The Role of London and Frankfurt in Supporting the Internationalization of the Renminbi." *New Political Economy* 24, no. 4: 530–545.

Pacheco Pardo, Ramon, and Jeong-ho Lee. 2020. "South Korea's COVID-19 Success: The Role of Advanced Preparations." KF-VUB Korea Chair Policy Brief. May 28, 2020. https://csds.vub.be/wp-content/uploads/2023/08/South-Koreas-COVID-19 -Success.pdf.

Pacheco Pardo, Ramon, and Pradumna B. Rana. 2015. "Complementarity between Regional and Global Financial Governance Institutions: The Case of ASEAN+3 and the Global Financial Safety Net." *Global Governance: A Review of Multilateralisms* 21, no. 3: 413–433.

Palmer, Scott. 1983. "Panic in Silicon Valley: The Semiconductor Industry's Cry for Help." *Cato Institute Policy Analysis,* no. 31. December 21, 1983. https://www .cato.org/sites/cato.org/files/pubs/pdf/pa031.pdf.

Pan, Che, Iris Deng, and Bien Perez. 2023. "Tech War: Huawei Helps China Win 'Symbolic' Victory in Defying Washington's Sanctions with Mate 60 Pro but Head-

winds Remain." *South China Morning Post*, September 5, 2023. https://www
.scmp.com/tech/tech-war/article/3233514/tech-war-huawei-helps-china-win
-symbolic-victory-defying-washingtons-sanctions-headwinds-remain.

Pan, Fenghua, Fangzhu Zhang, and Fulong Wu. 2021. "State-Led Financialization in
China: The Case of the Government-Guided Investment Fund." *China Quarterly*
247: 749–772.

Pandey, I. M., and Angela Jang. 1996. "Venture Capital for Financing Technology in
Taiwan." *Technovation* 16, no. 9.

Park, Chisung, Jooha Lee, and Changho Chung. 2015. "Is 'Legitimized' Policy Always Successful? Policy Legitimacy and Cultural Policy in Korea." *Policy Sciences* 48: 319–338.

Park, Edward. J. W. 2009. "Korean Americans and the U.S. High Technology Industry:
From Ethnicity to Transnationalism." In *Korean American Economy & Community in the 21st Century*, edited by E. Y. You, H. Kim, K. Park, and M. D. Oh,
293–314. Los Angeles: Korean American Economic Development Center.

Park, Gene. 2004. "The Political-Economic Dimension of Pensions: The Case of Japan."
Governance 17: 549–72.

Park, Hong Y., Geon-Cheol Shin, and Sung Hahn Shu. 2008. "Advantages and Short-
comings of Korean Chaebols." *International Business & Economics Research Journal* 7, no. 1. https://doi.org/10.19030/iber.v7i1.3210.

Park, Ju-min, and Hyunjoo Jin. 2018. "No Uber or Airbnb in South Korea—Red tape,
Risk-Aversion Hobble Startups." Reuters, December 17, 2018.

Park, Kate. 2023. "6 Investors Explain Why They Are Bullish about Japan's Startup Scene
Despite an Uncertain Economy." *TechCrunch*, June 5, 2023. https://techcrunch
.com/2023/06/05/japan-investor-survey/.

Park, Sam Ock, and Do Chai Chung. 2014. "The Evolution of an Industrial Cluster and
Its Policy Framework: The Case of Gumi City, Korea." In *Architects of Growth:
Sub-National Governments and Industrialization in Asia*, edited by Francis E.
Hutchinson, 279–304. Singapore: ISEAS.

Park, Shinok. 1996. "Korean Entrepreneurship in Silicon Valley." International Policy
Studies (June).

Park, Yong Soo. 2011. "Revisiting the Korean Developmental State after the 1997 Financial Crisis." *Australian Journal of International Affairs* 65, no. 5: 590–606.

Pearson, Margaret M., Meg Rithmire, and Kellee Tsai. 2023. *The State and Capitalism in
China*. Cambridge, UK: Cambridge University Press.

Pekkanen, Robert. 2004. "After the Developmental State: Civil Society in Japan." *Journal
of East Asian Studies* 4, no. 3: 363–388.

Pempel, T. J. 1982. *Policy and Politics in Japan: Creative Conservatism*. Philadelphia:
Temple University Press.

Pempel, T. J. 1998. *Regime Shift: Comparative Dynamics of the Japanese Political Economy*. Ithaca, NY: Cornell University Press.

Pempel, T. J. 2021. *A Region of Regimes: Prosperity and Plunder in the Asia-Pacific*.
Ithaca, NY: Cornell University Press.

Pempel, T. J., and Keiichi Tsunekawa (eds.). 2015. *Two Crises, Different Outcomes: East
Asia and Global Finance*. Ithaca, NY: Cornell University Press.

Peng, Lifang, Jen-Her Wu, Yi-Cheng Chen, and Chun Cheng. 2019. "The Performance
and Value Creation of E-commerce Ecosystems in Rural China: A Perspective of
Systems Theory." Paper presented at the Twenty-Third Pacific Asia Conference
on Information Systems, China.

Peng. Yaya. 2011. "A Review of 'Going out' Strategy's 10 Years: Achievements and Challenges." *Contemporary International Relations*, no. 8 (August): 77–78.

Perez, Carlota. 2002. *Technological Revolutions and Financial Capital: The Dynamics of Bubbles and Golden Ages.* Cheltenham, UK: Edward Elgar.

Perez, Carlota. 2016. "Capitalism, Technology and a Green Global Golden Age: The Role of History in Helping to Shape the Future." In *Rethinking Capitalism: Economics and Policy for Sustainable and Inclusive Growth*, edited by Michael Jacobs and Mariana Mazzucato, 191–217. Chichester, UK: Wiley Blackwell.

Perren, Lew, and Jonathan Sapsed. 2013. Innovation as Politics: The Rise and Reshaping of Innovation in UK Parliamentary Discourse 1960–2005. *Research Policy* 42, no. 10: 1815–1828.

Pesek, William. 2023. "Alibaba Share Sale a Sign of SoftBank Trouble." *Asia Times*, April 15, 2023.

Peters, Michael, and Fabrizio Zilibotti. 2023. "Creative Destruction, Distance to Frontier, and Economic Development." In *The Economics of Creative Destruction: New Research on Themes from Aghion and Howit*, edited by Ufuk Akcigit and John Van Reenen, 475–519. Cambridge, MA: Harvard University Press.

Pettis, Michael. 2013. *Avoiding the Fall: China's Economic Restructuring.* Washington, DC: Brookings Institution.

Pham, Cong S., Xuan Nguyen, Pasquale Sgro, and Xueli Tang. 2016. "Has China Displaced Its Competitors in High-Tech Trade?" *World Economy* 40, no. 8: 1569–1596.

Phang, Hanam. 2010. "Building Private and Occupational Pension Schemes in Korea." In *Retirement, Work and Pensions in Ageing Korea*, edited by Jae-jin Yang and Thomas R. Klassen, 96–108. Abingdon, UK: Routledge.

Philippon, Thomas. 2019. *The Great Reversal: How America Gave Up on Free Markets.* Cambridge, MA: Belknap/Harvard University Press.

Pierson, Paul. 2000. "Increasing Returns, Path Dependence and the Study of Politics." *American Political Science Review* 94, no. 2: 251–267.

Pirie, Iain. 2005. "The New Korean State." *New Political Economy* 10, no. 1: 25–42.

Pirie, Iain. 2018. "Korea and Taiwan: The Crisis of Investment-Led Growth and the End of the Developmental State." *Journal of Contemporary Asia* 48, no. 1: 133–158.

PKF. 2015. *Japan Tax Guide: 2015/16.* Accessed October 26, 2020. https://www.pkf.com/media/10026008/japan-tax-guide-2015-16.pdf.

Plantin, Jean-Christophe, and Gabriele de Seta. 2019. "WeChat as Infrastructure: The Techno-Nationalist Shaping of Chinese Digital Platforms." *Chinese Journal of Communication* 12, no. 3: 257–273.

Porter, Michael E. 1998. *Competitive Advantage: Creating and Sustaining Superior Performance.* New York: Free Press.

Porter, Michael E., Hirotaka Takeuchi, and Mariko Sakakibata. 2000. *Can Japan Compete?* Cambridge, MA: Perseus.

Provan, Sarah. 2019. "Huawei to Build Chip Plant Near Arm Holdings HQ in Cambridge." *Financial Times*, May 4, 2019.

Pulse News. 2023. "Korean Government Packages $7.9 bn Aids for Startups with Liquidity Bottleneck." *Maeil Business News Korea*, April 21, 2023.

Qing, Koh Gui, and Salvador Rodriguez. 2018. "In Silicon Valley, Chinese 'Accelerators' Aim to Bring Startups Home." Reuters, May 17, 2018. https://ca.reuters.com/article/businessNews/idCAKCN1II0UG-OCABS.

Qu, Tracy, and Ann Cao. 2023. "Former Alibaba CEO Daniel Zhang Steps Down from Cloud Unit in Surprise Exit amid Leadership Transition." *South China Morning Post*, September 11, 2023. https://www.scmp.com/tech/big-tech/article/3234066/former-alibaba-ceo-daniel-zhang-steps-down-cloud-unit-surprise-move-amid-leadership-transition?module=more_top_stories_int&pgtype=homepage.

Rahman, K. Sabeel., and Kathleen Thelen. 2019. "The Rise of the Platform Business Model and the Transformation of Twenty-First-Century Capitalism." *Politics & Society* 47, no. 2: 177–204.

Rajan, Ramkishen S. 2012. "Managing of Exchange Rate Regimes in Emerging Asia." *Review of Development Finance* 2, no. 2: 53–68.

Rao, Madanmohan. 2020. "Startup Guide Tokyo: How This Global Tech Hub Is Reinventing Itself for a New Wave of Entrepreneurs." March 11, 2020. https://your story.com/2020/03/startup-guide-tokyo-book-review.

Reslinger, Coralie. 2013. "Is There an Asian Model of Technological Emergence?" *Socio-Economic Review* 11, no. 2: 371–408.

Rethel, Lena. 2010. "The New Financial Development Paradigm and Asian Bond Markets." *New Political Economy* 15, no. 4: 493–517.

Richardson, Bradley M. 1997. *Japanese Democracy: Power, Coordination, and Performance.* New Haven, CT: Yale University Press.

Rigby, John, and Ronnie Ramlogan. 2013. "The Impact and Effectiveness of Entrepreneurship Policy." Nesta Working Paper 13/01.

Rithmire, Meg, and Hao Chen. 2021. "The Emergence of Mafia-like Business Systems in China." *China Quarterly.*

Rivera, Fernando Moncada. 2023. "CVC Unplugged: Why Microsoft Changed How It Invests in Startups." Global Corporate Venturing, September 11, 2023. https:// globalventuring.com/corporate/information-technology/cvc-unplugged-why -microsoft-changed-how-it-invests-in-startups/.

Robertson, Justin. 2007. "Reconsidering American Interests in Emerging Market Crises: An Unanticipated Outcome to the Asian Financial Crisis." *Review of International Political Economy* 14, no. 2: 276–305.

Robertson, Justin. 2010. "Private Equity and Asian Political Economy: 'Domestic' Private Equity Funds and New Actors." *Asian Survey* 50, no. 2: 356–377.

Rodrik, Dani, Arvind Subramanian, and Francesco Trebbi. 2002. "Institutions Rule: The Primacy of Institutions over Geography and Integration in Economic Development." NBER Working Paper Series 9305.

Roland, Gerard. 2023. "Socialism, Capitalism, State Capitalism, and Innovation." In *The Economics of Creative Destruction: New Research on Themes from Aghion and Howitt,* edited by Ufuk Akcigit and John Van Reenen, 520–532. Cambridge, MA: Harvard University Press.

Rowen, Henry S., and A. Maria Toyoda. 2002. "From *Keiretsu* to Startups: Japan's Push for High Tech Entrepreneurship." Asia/Pacific Research Center (October).

Rozelle, Scott, and Natalie Hell. 2020. *Invisible China: How the Urban-Rural Divide Threatens China's Rise.* Chicago: University of Chicago Press.

Rubinstein, Murray A. 2013. "The Evolution of Taiwan's Economic Miracle 1945–2000: Personal Accounts and Political Narratives." In *Technology Transfer Between the US, China and Taiwan: Moving Knowledge,* edited by Douglas Fuller, 25–46. London: Routledge.

Ruehl, Mercedes. 2019. "China VC Investment in South-East Asia Surges Fourfold." *Financial Times,* July 10, 2019.

Ruehl, Mercedes. 2020. "US Blacklisting Fails to Derail Ambitions of Chinese AI Startups." *Financial Times,* July 29, 2020.

Russell, Jon. 2019. "500 Startup Japan Becomes Coral Capital with a New $45M Fund." *TechCrunch,* March 5, 2019.

Ryan, Maria. 2022. "Taiwan Dominates the World's Supply of Computer Chips—No Wonder the US Is Worried." *Conversation,* August 4, 2022. https://theconversa

tion.com/taiwan-dominates-the-worlds-supply-of-computer-chips-no-wonder -the-us-is-worried-188242.

Salmon, Andrew. 2019. "As Unicorns Spawn, South Korea's Anti-entrepreneurial Practices Evaporate." *Asia Times*, June 8, 2019.

Samsung. 2018. "Three New Projects Spin Off from Samsung Electronics' C-Lab." Samsung Newsroom, June 6, 2018.

Samuels, Richard J. 2008. *Securing Japan: Tokyo's Grand Strategy and the Future of East Asia*. Ithaca, NY: Cornell University Press.

Samuels, Richard J. 2019. *Special Duty: A History of the Japanese Intelligence Community*. Ithaca, NY: Cornell University Press.

Sandulli, Francesco D., Jose Fernandez-Menendez, Antonio Rodriquez-Duarte, and Jose Ignacio Lopez-Sanchez. 2012. "Testing the Schumpeterian Hypothesis on an Open Innovation Framework." *Management Decision* 50, no. 7: 1222–1232.

Satoh, Ryohtaroh. 2023. "Aging Japan Wants Foreign Workers, but Will They Come?" *Nikkei Asia*, June 13, 2023.

Sauvant, Kari P., and Victor Zitian Chen. 2014. "China's Regulatory Framework for Outward Foreign Direct Investment." *China Economic Journal* 7, no. 1:141–163.

Saxenian, AnnaLee. 2002. "Transnational Communities and the Evolution of Global Production Networks: The Cases of Taiwan, China, and India." *Industry & Innovation* 9, no. 3: 183–202.

Saxenian, AnnaLee. 2006. *The New Argonauts: Regional Advantage in a Global Economy*. Cambridge, MA: Harvard University Press.

Saxenian, AnnaLee, and Chuen-Yueh Li. 2002. "Bay-to-Bay Strategic Alliances: The Network Linkages between Taiwan and the US Venture Capital Industries." *International Journal of Technology Management* 25, no. 1-2: 136–150.

Saxenian, AnnaLee, and Jinn-Yuh Hsu. 2001. "The Silicon Valley-Hsinchu Connection: Technical Communities and Industrial Upgrading." *Industrial and Corporate Change* 10, no. 4: 893–920.

Scarlatoiu, Greg. 2012. "Low Carbon, Green Growth Korea." In *Korean Science and Technology in an International Perspective*, edited by Jorg Mahlich and Werner Pascha, 239–258. Heidelberg: Springer.

Schaede, Ulrike. 2020. *The Business Reinvention of Japan: How to Make Sense of the New Japan and Why It Matters*. Palo Alto, CA: Stanford Business.

Scharpf, Fritz. 1999. *Governing in Europe: Effective and Democratic?* Oxford: Oxford University Press.

Schneider, Ben Ross. 2013. *Hierarchical Capitalism in Latin America: Business, Labor, and the Challenges of Equitable Development*. Cambridge, UK: Cambridge University Press.

Schoof, Ulrich. 2006. "Stimulating Youth Entrepreneurship: Barriers and Incentives to Enterprise Startups by Young People." SEED Working Paper 76.

Schoppa, Leonard J. 2006. *Race for the Exits: The Unraveling of Japan's System of Social Protection*. Ithaca, NY: Cornell University Press.

Schot, Johan, and W. Edward Steinmueller. 2018. "Three Frames for Innovation Policy: R&D, Systems of Innovation and Transformative Change." *Research Policy* 47, no. 9: 1554–1567.

Schuller, Margot, Marcus Conle, and David Shim. 2012. "Korean Innovation Governance under Lee Myung-Bak—A Critical Analysis of Governmental Actor's New Division of Labor." In *Korean Science and Technology in an International Perspective*, edited by Jorg Mahlich and Werner Pascha, 109–128. Heidelberg: Springer.

Schumacher, E. F. 1973. *Small Is Beautiful: A Study of Economics As If People Mattered*. New York: Vintage.

Schumpeter, Joseph. 1934. *The Theory of Economic Development*. Cambridge, MA: Harvard University Press.

Schumpeter, Joseph. 1942. *Capitalism, Socialism, and Democracy*. New York: Harper.

Schumpeter, Joseph. 1947. "The Creative Response in Economic History." *Journal of Economic History* 7, no. 2: 149–159.

Schwab, Klaus. 2021. *Stakeholder Capitalism: A Global Economy That Works for Progress, People and Planet*. Hoboken, NJ: John Wiley.

Segal, Adam. 2003. *Digital Dragon: High-Technology Enterprises in China*. Ithaca, NY: Cornell University Press.

Seki, Tomohiro. 2008. "What Are the SME Policies and Measures in Japan? The Outline of SME Promotion Policies in Japan." *JAIRO* 44, no. 1: 173–190.

Sender, Henny. 2019. "Leading China Health Tech Startup Ensnared by Cfius [Committee on Foreign Investment in the United States]." *Financial Times*, May 22, 2019.

Senor, Dan, and Saul Singer. 2009. *Startup Nation: The Story of Israel's Economic Miracle*. New York: Hachette.

Seong, Jieun, and Wichin Song. 2008. "Innovation Policy and Administration System in the Era of Post Catch-up: The Case of the Roh Moo-hyun Administration's Innovation Policy." *Asian Journal of Technology Innovation* 16, no. 2: 25–46.

Seoul Metropolitan Government. 2019. "Seoul to Establish a Fast Track to Become One of the Global Top Five Cities of Startup." April 4, 2019. http://english.seoul.go.kr/seoul-to-establish-a-fast-track-to-become-one-of-the-global-top-five-cities-of-startup/.

Sharif, Naubahar, and Yu Huang. 2019. "Industrial Automation in China's 'Workshop of the World.'" *China Journal* 81: 1–22.

Sheahan, Maria. 2016. "China's Fujian Drops Aixtron Bid after Obama Blocks Deal." Reuters, December 8, 2016.

Shih, Victor. 2020. "Financial Liberalization in China: The Contradiction Between Opening and Guaranteed Outcomes." *China Leadership Monitor*, March 1, 2020.

Shih, Victor. 2022. *Coalition of the Weak: Elite Politics in China from Mao's Stratagem to the Rise of Xi*. Cambridge, UK: Cambridge University Press.

Shin, Ha-Nee. 2023. "Venture Firms, Government Create $6.2 Billion Fund for Startups." *Korea JoongAng Daily*, July 24, 2023. https://koreajoongangdaily.joins.com/2023/07/24/business/economy/Korea-Venture-capital-CVC/20230724155009100.html.

Shivakumar, Sujai, Charles Wessner, and Thomas Howell. 2023. "Japan Seeks to Revitalize its Semiconductor Industry." Center for Strategic & International Studies, August 25, 2023. https://www.csis.org/analysis/japan-seeks-revitalize-its-semiconductor-industry.

Silicon Catalyst. 2021. "Silicon Catalyst Partners with Sony Semiconductor Solutions to Accelerate Semiconductor Startups." November 29, 2021. https://siliconcatalyst.com/silicon-catalyst-partners-with-sony-semiconductor-solutions-to-accelerate-semiconductor-startups.

Sim, Dewey. 2019. "How Chinese Money Is Driving Southeast Asia's Tech Startup Scene." *South China Morning Post*, October 6, 2019.

Simon, Denis Fred, and Merle Goldman, eds. 1989. *Science and Technology in Post-Mao China*. Cambridge, MA: Harvard University Press.

Simon, Denis Fred, and Michael Y. M. Kau. 1992. *Taiwan: Beyond the Economic Miracle*. London: Routledge.

Sivan, Yesha. 2014. "The Venture Ecosystem Framework: Messy, Fast, and Global." *Coller Venture Review* 1: 6–18.

REFERENCES 217

SK Telecom. 2011. *Partner for New Possibilities. 2011 SK Telecom Sustainability Report.* Seoul: SK Telecom.

Slodkowski, Antoni. 2022. "SoftBank Cuts Top Executives' Pay after Vision Fund Posts Record Loss." *Financial Times*, May 30, 2022.

Slodkowski, Antoni, and Eri Sugiura. 2022. "Japan to Tap Vast Pension Fund in Drive to Create More Start-Ups." *Financial Times*, June 10, 2022.

Smart, Alan, and Jinn-Yuh Hsu. 2014. "The Chinese Diaspora, Foreign Investment and Economic Development in China." *Review of International Affairs* 3, no. 4: 544–566.

Sohn, JiAe. 2017. "President Emphasizes 'People-Centered Fourth Industrial Revolution.'" *Cheong Wa Dae*, October 12, 2017.

Song, Jesook. 2009. *South Koreans in the Debt Crisis: The Creation of a Neoliberal Welfare Society.* Durham, NC: Duke University Press.

Song, Ligang. 2018. "State-Owned Enterprise Reform in China." In *China's 40 Years of Reform and Development: 1978–2018*, edited by Ross Garnaut, Ligang Song, and Cai Fang, 345–374. Canberra: ANU University Press.

Soni, Jimmy. 2022. *The Founders: Elon Musk, Peter Thiel and the Company that Made the Modern Internet.* New York: Atlantic.

Srnicek, Nick. 2016. *Platform Capitalism.* Cambridge, UK: Polity.

Stancati, Margherita, Mayumi Negishi, and Nicolas Parasie. 2017. "SoftBank, Saudis Launch $100 Billion Tech Fund." *Wall Street Journal*, May 2017.

Standing Committee of the National People's Congress. 2001. Trademark Law of the People's Republic of China (2001 Amendment). Accessed June 26, 2024. http://www.lawinfochina.com/display.aspx?lib=law&id=2107.

Standing Committee of the National People's Congress. 2002a. Law of the People's Republic of China on Popularization of Science and Technology. Accessed September 9, 2020. https://en.ustc.edu.cn/2011/0510/c5381a49673/pagem.htm.

Standing Committee of the National People's Congress. 2002b. Law of the People's Republic of China on the Promotion of Small and Medium-Sized Enterprises. Accessed June 26, 2024. http://www.lawinfochina.com/display.aspx?lib=law&id=2385&CGid=7.

STAR. 2020. "Overview." Accessed June 26, 2024. http://star.sse.com.cn/star/en/getting started/overview/.

Startup Genome. 2020. *The Global Startup Ecosystem Report GSER 2020*: 165–166.

Startup Genome. 2022. *The Global Startup Ecosystem Report GSER 2022.*

State Council Information Office of the PRC. 2016. "SCIO Press Conference on Stabilizing Industry Growth and Readjusting Structure." Accessed June 26, 2024. http://www.scio.gov.cn/32618/Document/1469891/1469891.htm.

State Council of the PRC. 2008. "Guiding Opinions on Promoting Employment through Entrepreneurship." [In Chinese.] Accessed June 26, 2024. http://www.gov.cn/gongbao/content/2008/content_1139413.htm.

State Council of the PRC. 2014. "Notice on the Plan for Deepening the Reform of Management of Centrally-Financed S&T Projects." [In Chinese.] Accessed June 26, 2024. http://www.gov.cn/zhengce/content/2015-01/12/content_9383.htm.

State Council of the PRC. 2015a. "Opinion on Several Policies and Measures to Vigorously Advance the Mass Entrepreneurship and Innovation Initiative." [In Chinese.] Accessed June 26, 2024. http://www.gov.cn/zhengce/content/2015-06/16/content_9855.htm.

State Council of the PRC. 2015b. "Opinion of the State Council on Furthering the Work on Employment and Entrepreneurship under New Conditions." [In Chinese.] Accessed June 26, 2024. http://www.gov.cn/zhengce/content/2018-09/26/content_5325472.htm.

State Council of the PRC. 2016a. "China's High-Tech Innovation Catching Up with Silicon Valley." August 6, 2016. http://english.www.gov.cn/news/top_news/2016/08/05/content_281475409885715.htm.

State Council of the PRC. 2016b. "Provisions Concerning the Establishment of Foreign-Funded Venture Capital Enterprises." [In Chinese.] Accessed June 26, 2024. http://www.gov.cn/zhengce/2016-03/15/content_5053562.htm.

State Council of the PRC. 2018. "Opinions on Promoting the High-Quality Development and the Establishment of an Upgraded Version of 'Mass Innovation and Entrepreneurship.'" [In Chinese.] Accessed June 26, 2024. http://www.gov.cn/zhengce/content/2018-09/26/content_5325472.htm.

State Council of the PRC. 2019. "Premier Stresses Mass Entrepreneurship and Innovation." June 13, 2019. http://english.www.gov.cn/premier/news/2019/06/13/content_281476713826116.htm.

State Development Planning Commission and MoST. 2001. "The State Planning Commission and the Ministry of Science and Technology Issued the National Economic and the Tenth Five-Year Plan for Social Development Special Plan (Science and Technology Development Plan) Notice." [In Chinese.] Accessed June 26, 2024. http://www.gov.cn/gongbao/content/2002/content_61374.htm.

Storz, Cornelia, Bruno Amable, Steven Casper, and Sebastien Lechevalier. 2013. "Bringing Asia into the Comparative Capitalism Perspective." *Socio-Economic Review* 11, no. 2: 217–232.

Storz, Cornelia, and Sebastian Schafer. 2011. *Institutional Diversity and Innovation: Continuing and Emerging Patterns in Japan and China*. London: Routledge.

Streeck, Wolfgang. 2009. *Re-Forming Capitalism: Institutional Change in the German Political Economy*. Oxford: Oxford University Press.

Streeck, Wolfgang, and Kozo Yamamura. 2003. "Introduction: Convergence or Divergence? Stability and Change in German and Japanese Capitalism." In *The End of Diversity? Prospects, for German and Japanese Capitalism*, edited by Wolfgang Streeck and Kozo Yamamura, 1–50. Ithaca, NY: Cornell University Press.

Stubbs, Richard. 2009. "What Ever Happened to the East Asian Developmental State? The Unfolding Debate." *Pacific Review* 29, no. 1: 1–22.

Stubbs, Richard. 2012. "The East Asian Developmental State and the Great Recession: Evolving Contesting Coalitions." In *East Asia and the Global Crisis*, edited by Shaun Breslin, 43–58. London: Routledge.

Stubbs, Richard. 2017. "The Origins of East Asia's Developmental States and the Pressures for Change." In *Asia after the Developmental State: Disembedding Autonomy*, edited by Toby Carroll and Darryl S. L. Jarvis, 51–71. Cambridge, UK: Cambridge University Press.

Studwell, Joe. 2014. *How Asia Works: Success and Failure in the World's Most Dynamic Region*. London: Profile.

Su, Fubing, Ran Tao, and Dail L. Yang. 2018. "Rethinking the Institutional Foundations of China's Hypergrowth: Official Incentives, Institutional Constraints, and Local Developmentalism." In *The Oxford Handbook of the Politics of Development*, edited by Carol Lancaster and Nicolas van de Walle, 626–651. Oxford: Oxford University Press.

Suchard, Jo-Ann, Mark Humphrey-Jenner, and Xiaping Cao. 2021. "Government Ownership and Venture Capital in China." *Journal of Banking & Finance* 129: 106–164.

Sugihara, Junichi. 2022. "Japan's Top Business Lobby Wants to See 100 Unicorns by 2027." *Nikkei Asia*, March 12, 2022.

Sugihara, Kaoru. 2004. "East Asian Path." *Economic & Political Weekly* 39, no. 34: 21–27.

Sugita, Yoneyuki. 2016. "The Yoshida Doctrine as a Myth." *Japanese Journal of American Studies* 27: 123–143.

Sull, Donald. 2005. *Made in China: What Western Managers Can Learn from Trailblazing Chinese Entrepreneurs*. Cambridge, MA: Harvard Business Review.

Sumitomo Corporation. 2021. "Selected as 'Noteworthy DX Company 2021' and 'DX Certified Business Operator.'" June 7, 2021. https://www.sumitomocorp.com/en /jp/news/topics/2021/group/20210607.

Sumitomo Corporation. 2022. "Promoting Cutting-Edge Innovation through Collaboration with Startups." Accessed June 26, 2024. https://www.sumitomocorp.com /en/europe/business/case/group/presidio.

Summers, Tim. 2018. *China's Regions in an Era of Globalization*. London: Routledge.

Sung, Chang-Yong, Ki-Chan Kim, and Sunyoung In. 2016. "Small and Medium-Sized Enterprises Policy in Korea from the 1960s to the 2000s and Beyond." *Small Enterprise Research* 23, no. 3: 262–275.

Suzuki, Kenjiro, and Narushi Nakai. 2022. "Japan's Midcareer Job Seekers Flock to Startups." *Nikkei Asia*, March 13, 2022.

Suzuki, Wataru. 2018. "Silicon Valley Wants to Groom Next Chinese Unicorn—in China." *Nikkei Review*, October 23, 2018.

Suzuki, Wataru. 2022. "Japan Startups See Kishida's 'New Capitalism' as Road without Map." *Nikkei Asia*, June 21, 2022.

Swanson, Ana. 2023. "Biden to Restrict Investments in China, Citing National Security Threats." *New York Times*, August 8, 2023. https://www.nytimes.com/2023 /08/08/business/economy/biden-china-companies-restrictions.html?smid= nytcore-ios-share&referringSource=articleShare.

Symons, Tom. 2015. "Startups Get Less than 3% of Government Spending, This Must Change." *Guardian*, August 19, 2015.

SZSE. 2020. "About ChiNext." Accessed June 26, 2024. http://www.szse.cn/English /products/equity/ChiNext/index.html.

Taipei Exchange. 2022. "The Introduction to the Emerging Stock Market." Accessed June 26, 2024. https://www.tpex.org.tw/web/regular_emerging/apply_way/stan dard/intro.php?l=en-us.

Taipei Times. 2017. "President Tsai Responds to Morris Chang Criticism." October 4, 2017.

TAITRA. 2020. "Taiwan Startup Ecosystem Map." August 10, 2020. https://london.tai wantrade.com/news/detail?id=30207.

Takeuchi, Kosuke. 2023. "Japan to Remove Limit on Overseas Investment by Startup Funds." *Nikkei Asia*, January 23, 2023.

Takeuchi, Yusuke. 2019. "Japan to Help Channel Capital into Southeast Asia Inc." *Nikkei Asian Review*, November 6, 2019.

Takeuchi, Yusuke. 2022. "Japan Seeks to Boost Startup Economy with New Cabinet Post." *Nikkei Asia*, July 4, 2022.

Tan, Felix Ter Chian, Shan L. Pan, and Lili Cui. 2016. "IT-Enabled Social Innovation in China's Taobao Villages: The Role of Netrepreneurs." Paper presented at the Thirty Seventh International Conference on Information Systems, Dublin.

Tate, John Jay. 1995. *Driving Production Innovation Home: Guardian State Capitalism and the Competitiveness of the Japanese Automobile Industry*. Berkeley, CA: Berkeley Roundtable on the International Economy.

Taylor, Mark Zachary. 2004. "Empirical Evidence against Varieties of Capitalism's Theory of Technological Innovation." *International Organization* 58, no. 3: 601–631.

Taylor, Mark Zachary. 2016. *The Politics of Innovation: Why Some Countries Are Better Than Others at Science and Technology*. Oxford: Oxford University Press.

Tech Incubation Program for Startup (Korea). 2022. "Partners and Accelerators." Accessed June 26, 2024. http://www.jointips.or.kr/bbs/board.php?bo_table=eng_company.

Tepper, Jonathan. 2023. *The Myth of Capitalism: Monopolies and the Death of Competition.* Hoboken, NJ: Wiley.

Thelen, Kathleen. 2018. "Regulating Uber: The Politics of the Platform Economy in Europe and the United States." *Perspectives on Politics* 16, no. 4: 938–953.

Thelen, Kathleen, and James Mahoney. 2015. "Comparative-Historical Analysis in Contemporary Political Science." In *Advances in Comparative-Historical Analysis*, edited by James Mahoney and Kathleen Thelen, 3–37. Cambridge, UK: Cambridge University Press.

Thomas, Christopher A. 2021. "Lagging but Motivated: The State of China's Semiconductor Industry." *Brookings Institute: Tech Stream*, January 7, 2021.

Thomas, Leigh. 2020a. "France to Tighten Controls on Non-EU Foreign Investment." Reuters, April 29, 2020.

Thomas, Owen. 2020b. "SoftBank Has Pumped Up Silicon Valley Twice. Will We Ever Learn?" *San Francisco Chronicle*, January 8, 2020.

Thorbecke, Willem. 2023. *The East Asian Electronics Sector.* Cambridge, UK: Cambridge Elements.

Thorsen, Anna. 2019. "Why Is China Investing So Much in Europe?" *Valuer*, February 12, 2019. https://www.valuer.ai/blog/why-is-china-investing-so-much-in-europe.

Thurbon, Elizabeth. 2016. *Developmental Mindset: The Revival of Financial Activism in Korea.* Ithaca, NY: Cornell University Press.

Thurbon, Elizabeth, Sung-Young Kim, Hao Tan, and John A. Matthews. 2023. *Developmental Environmentalism: State Ambition and Creative Destruction in East Asia's Green Energy Transition.* Oxford: Oxford University Press.

Thurbon, Elizabeth, and Linda Weiss. 2006. "Investing in Openness: The Evolution of FDI Strategy in South Korea and Taiwan." *New Political Economy* 11, no. 1: 1–22.

Thurbon, Elizabeth, and Linda Weiss. 2021. "Economic Statecraft at the Frontier: Korea's Drive for Intelligent Robotics." *Review of International Political Economy* 28, no. 1: 103–127.

Tiberghien, Yves. 2007. *Entrepreneurial States: Reforming Corporate Governance in France, Japan, and Korea.* Ithaca, NY: Cornell University Press.

Tipton, Frank B. 2009. "Southeast Asian Capitalism: History, Institutions, States, and Firms." *Asia Pacific Journal of Management* 26, no. 3: 401–434.

Titcomb, James. 2019. "The Trade War Silicon Valley Should Be Worried about Isn't Between the US and China." *Daily Telegraph*, July 29, 2019.

To, Yvette. 2023. "Friends and Foes: Rethinking the Party and Chinese Big Tech." *New Political Economy* 28, no. 2: 299–314.

Tokyo Metropolitan Government. 2023. "Outbound Program." [In Japanese.] Accessed June 26, 2024. https://www.x-hub-tokyo.metro.tokyo.lg.jp/outbound_program.

Tong, Sarah Y., and Wan Jing. 2017. *China's Economy in Transformation under the New Normal.* Singapore: World Scientific.

Toto, Serkan. 2008. "Why Yahoo Japan Is Worth Nearly As Much As Yahoo." *TechCrunch*, August 24, 2008.

Toyota. 2023. "Toyota Open Labs Launches to Connect Innovative Startups with Global Opportunities for a Sustainable Future." August 29, 2023. https://newsroom.toyota.eu/toyota-open-labs-launches-to-connect-innovative-startups-with-global-opportunities-for-a-sustainable-future/.

Tsai, Kellee. 2002. *Back-Alley Banking: Private Entrepreneurs in China.* Ithaca, NY: Cornell University Press.

Tsai, Kuen-Hung, and Jiann-Chyuan Wang. 2004. "The Innovation Policy and Performance of Innovation in Taiwan's Technology-Intensive Industries." *Problems and Perspectives in Management*. 2, no. 1: 62–75.

Tsai, Lucas. 2022. "TSMC: Enabling Startups to Unleash New Semiconductor Innovation." *TSMC Blog*, April 18, 2022. https://www.tsmc.com/english/news-events /blog-article-20220418.

Tsai, Pan-Long. 1999. "Explaining Taiwan's Economic Miracle: Are the Revisionists Right?" *Agenda: A Journal of Policy Analysis and Reform* 6, no. 1: 69–82.

Tsuchikawa, Gen. 2020. Sony Innovation Fund Presentation. Global Corporate Venturing, June 4, 2020.

Tyler, Patrick E. 1995. "Chen Yun, Who Slowed China's Shift to Market, Dies at 89." *New York Times*, April 12, 1995.

Uesugi, Iichiro. 2006. "SME Financing in Japan: What We Have Found." Research Institute of Economy, Trade and Industry, 2006/01 Research & Review.

UNCTAD. 1995. *World Investment Report 1995: Transnational Corporations and Competitiveness*. New York: United Nations.

US Department of the Treasury. 2017. "Statement on the President's Decision Regarding Lattice Semiconductor Corporation." September 13, 2017. https://www.treasury .gov/press-center/press-releases/Pages/sm0157.aspx.

van Dijck, J. 2021. "Seeing the Forest for the Trees: Visualizing Platformization and Its Governance." *New Media & Society* 23, no. 9: 2801–2819.

van Romburgh, Marlize, and Gene Teare. 2023. "Chinese Startup Investors Are Stepping Up With Capital As American VCs Retreat." Crunchbase, August 10, 2023. https:// news.crunchbase.com/venture/china-us-vc-startup-investment-biden-order -data/?utm_source=cb_daily&utm_medium=email&utm_campaign=20230 811&utm_content=intro&utm_term=content&utm_source=cb_daily&utm _medium=email&utm_campaign=20230703.

Vitols, Sigurt. 2003. "From Banks to Markets: The Political Economy of Liberalization of the German and Japanese Financial Systems." In *The End of Diversity? Prospects for German and Japanese Capitalism*, edited by Kozo Yamamura and Wolfgang Streeck, 240–260. Ithaca, NY: Cornell University Press.

Vogel, Ezra F. 2011. *Deng Xiaoping and the Transformation of China*. Cambridge, MA: Harvard University Press.

Vogel, Steven K. 2006. *Japan Remodeled: How Government and Industry Are Reforming Japanese Capitalism*. Ithaca, NY: Cornell University Press.

Vogel, Steven K. 2018. *Marketcraft: How Governments Make Markets Work*. Oxford: Oxford University Press.

Vu, Tuong. 2010. *Paths to Development in Asia: South Korea, Vietnam, China, and Indonesia*. Cambridge, UK: Cambridge University Press.

Wade, Robert H. 1990. *Governing the Market: Economic Theory and the Role of Government in East Asian Industrialization*. Princeton, NJ: Princeton University Press.

Wade, Robert H. 1998. "From 'Miracle' to 'Cronyism': Explaining the Great Asian Slump." *Cambridge Journal of Economics* 22, no. 6: 693–706.

Wade, Robert H. 2003. "What Strategies Are Viable for Developing Countries Today? The World Trade Organization and the Shrinking of 'Development Space.'" *Review of International Political Economy* 10, no. 4: 621–644.

Wade, Robert H. 2016. "Industrial Policy in Response to the Middle-Income Trap and the Third Wave of the Digital Revolution." *Global Policy* (August).

Wade, Robert H. 2017. "The American Paradox: Ideology of Free Markets and Practice of Directional Thrust." *Cambridge Journal of Economics* 41, no. 3: 859–880.

Wade, Robert H. 2018. "The Developmental State: Dead or Alive?" *Development and Change* 49, no. 2: 518–546.

Wakasugi, Tomoko. 2023. "Alibaba Founder Jack Ma Starts Ready-Made Food Company." *Nikkei Asia*, November 25, 2023.

Walter, Andrew. 2006. *Governing Finance: East Asia's Adoption of International Standards*. Ithaca, NY: Cornell University Press.

Walter, Andrew, and Xiaoke Zhang. 2012. *East Asian Capitalism: Diversity, Continuity and Change*. Oxford: Oxford University Press.

Walter, Carl E., and Fraser J. T. Howie. 2012. *Red Capitalism: The Fragile Financial Foundation of China's Extraordinary Rise*. Singapore: Wiley.

Wan, Ming. 2008. *The Political Economy of East Asia: Striving for Wealth and Power*. Washington, DC: CQ.

Wang, Chengang, Yingqi Wei, and Xiaming Liu. 2007. "Does China Rival Its Neighbouring Economies for Inward FDI?" *Transnational Corporations* 16, no. 3: 35–60.

Wang, Emily Xiaoxia. 2013. "Entrepreneurship Financing: Innofund." In *Entrepreneurship and Economic Growth in China*, edited by Ting Zhang and Roger Stough, 131–163. Singapore, World Scientific.

Wang, Eudora. 2021. "Taiwan's AppWorks Raises $114m to Expand Investment in ASEAN." *Nikkei Asia*, March 4, 2021.

Wang, Huiyao, David Zweig, and Xiaohua Lin. 2011. "Returnee Entrepreneurs: Impact on China's Globalization Process." *Journal of Contemporary China* 20, no. 70: 413–431.

Wang, Jenn-Hwan. 2007. "From Technological Catch-Up to Innovation-Based Economic Growth: South Korea and Taiwan Compared." *Journal of Development Studies* 43, no. 6: 1084–1104.

Wang, Lanfang, and Susheng Wang. 2011. "Cross-Border Venture Capital Performance: Evidence from China." *Pacific-Basin Finance Journal* 19, no. 1: 71–97.

Wang, Lee-rong. 1995. "Taiwan's Venture Capital: Policies and Impacts." *Journal of Industry Studies* 2, no. 1: 83–94.

Wang, Serenitie, and Daniel Shane. 2019. "Jack Ma Endorses China's Controversial 12 Hours a Day, 6 Days a Week Work Culture." *CNN*, April 16, 2019.

Wang, Tongtao. 2017. "Chinese Technology Companies 'Going Global': Issues and Suggestions." *Advances in Social Sciences, Education and Humanities Research* 105: 449–454.

Wang, Yanbo, Jizhen Li, and Jeffrey L. Furman. 2017. "Firm Performance and State Innovation Funding: Evidence from China's Innofund Program." *Research Policy* 46, no. 6: 1141–1161.

Wang, Zhaoxing, Qile He, Senmao Xia, David Sarpong, Ailun Xiong, and Gideon Maas. 2020. "Capacities of Business Incubators and Regional Innovation Performance." *Technological Forecasting & Social Change* 158: 1–13.

Warwick, Ken, and Alistair Nolan. 2014. *Evaluation of Industrial Policy: Methodological Issues and Policy Lessons*. Paris: OECD.

Wattles, Jackie. 2018. "How Jack Ma Went from English Teacher to Tech Billionaire." *CNN*, September 9, 2018.

Weiblen, Tobias, and Henry W. Chesbrough. 2015. "Engaging with Startups to Enhance Corporate Innovation." *California Management Review*, 57, no. 2: 66–90. https://doi.org/10.1525/cmr.2015.57.2.66.

Weiss, Linda. 2003. "Guiding Globalization in East Asia: New Roles for Old Developmental States." In *States in the Global Economy*, edited by Linda Weiss, 245–270. Cambridge, UK: Cambridge University Press.

Weiss, Linda. 2014. *America Inc.? Innovation and Enterprise in the National Security State*. Ithaca, NY: Cornell University Press.

Welch, David, John Lippert, and Yan Zhang. 2018. "Nissan-Renault Plans $1 Billion Fund for Auto Tech Startups." *Industry Week*, January 10, 2018. https://www.industryweek.com/leadership/article/22024898/nissanrenault-plans-1-billion-fund-for-auto-tech-startups.

Wells, Peter. 2017. "INCJ Bails Out Failing Giants but Minnows Struggle." *Financial Times*, October 18, 2017.

Wen, Chao-Tung, and Jun-Ming Chen. 2014. "Taiwan: Linkage-Based Clusters of Innovation—The Case of Taiwan's IT Industry." In *Global Clusters of Innovation: Entrepreneurial Engines of Economic Growth around the World*, edited by Jerome S. Engel, 222–246. London: Elgar.

Westney, D. Eleanor. 1987. *Imitation and Innovation: The Transfer of Western Organizational Patterns to Meiji Japan*. Cambridge, MA: Harvard University Press.

White, Edward, and Lucy Hornby. 2019. "South Korean Shipbuilders Brace for Fight after China Mega-mergers." *Financial Times*, August 6, 2019.

Whiting, Susan H. 2001. *Power and Wealth in Rural China: The Political Economy of Institutional Change*. Cambridge, UK: Cambridge University Press.

Whitley, Richard. 1992. *Business Systems in East Asia*. London: Sage.

Whitley, Richard. 1999. *Divergent Capitalisms. The Social Structuring and Change of Business Systems*. Oxford: Oxford University Press.

Whitley, Richard. 2007. *Business Systems and Organizational Capabilities: The Institutional Structuring of Competitive Competences*. Oxford: Oxford University Press.

Whitley, Richard, and Xiaoke Zhang. 2016. *Changing Asian Business Systems: Globalization, Socio-Political Change, and Economic Organization*. Oxford: Oxford University Press.

Whittaker, Hugh. 2001. "Crisis and Innovation in Japan: A New Future through Techno-entrepreneurship?" ESRC Centre for Business Research, University of Cambridge, Working Paper 193 (March). Accessed June 26, 2024. https://www.cbr.cam.ac.uk/wp-content/uploads/2020/08/wp193.pdf.

Whittaker, Hugh, Tianbiao Zhu, Timothy Sturgeon, Mon Han Tsai, and Toshie Okita. 2010. "Compressed Development." *Studies in Comparative International Development* 45, no. 4: 439–467.

Williams, Jack, and Ch'ang-yi David Chang. 2008. *Taiwan's Environmental Struggle: Toward a Green Silicon Island*. London: Routledge.

Wilson, Jeanne. 2007. "China's Transformation toward Capitalism." In *Varieties of Capitalism in Post-Communist Countries*, edited by David Lane and Martin Myant, 239–257. London: Palgrave Macmillan.

Winckler, Edwin A., and Susan Greenhalgh, eds. 1988. *Contending Approaches to the Political Economy of Taiwan*. Armonk, NY: East Gate Book.

Witt, Michael A., and Gordon Redding. 2013. *The Oxford Handbook of Asian Business Systems*. Oxford: Oxford University Press.

Witt, Michael A., Luiz Ricardo Kabbach de Castro, Kenneth Amaeshi, Sami Mahroum, Dorothee Bohle, and Lawrence Saez. 2018. "Mapping the Business Systems of 61 Major Economies: A Taxonomy and Implications for Varieties of Capitalism and Business Systems Research." *Socio-Economic Review* 16, no. 1: 5–38.

Wladawsky-Berger, Irving. 2020. "Why the "Techlash" Is a Threat to Growth and Progress." *Wall Street Journal*, June 6, 2020.

Wong, Christine. 2011. "The Fiscal Stimulus Program and Public Governance Issues in China." *OECD Journal on Budgeting* 11, no. 3. http://dx.doi.org/10.1787/budget-11-5kg3nhljqrjl.

Wong, Jacky. 2016. "SoftBank-ARM: These Chips Don't Come Cheap." *Wall Street Journal*, July 18, 2016.

Wong, Joseph. 2004. "The Adaptive Developmental State." *Journal of East Asian Studies* 4, no. 3: 345–362.

Wong, Joseph. 2005. "Re-Making the Developmental State in Taiwan: The Challenges of Biotechnology." *International Political Science Review* 26, no. 2: 169–191.

Wong, Joseph. 2011. *Betting on Biotech: Innovation and the Limits of Asia's Developmental State*. Ithaca, NY: Cornell University Press.

Woo, Jung-en. 1991. *Race to the Swift: State and Finance in the Industrialization of Korea*. New York: Columbia University Press.

Woo-Cumings, Meredith, ed. 1999. *The Developmental State*. Ithaca, NY: Cornell University Press.

World Bank. 1993. *The East Asian Miracle: Economic Growth and Public Policy*. New York: Oxford University Press.

World Bank. 2020a. "China—Country Dashboard." Accessed July 25, 2020. http://data topics.worldbank.org/jobs/country/china.

World Bank. 2020b. "GDP Growth (Annual %)—China." Accessed August 28, 2020. https://data.worldbank.org/indicator/NY.GDP.MKTP.KD.ZG?locations=CN.

World Bank. 2020c. "Labor Force Participation Rate, Female (% of Female Population Ages 15+." https://data.worldbank.org/indicator/SL.TLF.CACT.FE.ZS.

Wright, Lisa, Shweta Vasani, and Nele Dhondt. 2019. "Expansion of Foreign Investment Controls in the UK and Beyond—Latest Developments." *Slaughter and May* (November). Accessed June 26, 2024. https://prodstoragesam.blob.core.windows .net/highq/2537714/expansion-of-foreign-investment-controls-in-the-uk-and -beyond.pdf.

X-Hub TOKYO. 2017. "Ask the Person in Charge of Tokyo, What You Want to Tell the Participants about the Aim of Launching X-HUB TOKYO." [In Japanese.] November 1, 2017. https://x-hub.tokyo/contents/361.

Xinhua. 2017. "China Focus: Xi Steers Chinese Economy toward High-Quality Development." December 21, 2017.

Xinhua. 2018. "China to Upgrade Mass Entrepreneurship and Innovation." September 6, 2018.

Xinhua. 2019. "GEM 10th Anniversary: Over 90% of High-Tech Enterprises, It's Time for Comprehensive Reform." [In Chinese.] October 30, 2019.

Xinhua. 2020. "China Stresses Advancing Entrepreneurship, Innovation, Enhancing Employment." July 16, 2020.

Xinhua. 2023. "China Extends Tax Incentives to Encourage Investment in Startups." August 2, 2023.

Xu, Nadeem. 2020. "China's High-Tech Zones Keep Growing in Epidemic." *Asia Times*, July 24, 2020.

Xu, Wei. 2017. *China to Further Promote Innovation and Entrepreneurship*. Accessed August 28, 2020. http://english.www.gov.cn/premier/news/2017/07/12/content _281475723086902.htm.

Xue, Lan, and Zheng Liang. 2010. "Relationships between IPR and Technology Catch-Up: Some Evidence from China." In *Intellectual Property Rights, Development, and Catch-Up: An International Comparative Study*, edited by Hiroyuki Odagiri, Akira Goto, Atsushi Sunami, and Richard R. Nelson, 317–360. Oxford: Oxford University Press.

Yamamura, Kozo. 2003. "Germany and Japan in a New Phase of Capitalism: Confronting the Past and the Future." In *The End of Diversity? Prospects for German and Japanese Capitalism*, edited by Kozo Yamamura and Wolfgang Streeck, 115–146. Ithaca, NY: Cornell University Press.

Yamawaki, Hideki. 2002. "The Evolution and Structure of Industrial Clusters in Japan." *Small Business Economics* 18: 121–140.

Yang, Lijun. 2018. "Higher Education Expansion and Post-college Unemployment: Understanding the Roles of Fields of Study in China." *International Journal of Educational Development* 62: 62–74.

Yang, Sophia. 2018. "Taiwan's First-Ever Coworking Space for Fintech Startups Kicks Off in Taipei." *Taiwan News*, September 18, 2018.

Yao, Xiaofang, Xiyue Wu, and Dan Long. 2016. "University Students' Entrepreneurial Tendency in China: Effect of Students' Perceived Entrepreneurial Environment." *Journal of Entrepreneurship in Emerging Economies* 8, no. 1: 60–81.

Yao, Yang. 2004. "Government Commitment and the Outcome of Privatization in China." In *Governance, Regulation, and Privatization in the Asia-Pacific Region*, edited by Takatoshi Ito and Anne O. Krueger, 251–276. Chicago, University of Chicago Press.

Ye, Min. 2009. "Policy Learning or Diffusion: How China Opened to Foreign Direct Investment." *Journal of East Asian Studies* 9, no. 3: 399–431.

Yeh, Thomas M. F. 2006. "Venture Capital Industry Development in Taiwan." 14th Conference on Pacific Basin Finance, Economics and Accounting, July 14, 2006.

Yen, William. 2021. "Tsai Awards 9 Startups Chosen to Promote Taiwan as 'Startup Island.'" *Focus Taiwan*, October 19, 2021.

Yeo, Yukyung, and Martin Painter. 2011. "Diffusion, Transmutation, and Regulatory Regime in Socialist Market Economies: Telecoms Reform in China and Vietnam." *Pacific Review* 24, no. 4: 375–395.

Yeung, Henry Wai-chung. 2014. "Governing the Market in a Globalizing Era: Developmental States, Global Production Networks and Inter-firm Dynamics in East Asia." *Review of International Political Economy* 21, no. 1: 70–101.

Yeung, Henry Wai-chung. 2016. *Strategic Coupling: East Asian Industrial Transformation in the New Global Economy*. Ithaca, NY: Cornell University Press.

Yeung, Henry Wai-chung. 2017. "State-Led Development Reconsidered: The Political Economy of State Transformation in East Asia since the 1990s." *Cambridge Journal of Regions, Economy and Society* 10, no. 1: 83–98.

Yip, George S., and Bruce McKern. 2016. *China's Next Strategic Advantage: From Imitation to Innovation*. Cambridge, MA: MIT Press.

Yip, Waiyee. 2021. "China Steps in to Regulate Brutal '996' Work Culture." *BBC News*, September 2, 2021.

Yonekura, Seiichiro, and Michael Lynskey. 2000. "Why Japan Needs Startups." *Journal of Japanese Trade and Industry* 19, no. 4: 10–13.

Yonhap. 2018a. "Moon Urges All-out Efforts to Turn Tide of 'Disastrous' Youth Unemployment." March 15, 2018.

Yonhap. 2018b. "S. Korea's 3rd Bourse Marks Solid Growth in 2018." December 30, 2018.

Yoon, Donghun. 2017. "The Regional-Innovation Cluster Policy for R&D Efficiency and the Creative Economy: With Focus on Daedeok Innopolis." *Journal of Science and Technology Policy* 8, no. 2: 206–226.

You, Jong-sung. 2016. *Democracy, Inequality and Corruption: Korea, Taiwan and the Philippines Compared*. Cambridge, UK: Cambridge University Press.

Yu, Tony Fu-Lai. 2012. *Entrepreneurship and Taiwan's Economic Dynamics*. London: Springer.

Yu, Tony Fu-Lai, and Ho-Don Yan, eds. 2015. *Handbook of East Asian Entrepreneurship*. London: Routledge.

Yu, Xie, Elaine Yu, and Jing Yang. 2021. "Didi Shares Plunge as China's Probes of U.S.-Listed Firms Jolt Investors." *Wall Street Journal*, July 6, 2021.

Yuan, Li. 2023. "Beijing Offers Love, but Chinese Entrepreneurs Aren't Buying It." *New York Times*, July 22, 2023.

Yuan, Zhenhuan. 2004. "Land Use Rights in China." *Cornell Real Estate Review* 3: 73–78.

Yuasa, Taishu. 2023. "Japan Moves to Let Foreign Trainees Change Jobs after 1 Year." *Nikkei Asia*, October 19, 2023.

Yusuf, Shahid, and Kaoru Nabeshima. 2009. *Growth through Innovation: An Industrial Strategy for Shanghai (vol. 3): Full Report.* Washington, DC: World Bank Group.

Zehavi, Amos, and Dan Breznitz. 2017. Distribution Sensitive Innovation Policies: Conceptualisation and Empirical Examples. *Research Policy* 46: 327–336.

Zeitlin, Jonathan, and Gary Herrigel, eds. 2000. *Americanization and its Limits: Reworking U.S. Technology and Management in Postwar Europe and Japan.* Oxford: Oxford University Press.

Zeng, Douglas Zhihua. 2011. "How Do Special Economic Zones and Industrial Clusters Drive China's Rapid Development?" World Bank Policy Research Working Paper 5583.

Zhai, Keith, and Liza Lin. 2022. "China to Conclude Didi Cybersecurity Probe, Lift Ban on New Users." *Wall Street Journal*, June 6, 2022.

Zhang, Erchi, Wen Simin, Wei Yiyang, and Han Wei. 2019. "In Depth: Southeast Asia Becomes Region's Next Tech Battleground." *Caixin Global*, November 18, 2019.

Zhang, Jing, Wei Zhang, Andreas Schwab, and Sipei Zhang. 2017. "Institutional Environment and IPO Strategy: A Study of ChiNext in China." *Management and Organization Review* 13, no. 2: 399–430.

Zhang, Lin. 2023. *The Labor of Reinvention: Entrepreneurship in the New Chinese Digital Economy.* New York: Columbia University Press.

Zhen, Lui. 2023. "From AI to Data Leaks, Cyber Dangers Threaten China's Infrastructure, State Security Chief Warns." *South China Morning Post*, September 27, 2023. https://www.scmp.com/news/china/politics/article/3235893/ai-data-leaks -cyber-dangers-threaten-chinas-infrastructure-state-security-chief-warns.

Zheng, Shilin, and Zhaochen Li. 2020. "Pilot Governance and the Rise of China's Innovation." *China Economic Review* 63: 101521.

Zheng, Yongnian, and Minjia Chen. 2009. "China's State-Owned Enterprise Reform and Its Discontents." *Problems of Post-Communism* 56, no. 2: 36–42.

Zheng, Yongnian, and Yanjie Huang. 2018. *Market in State: The Political Economy of Domination in China.* Cambridge, UK: Cambridge University Press.

Zhi, Qiang, and Margaret M. Pearson. 2016. "China's Hybrid Adaptive Bureaucracy: The Case of the 863 Program for Science and Technology." *Governance* 30, no. 3: 407–424.

Zhong, Ramond. 2020. "In Halting Ant's I.P.O., China Sends a Warning to Business." *New York Times*, December 24, 2020.

Zhou, Cissy. 2023. "Clouds Gather over Alibaba's Key Unit after IPO Plans Shelved." *Nikkei Asia*, December 1, 2023.

Zhou, Yu, and Xielin Liu. 2016. "Evolution of Chinese State Policies on Innovation." In *China as an Innovation Nation*, edited by Yu Zhou, William Lazonick, and Yifei Sun, 33–67. Oxford, Oxford University Press.

Zhou, Zhong-guo, Monica Hussein, and Qi Deng. 2021. "ChiNext IPOs' Initial Returns before and after the 2013 Stock Market Reform: What Can We Learn?" *Emerging Markets Review* 48: 100817.

Zhu, Julie, Meg Shen, and Greg Roumeliotis. 2020. "China Slams the Brakes on Ant Group's US$ 37 Billion Listing." Reuters, November 3, 2020.

Zider, Bob. 1998. "How Venture Capital Works." *Harvard Business Review* (November–December).

Zuo, Manda, and He Huifeng. 2023. "Death and Debt in China: How a 'Half-Baked' Bankruptcy Law Offers Few Individuals a Fresh Start." *South China Morning Post,* September 11, 2023. https://www.scmp.com/economy/china-economy/article /3233923/death-and-debt-china-how-half-baked-bankruptcy-law-offers-few -individuals-fresh-start.

Zweig, David. 2002. *Internationalizing China: Domestic Interests and Global Linkages.* Ithaca, NY: Cornell University Press.

Zysman, John. 1983. *Governments, Markets, and Growth: Financial Systems and the Politics of Industrial Change.* Ithaca, NY: Cornell University Press.

Index

Note: Page numbers followed by letters f and t refer to figures and tables, respectively.

Post Bank (Japan), 41, 52
Presidio Ventures, 50
ProLogium, 5

quantum computing, startups and, 4, 5, 113

radical innovation: changes over time, 172n10;
China's policies supporting, 21, 114,
116–17, 120, 120f, 122, 123; East Asian
countries' convergence toward, 34, 129–
30, 129f, 131; Japan's policies supporting,
52–55, 57, 58f, 59, 125f, 126, 131; Korea's
policies supporting, 75, 78, 80–81, 125f,
126; liberal market economy (LME) and,
3, 6, 23; Mark I paradigm and, 25f, 33;
and national security, 35–36; Taiwan's
policies supporting, 83–84, 93–95, 99,
125f, 127–28
Rapidus (joint venture), 56–57
regional development, startup policies focused
on, 143; in China, 105–6, 117–19, 122,
134; in Korea, 66
Renault, 51
renewable energy sector, China's efforts to
develop, 116, 128
Riney, James, 51
Robinson, James, 24
robotics: China's policies supporting, 119,
122; startup policies and, 4, 34; Taiwan's
policies supporting, 94
Roh Moon-hyun, 74, 76
Roh Tae-woo, 64, 65
Roland, Gerard, 35

Samsung: and C-Lab (Creative Lab), 66;
scandal involving, 175n4; as VC investor,
4, 80, 174n1
Saxenian, AnnaLee, 88
Schaede, Ulrike, 135, 174n14
Schumacher, E. F., 143
Schumpeter, Joseph, on innovation patterns, 5,
8–9, 14, 24, 140–41, 143
secondments, at startups, 29, 48, 49, 58,
133
Seko, Hiroshige, 38
semiconductor industry: China's policies on,
21, 102, 106, 116, 119, 121, 122, 128,
172n5; Japan's efforts to promote, 56–57,
59, 131; and national security, 35–36;
startups considered as resources for big
business in, 4; Taiwan's dominance in,
4, 82, 88, 89, 94–95, 96, 99, 100, 127,
176n14; US policies on, 138

Semiconductor Manufacturing International
Corporation (SMIC, China), 106, 116,
119, 172n5; state and, 21, 102, 121, 128
Sequoia China, 108, 113
Shanghai Stock Exchange, 104, 107; STAR
market of, 113, 122, 132
Shen, Neil, 107, 113
Shenzhen Stock Exchange (SZSE), 104, 111,
112; ChiNext, 112, 113, 122, 178n15
Silicon Catalyst, 57
Silicon Valley: challenges to myth of, 2, 22,
139; Chinese policies modeled on, 103,
177n3; incumbent dominance in, 139;
international efforts modeled on, 137,
139; investments in China, 113–14;
Japanese policies inspired by, 53; Japan's
partnerships with, 4, 48, 56, 57; Korea's
partnerships with, 71, 74; negative
reaction to growing power of, 142–43;
Taiwanese engineers returning from,
88–89, 176n8; Taiwan's partnerships with,
86, 88–89, 90, 176n11
size of firms: in China, 103, 106–8, 120–21,
120f, 125f, 128; developmental state and,
7, 15, 26–27, 171n1, 174n2; in Japan, 26,
39, 42–45, 57–59, 58f, 125f, 126; in Korea,
26, 61, 65–68, 79, 79f, 125f, 126, 130; in
Mark I paradigm, 8, 10, 25f, 27–28; in
Mark II paradigm, 9, 10, 25f, 26–27; in
study of startup capitalism, 19, 23–24, 28;
in Taiwan, 4, 28, 82–83, 84, 85–87, 94,
97, 98, 98f, 125f, 127, 128, 130. See also
large companies; small- and medium-size
enterprises (SMEs)
SK Telecom, and startup partnerships, 66
small- and medium-size enterprises (SMEs):
in China, and innovation activities, 103;
in developmental state, 171n1, 174n2;
Taiwan's support for, 4, 28, 82–83, 84,
85–87, 94, 97, 98, 98f, 125f, 127, 128, 130
Small Business Innovation Research program
(SBIR): Chinese version of, 111; Japanese
version of, 53
SME Administration (Taiwan), 85–86, 89–90,
97
SMRJ Venture Fund (Japan), 49, 56
social inclusion, startup policies promoting,
134, 143; in China, 118–19, 134; in Japan,
56, 134; in Korea, 134; in Taiwan, 97. See
also women
social purpose, 34–36; assessment of,
approaches to, 18; China's innovation
policies and, 35, 105–6, 117–19, 120,